French Poetry Today

French Poetry Today

A bilingual anthology

Edited and with an introduction by

SIMON WATSON TAYLOR
and EDWARD LUCIE-SMITH

SCHOCKEN BOOKS · NEW YORK

Published in U.S.A. in 1971
by Schocken Books Inc.
67 Park Avenue, New York, N.Y. 10016

Copyright © 1971 by Simon Watson Taylor and Edward Lucie-Smith

Library of Congress Catalog Card No. 71-163335

Printed in Great Britain

Contents

BORIS VIAN

Acknowledgements

Acknowledgement is made to the following who have kindly granted permission to reprint the poems included in this volume:

Monsieur Marc Alyn for his poems 'Trahison du fruit' and 'Le Poème au poète' from *Délébiles* (1962). Monsieur Louis Aragon for his poems 'L'Entreinte', which has appeared in *Lettres françaises* and 'L'Homme seul', from *Poètes d'aujourd'hui: Aragon*. L'Arbalète Marc Barbezat for 'L'Éhontee', 'Menu òu la quinte' and 'Compte tu' from *L'Arbre à lettres* (1966) and 'Vendange' from *Rien voilà l'ordre* (1959), all by Olivier Larronde. Monsieur Julien Blaine for his poems 'Quatrième', 'Onzième', 'Treizième' and 'Quatorzième' from *W M Quinzième* (1966), Madame Edith Boissonnas for her poems 'Le Regard', 'Accalmie' and 'Le Vide', which have previously appeared in *Nouvelle Revue française*. Monsieur Alain Bosquet for the translation by Samuel Beckett of 'Écrit en marge du poème', three extracts from his poem *Deuxième Testament*, which appeared in *Selected Poems* (1962), published by New Directions Publishing Corporation. Jonathan Cape Ltd for Anthony Rudolf's translations of 'The Dialogue of Anguish and Desire' and 'The Art of Poetry' by Yves Bonnefoy from *Selected Poems* (1968). Monsieur Jean Pierre Faye for extracts from his poem 'Le Change'. Editions Gallimard for 'Le Paresseux' by Aragon from *Elégie à Pablo Neruda* (1966); 'Origine' and 'L'Ami caillou' from *Quatre Téstaments* (1967) and 'Écrit en marge du poème', three extracts from *Deuxième Testament* (1959), all by Alain Bosquet; the extract from 'Dialogues des règnes' by Michel Butor from *Illustrations II* (1969); 'Le Ramier' and 'Tradition du météore' by René Char, both from *Dans la pluie giboyeuse* (1968); 'Prose' and 'L'Été l'hiver la nuit la nuit' by Michel Deguy, both from *Figurations* (1969); 'La Soif' from *L'Épervier*, 'Saccade' from *Saccades* (1962), and the extract from 'L'Issue dérobée' from *L'Embrasure* (1969), all by Jacques Dupin; 'Le Cri', 'Symboles du temps' and 'Art de la guerre' by Jean Follain, all from *D'après tout* (1967); 'Dans les lointains parages' from *Il n'y a pas de paradis* and 'Prise à partie' and 'Linge propre ou l'héritier' from *La Sainte Face* (1968), all by André Frénaud; 'Chant V' and 'Chant VI' by Jean Grosjean from

Hiver (1964); 'Dans un tourbillon de neige' from *L'Ignorant* (1957) and 'Sur les pas de la lune', 'Dans l'herbe à l'hiver survivant...' and 'Tout fleur n'est que de la nuit...' from *Airs* (1967), all by Philippe Jaccottet; 'Taupe Crevée sur la route', 'Le Prospecteur' and 'Promesse', all from *Une Somme de poésie: petit théâtre crépusculaire* (1963) by Patrice de La Tour du Pin; 'Chansons pour des fiançailles' by Jean Lescure from *Drailles* (1968); 'Parmi des langues étrangères' and 'Ginza' by Jean Pérol from *Le Coeur véhément* (1968); 'Des ennuis qu'il peut y avoir...' and 'Je ne saurais vous dire tout...' by Georges Perros, both from *Une Vie ordinaire* (1967); 'L'Usage de la nudité' by Andre Pieyre de Mandiargues from *Le Point où j'en suis* (1964); 'La Nouvelle Araignée' from *Le Grand Recueil* (1961) and 'L'Ardoise' from *Le Nouveau Recueil* (1967), both by Francis Ponge; 'Les Ombres' from *Histoires* (1946) and 'Comme par miracle' and 'Ce n'est pas moi qui chante...' from *Fatras* (1965), all by Jacques Prévert; 'Le Porc' from *Battre la campagne* (1968) and 'Buccin', 'Le Livre de bord' and 'Une traversée en 1922' from *Fendre les flots* (1969), all by Raymond Queneau; 'Le Bracelet perdu' and 'Matin d'octobre' by Jacques Réda from *Amén* (1968); 'Avec de grand gestes...' and 'Tou Fou' from *Le Monde d'une voix* (1968) by Armand Robin; 'Silencieuse et grandissante' by Jean-Philippe Salabreuil from *L'Inésperé* (1968); 'Harengs et bouleaux', 'Litanie' and 'La Mort du poète' by Jude Stefan, all from *Cyprès* (1967); 'Une femme un oiseau' and 'Mémoire morte' by Jean Tardieu, both from *Histoire obscure* (1961); 'Les Objets perdus' by Toursky from *Un Drôle d'air* (1963). Editions Bernard Grasset for 'Feux contre feux', 'Pourquoi serpent', 'Sans rien autour', and 'Transfert nocturne' by Armen Lubin, all from *Feux contre feux* (1968). Monsieur Eugene Guillevic for his poem 'Paliers', which has appeared in *Nouvelle Revue française*. Mercure de France for 'Le Dialogue d'angoisse et de désir' and 'Art de la poésie' by Yves Bonnefoy from *Pierre écrite* (1965); 'La Lumière de la lame' and 'Ajournement' by André du Bouchet from *Où le soleil* (1968); and 'Ces Livres' from *Poésie VII–IX: Langue* (1967), 'Vaisseau', 'Cheveux et miroirs' and 'Un Jour sera connu...', all from *Poésie X–XI: Mélodrame* (1967), 'Beauté', 'Je suis encore ému...' and 'Promenade' from *Poésie X–XI: Moires* (1967), all by Pierre Jean Jouve. Editions Albin Michel for 'Menteur' and 'Le Sablier' by Robert Sabatier from *Les Châteaux de millions d'années* (1969). Harry Mathews for his translation of 'Eros Possessed: theatricals', extracts from *Eros energumène* by Denis Roche. Editions Jean-Jacques Pauvert for 'Je voudrais pas crever' and 'Un Jour' by Boris Vian from *Je*

Voudrais pas crever (1962). Penguin Books Ltd for Simon Watson Taylor's translations of 'Levels' by Guillevic and 'I don't want to Croak' by Boris Vian from *French Writing Today* (1968). Rapp + Whiting Ltd for Keith Bosley's translations of 'These Books', 'Vessel', 'Beauty' and 'A Walk' by Pierre Jean Jouve from *An Idiom of Night* (1968). Monsieur Saint-Jean Perse for the extracts from his poem *Oiseaux*, which first appeared in *Nouvelle Revue française*. Editions du Seuil for 'Prière athée' from *Evangélaire* (1960), 'La Tour' from *Babel* (1952), 'Le Vent' from *Visage nuage* (1956), all by Pierre Emmanuel; 'Verdammnis ist im Wesen' from *Paysages en deux* (1964) and an extract from *Comme* (1965), both by Marcelin Pleynet; 'La Distance du feu' from *La Terre du sacre* (1966) and 'Récit 4' from *La Braise et la rivière* (1969), both by Jean-Claude Renard; and 'Théâtre des agissements d'Eros', extracts from *Eros energumène* (1968) by Denis Roche. Editions du Soleil Noir for '3e jour', 'Cri', 'De derrière les loups' by Jean-Pierre Duprey, all from *La Fin et la manière*, and the extract from *Adrianopol* by Alain Jouffroy from *Libertés de la liberté* (1970).

Introduction

French poetry today traces its descent directly from Gérard de Nerval (1808–55), and from Charles Baudelaire (1821–67). With the Nerval of *Aurélia* and *Les Chimères*, French poetry ceased to be a form of descriptive writing and became a new *language* based upon its own independent concepts and employing a scale of imaginary values unrelated to social norms. With the exception of Edgar Allen Poe (whose work duly aroused the enthusiasm of Baudelaire and his successors), neither English nor American poetry pursued a similar course. Here, Wordsworth's insistence upon the value of the language of everyday speech exerted a continuing influence, as did his parallel insistence that poetry was 'emotion recollected in tranquillity'.

For Nerval, intermittent madness provided a means of liberating the imagination, so that it might seize aspects of the unknown that had never hitherto been systematically recorded. Nerval was the first poet in modern times to treat dream as a superior reality. Coleridge, by contrast, only hints at such a possibility in the famous fragment 'Kubla Khan: or, a vision in a dream', and the fact that the poem remained a fragment is in itself significant. French poetry accepted the challenge that English poetry refused.

With Baudelaire, French poetry, in abandoning everyday reality, proposed instead a whole range of *symbolic* structures which were more or less accessible to interpretation by the reasoning mind, but only at reason's expense. Opium was sometimes the means by which Baudelaire exacerbated his senses in order to produce a poetic tension of unreason akin to Nerval's. Here, again, a comparison with Coleridge is instructive: Coleridge seems to have used laudanum simply as a means of escape from personal dilemmas which he could not resolve, though Thomas De Quincey was readier to explore the beauties and horrors of the world which opium made available to him. In Baudelaire's case,

17

as sometimes with De Quincey, the problem of the function of literature, and of the drug's effect upon the powers of the writer, became broadened into the more agonizing problem of human identity itself. It was a quest which he pursued with consummate art and a splendidly Byronic fatalism.

Nerval left no trace of immediate influence behind him. Indeed, it is only quite recently that the seminal importance of his small output of uneven but often astonishing verse has been recognized. Baudelaire, though he had no direct heirs, provided the initial inspiration for two very different poets: Stéphane Mallarmé (1842–98), and Arthur Rimbaud (1854–91). Rimbaud's attempts to attain a deliberately induced state of unreason by poetic means were summed up in two celebrated formulae which profoundly influenced successive generations: 'Le Poète se fait *voyant* par un long, immense et raisonné *dérèglement de tous ses sens*' ('The Poet transforms himself into a *seer* by means of a prolonged, comprehensive and deliberate *derangement of all his senses*)'; and 'Je est un autre' ('I is another [person]').

Together with the writings of the Comte de Lautréamont (Isidore Ducasse, 1847–70), who attacked, through his anti-hero Maldoror, the very concept of rational human identity, Rimbaud's determined effort to destroy the rational self in his search for a purely verbal (and delirious) reality provided – and especially through his use of free association – the basis for the whole theoretical structure of surrealism fifty years later.

But neither Nerval, Baudelaire, Lautréamont nor Rimbaud, however great their eagerness to overthrow the tangible and unacceptable universe, made any equivalent attempt to impose a revolution upon the *form* of their new language of revolt; the French syntactic, grammatical and semantic traditions remained largely unviolated. It was left to Mallarmé, in a long poem written at the very end of his life (*Un Coup de dé jamais n'abolira l'hasard*, 1897), to mount an assault on the accepted ordering of words, abandoning rhyme, grammar and logical thematic progression in favour of an artificially imposed architecture of musical suggestion and more or less hermetic allusion. Unfortunately, this experiment, bold as it seemed, was vitiated by a dehumanized perfectionism, and Mallarmé's work, taken as a whole, instead of ushering in an immediate new era served to bolster the preciosity and the vaporous posturings of second-generation symbolists, and thus initiated a condition of spiritual apathy which endured until well after the turn of the century.

During the last few decades of the nineteenth century, and at the beginning of the twentieth, there were, of course, points at which French and Anglo-American poetry were tangential. The prestige of French culture was sufficient to see to that. Unfortunately, these encounters were not always of the most fruitful kind. There were, for example, links between French symbolism in its 'decadent' phase and the English Decadents: Pater, Wilde, Beardsley, Symons and Swinburne. Apart from an evident community of ideas, it was at this time, as at almost no other, that we find poetry, criticism and the visual arts going hand in hand in England, just as they have usually done in France during the past century. But English Decadence, despite its element of protest against bourgeois rationalism, was, taken as a whole, a far more superficial phenomenon than French symbolism. The principal symbolist who wrote in English, the Anglo-Irish poet W. B. Yeats, turned symbolist doctrine to his own magnificent purposes just as the more serious poets in France were beginning to question and abandon it. The continuing influence of symbolism upon English verse was not through Yeats, who remained an isolated figure even in his own literature, but through the impact of two interesting if minor French poets, Tristan Corbière (1845–75) and Jules Laforgue (1860–87), upon the career of T. S. Eliot, who took from them what he needed and no more.

In England and America, Mallarmé's spatial and typographical experiments made no impact. In France, they were developed in a more vigorous context as a result of the new definitions of space and matter proposed by the cubist and futurist painters during the decade before the First World War. Guillaume Apollinaire (1880–1918), in particular, with the picture-poems he called 'calligrammes', and with his free verse celebrations of 'modernism', not only echoed the outlook of the artists who were his friends (his collection of art criticism, *Les Peintres Cubistes: méditations ésthétiques*, appeared in 1913), but also reflected an enthusiasm for the new thrusting forces, mechanical and urban, which had inspired Whitman and Verhaeren, and which were now exciting the polemical passions of F. T. Marinetti.

Though he had already gone well beyond the position assumed by the English 'pylon poets' (Auden, Spender and Day Lewis) in the 'thirties, Apollinaire's prosodic conceptions, under their veneer of eye-catching experimentalism, remained basically attached to romantic precedent, and were sometimes weakened by a sentimental approach. It was left to Hugo Ball, Tristan Tzara and the other Dada poets (writing in German as well as French) to do an effective demolition job on the form as well as the purpose of language. They accomplished this linguistic sabotage with fierce glee during the period of the First World War, when they were living a closely shared life of voluntary exile in Zurich, in neutral Switzerland. When Paris again became accessible, and some of the leading exponents of Dada, notably Tzara, migrated there, the Dada explosion petered out. In the war's aftermath the surrealists (not yet so called), under the leadership of André Breton, eliminated the Dadaists' heroic nihilism in favour of a coherent poetic adventure based upon socially responsible (though theoretically revolutionary) concepts.

If the surrealists carried the liberation of the imagination to unparalleled lengths, in a systematized application of Rimbaud's edict, 'Changer la vie', they may nevertheless be considered, paradoxically, to have exercised a reactionary influence. by returning the structure of poetic language to the accepted formulations from which, for their own very different purposes, Mallarmé, Apollinaire (spasmodically), Pierre-Albert Birot and Tzara had tried to extricate it. The most aggressive, hallucinatory or supposedly automatic poetic writing produced by the surrealists continued to be couched in a language that did not differ greatly from that of Victor Hugo, making use of a conventional vocabulary and normal syntax. And the *moral* tone was equally evident. Claudel and Breton, both of whom have been considered legitimate spiritual heirs of Rimbaud, although diametrically – indeed, violently – opposed in their vision of how, and in what sense, 'the world' should be 'changed', were both driven by a high moral concern (which led the one to catholicism, the other to surrealism); each expressed his deeply felt moral, philosophical and metaphysical arguments in a sonorous and splendid prosody anchored firmly in the French tradition. In that sense, there is a good deal of common ground, outrageous though the idea might seem to partisans of either camp, between Claudel's *Cinq grandes odes* and Breton's *Ode à Charles Fourier*.

The somewhat uncomfortable fact that the surrealists shared not only a moral awareness but even a poetic language with Claudel and his followers does not in the least detract from the importance, which is clearly a central one, of the surrealist movement in relation to the development of French poetry in the years between the two world wars, and especially during the decade 1925–35. Not only was Breton a poet, so too were most of his closest associates – Aragon, Robert Desnos, René Crevel, Philippe Soupault, Georges Ribemont-Dessaignes, among others. These men might – indeed, usually did, in time – quarrel with one another or, most often, with Breton, on personal grounds, or those of politics or the interpretation of surrealist doctrine. But they could call upon a cogent scheme of socio-literary principles upon which to base their writing. Surrealism brought together Freudian theories about the operation of the unconscious mind, and the 'revolution of sensibility' which had been evolving in French literature ever since Nerval. Some poets who accepted the label 'surrealist', such as Benjamin Péret, Antonin Artaud, Paul Eluard and René Char, threw themselves wholeheartedly into the 'official' movement's activities during some at least of those inter-war years.

Others, especially Michel Leiris, and the poets centred round the Grand Jeu group of René Daumal and Roger Gilbert-Lecomte, owed a great deal to surrealism while remaining aloof or engaging in rival activities. Others again, such as Henri Michaux, Jean Tardieu and Jacques Audiberti, practised surrealist precepts in their poetry, but retained an entirely individualist independence. In the end, the relative distance that poets preferred to put between themselves and Breton, the fiery nucleus of the movement's explosive and exigent activities, did not matter all that much. Interpreted in the broadest sense, surrealism provided many French modernists with common ground, a place to take root.

No such common ground existed in England or in America. Modernist experiments, such as those made by the Sitwells in England, were apt to seem both willed and wilful. In America, e. e. cummings's attempt to distort the language and bend it to his own purposes attracted attention but remained comparatively unproductive for a good reason: he had little that was truly original to express in the new forms he had invented. e. e. cummings was struggling with difficulties that Apollinaire had already encountered and partly overcome through his understanding of modernism as something which affected all the arts, not merely poetry. The isolation of a more gifted, and more committed experimentalist, Hart Crane, is symbolic of the fate which overtook American poetry. But Crane, at least, wrestled with the need to find his identity as a man, and not merely as an American.

In England, surrealism failed conspicuously to make inroads on poetic development. During the 'thirties, Auden and his school experimented tentatively with surrealist techniques (*The Orators*, by Auden himself, is perhaps the best-known example of such fieldwork), and they were certainly well aware of the importance of Freud's theories. But they had little sense of poetry as a language equipped with independent concepts and values which were unrelated to the 'real' world. Instead, political events increasingly lured them towards involvement with that world. They began to exhort, to preach, to satirize, and the foreign poet who influenced them most was Bertolt Brecht. Auden, again, is the most conspicuous example of Brecht's influence.

Poets of a slightly younger generation, David Gascoyne and Dylan Thomas, for instance, also failed to marry surrealism effectively to the English literary tradition, although Thomas's Celtic exuberance brought him a good deal closer to an accommodation with that exotic phenomenon than did Gascoyne's wooden imitations. In general, though, the graft was rejected quite simply because the main stock had been developing and fertilizing in quite a different way ever since the beginning of the nineteenth century. English poets had consistently chosen 'nature', as opposed to 'vision'.

We have seen how different the situation was in France between the wars. There, the ramifications of surrealism can be best appreciated if we consider that its spirit was present, in one form or another, in the work of a number of distinguished poets who had no connection whatsoever with the movement: Pierre Jean Jouve's sublimated eroticism, Jean Cocteau's witty fantastifica-tions, Saint-John Perse's mythological treatment of nature and history may all be perceived to contain specific references to surrealism.

Nevertheless, French poetry remained very much at the mercy of political events, and the outbreak of the Second World War led to the scattering of an already diminished surrealist force. Those poets who had once – or still – moved in Breton's orbit, and who now elected to stay in France (Aragon, Tzara, Eluard, Char, Desnos were the most important) felt compelled to express their patriotic fervour as Resistance poets, thus falling into the trap which the Spanish Civil War had opened for Auden and his associates in England. They did so mainly in unmemorable elegies and odes that had little to do with surrealism.

Those who chose exile never regained the moral ground they lost by being absent from the physical and spiritual travails of their occupied and partitioned country. After Breton's return to Paris in 1946, dispirited efforts were made to rebuild the official surrealist movement, but it remained a pale shadow of its former self. The surrealist paraphernalia of mystification and irrationalism had in any case come to seem redundant to those who confronted the perspectives of post-war France. Yet the most valuable part of surrealism survived: in concentrated form as pure automatism in the hands of a very few inspired poets such as Jean-Pierre Duprey; and as a residual influence in the work of a number of other writers such as Char, Michaux, Prévert, Tardieu, Jouffroy, Bosquet and Pieyre de Mandiargues. And there were, also, younger poets among the post-war generation who resumed and embellished the preoccupations of other authoritative figures, particularly Saint-John Perse and Francis Ponge. Both Aragon and Char, in their post-surrealist guise, made new disciples.

The major post-war influence, however, was provided by Sartre's existentialism, and this in turn had sprung from the disillusion and pessimism that gripped France during her years of defeat and national humiliation. The sense of revulsion that had crystallized into a philosophical existentialism produced three main tendencies in French poetry during the 'fifties. These have been usefully summarized by Alain Bosquet (in *Verbe et vertige*, 1961) as, first, a renewal of Dadaist influence; second, phenomenology (in the Husserlian sense); and third, a sort of cosmic counter-humanism.

In 1946 the poet Isidore Isou launched a movement which he christened Lettrism. This, in its wild and noisy reduction of language to a string of disjointed phonemes, recalled the calculated excesses of Dada. Lettrism's absurd and egomaniacal revolt was predictably ephemeral, but it served the useful purpose of shaking up received ideas about the nature of language, and hence prompted research into new forms of expression that would combine verbal, audio-visual, typographical and kinetic elements. Its legitimate offspring thus include genuinely international movements such as Concrete Poetry and Spatialist Poetry.

Newly aroused misgivings about language gave rise to what Nathalie Sarraute has called 'the age of suspicion', made manifest in a desire to 'objectify' man's relationship with his environment and consequently to eschew psychological analysis in approaching a theme, or metaphor in describing it. In prose, these preoccupations ushered in what was miscalled the *nouveau roman*, established around 1955 by Alain Robbe-Grillet, Michel Butor and others. But well before that date, this variety of 'lyrical phenomenology' (a term coined by Bosquet in the above-mentioned study) had provided the impetus for the poems of Guillevic and Jean Follain,

24

and for the short prose-essays by Ponge which proclaimed a new 'reign of the object'.

Ponge, in his turn, was to provide one of the poetic inspirations (the others were Artaud and Georges Bataille) behind the formation, in 1960, of the *Tel Quel* group of writers, and of the review of that name (its subtitle, 'Science/Littérature'). The group has latterly included Marcelin Pleynet, Philippe Sollers, Denis Roche, Jean Ricardou and Jean Thibaudeau among the poets/novelists; Roland Barthes, Jacques Derrida, Michel Foucault and Julia Kristeva among the theorists/critics. The elaborate and highly sophisticated theories of language proposed by the *Tel Quel* group derive substantially from a Marxist epistemology oriented towards the linguistic researches of the Russian futurists of the early revolutionary period (Tretiakov, etc.), the later structuralist proposals of the psychoanalyst Lacan and others, Derrida's 'grammatology', and Saussure's semiology as refurbished by Kristeva. *Tel Quel* pronouncements abound in *mots d'ordre* such as 'Writing [*l'écriture*] is a function of social transformation', or 'To challenge the system of rhetoric, the narrative forms, imposed upon language by capitalism is in itself to question bourgeois ideology and the bourgeois concept of the world as a "sensible", discursive, accumulative hierarchy'.

The quality of the writing to emerge from this highly formalistic approach to poetry has been variable, though, at least in the case of Pleynet and Roche, sheer poetic ebullience seems to have successfully conquered the alarming mass of theory. One of the most talented founder-members of *Tel Quel*'s editorial committee, Jean Pierre Faye, broke away in 1967 to found his own review *Change*, which has since offered a more supple and less austere view of structural linguistics (Faye himself, and at least two of his chief collaborators, Maurice Roche and Jacques Roubaud, are blessed with a well-developed sense of non-bourgeois humour).

The highly intellectual approach to linguistic problems exemplified by the poet-theoreticians of *Tel Quel* and *Change* is paralleled, at least in density of philosophical speculation, by the investigations into the nature of language conducted during the last decade by Michel Deguy. In a series of erudite and far-ranging

25

'theme-books' (*Fragments du cadastre, Actes, Figurations*), Deguy has sought to bring together, both theoretically and by practical application, the experience that produces poetry, '*le* poétique', and the language of that experience, '*la* poétique'. Increasingly, therefore, his own poems have tended to appear in the guise of exemplars of his theory of metaphor: comparison as the essential link between language and human reality.

The third recognizable tendency to make itself felt in French poetry during the early fifties was what we have called a 'cosmic counter-humanism', a poetry manifesting itself in a metaphysical abstraction of thought and in a concomitant *occultation* of language. Here the conjoined influences of Char, Saint-John Perse and Jouve are paramount. 'René Charism', as it has been unkindly labelled (Jean Paulhan went so far as to call it, ironically, '*la grande terreur*'), was characterized by a preciosity of feeling expressed with an elliptic and sybilline concision which provided further opportunity for mystery. The style has not only fascinated the younger generation of poets, but has proven fairly easy to imitate, and a small army of epigones has continued to produce laconic facsimiles of the original models. The more fruitful aspects of Char's cosmic and elemental preoccupations exercised a powerful influence on a few first-rate poets, notably Jacques Dupin and André du Bouchet, who have since eased themselves out of this somewhat constrictive pattern of thought. Meanwhile, Char's charisma seems to hover still over the pages of *L'Ephémère*, the handsome review founded in 1965 by du Bouchet, the novelist-poet Louis René des Forêts, the critic Gaëtan Picon, and Yves Bonnefoy. About Bonnefoy (perhaps the poet of his generation who is best known abroad) it will be necessary to say more in a moment.

The eloquent and erudite rhetoric of Saint-John Perse, although seemingly as far removed as possible from Char's tightly reined language, demonstrates the same qualities (some may well find them exasperating) of ambiguity and obscurity beneath a richly imaged texture of great allegorical and mythological themes. Not surprisingly, the panoramic splendour of the verse has set its mark on the early work of poets who are themselves as different

26

as Alain Bosquet and Alain Jouffroy. Saint-John Perse is still capable of exercising an influence over much younger writers, such as the late Jean-Pierre Salabreuil. Meanwhile, he is duly consecrated a 'great writer' by a public which seldom reads poetry, and now occupies the place in the French literary pantheon once reserved for Claudel.

A livelier and deeper influence on the development of French poetry since 1950 has been that of Pierre Jean Jouve, a great and solitary figure whose importance is as yet scarcely appreciated outside France. Nothing could better sum up Jouve's mystical yet carnal perception of life than his own comment: 'Revolution, like the religious deed, has need of love. Poetry is an inner vehicle of love.' Not obscurity but true mystery – the mystery of grace, a physical as well as a spiritual grace – lies at the heart of Jouve's poetry. As an essentially religious poet whose faith has been fortified rather than weakened by his study of psychoanalytic theory, Jouve's impact on those poets of the post-war era whose Christianity is explicit in their work (and in France these are a surprisingly numerous as well as a surprisingly distinguished company) has been more salubrious than that of Claudel. If Jouve's influence may be seen most directly at work in the case of Pierre Emmanuel, it is also doubtless true that the element of broad and generous belief which informs the poetry of Jean Grosjean and Jean-Claude Renard derives ultimately from Jouve rather than from the massive orthodoxy of Claudel, whom most critics name as the mentor of this group. It is Patrice de La Tour du Pin, rather, who continues the Claudelian tradition.

Jouve's influence is to be seen plainly in the first published work of Yves Bonnefoy; but only Jouve's darker side seems to be present. We find Jouve's spiritual anguish, but not his redeeming faith; his premonitions of death but not his joyful awareness of sexuality. Bonnefoy's increasingly subjective vision has expressed itself in a language moulded to pure ideas divorced from sensuous reality. This rigorously anti-intellectual and despairingly anti-humanist poetry has enjoyed the admiration of a number of younger French poets, as well as, more surprisingly, of that part of the Anglo-American literary community which pays any attention to contemporary French verse. Surprisingly, because one must acknowledge the justice of Michael Hamburger's remark (in *The Truth of Poetry*, 1970) that 'Bonnefoy's [poetry] is remote from almost every idiom of contemporary English or American poetry, because its language functions in a radically different way, its movement proceeds in a radically different direction; and above all, because it assumes an order of pure ideas, of pure subjectivity, that can be evoked poetically with a minimum of sensuous substantiation.' One must also point out, however, that Bonnefoy can seem obscure and captious even in French terms, and not merely in comparison with another literature.

There can be no doubt, though, that an opinion has gradually gained currency in England and in America, according to which French poetry today is held to be an isolated phenomenon, cut off from international trends, lacking in recognizable social content, and prone to indulge in inflated rhetoric and flashy metaphysical conceits.

Such an image is, needless to say, a caricature. Indeed, there are plenty of French poets who have remained apart from the influences we have just been discussing, and who are readily assimilable by English and American readers. In particular, there is the vigorous populist tradition which has always been an important strand in the skein of French poetry, from the time of Villon onwards. It is as important now as it has ever been. The poetry of Jacques Prévert, Raymond Queneau, Boris Vian, among others, has become as familiar to the French public at large through the medium of gramophone record, radio, and the musical renderings of the *chansonniers* as much as through the printed word. And the lighthearted but entirely serious poems of Prévert have sold in their hundreds of thousands in paperback editions. It might be added that this popular tradition has none of the self-consciousness of Anglo-American 'pop' poetry: French poets do not have to strain to reach their audience, nor make concessions to its taste.

In addition, the French contemporary scene offers much heartening evidence of the existence of a thoroughly accessible poetry, based upon universal human situations. There is the noble, if sometimes inflated, romanticism of Aragon; the essential humanism, the impassioned involvement in life, however unjust or unhappy circumstances may be, of Armen Lubin, Jacques Réda and Armand Robin; the wry humour or delicate irony of Jean Lescure, Jean Pérol, Georges Perros, Robert Sabatier, Jude Stéfan and Toursky; the artlessly artful simplicity of Philippe Jaccottet; the sarcastic and burlesque tragicomedies of Raymond Queneau....

Queneau, as it happens, is a supreme example of the impossibility of fitting some of the best contemporary French poets into a convenient category. He is certainly populist in the sense that, in his verse as in his prose, he has consistently sought to formulate both a style and an imaginative approach which would narrow the gulf separating the French written language from the spoken, colloquial word. At the same time, Queneau's 'populism' is very far from being simplistic: his corrosive wit, his humour which can be 'black' as well as sunny, his feeling for an eroticism which sometimes flirts deliberately with obscenity – all of these bring him close to Alfred Jarry and his science of 'pataphysics' (or imaginary solutions). With Queneau, as with Jarry, seriousness and the mockery of seriousness are inextricably mixed.

The anguish which is never far beneath the surface of Queneau's apparently gentle allegories is more obviously present in the existential fables of Edith Boissonnas, whose imagery has some of the same strength and occasional quirkiness.

The baroque imagination of Olivier Larronde, too, gave him some affinity to Queneau, at least in those of his poems which best show his malicious and often self-mocking humour, and his mercurial alternation of mood, within the same text, of the serious and the frivolous. His more pretentious personae echoed influences as divergent as Cocteau and Mallarmé.

French poetry, then, can be as lyrical, as down-to-earth, as wildly eccentric, as unpredictable, as wilful, as full of surprises as anything being produced currently in England and America. But there is a difference, and it is one of background and formation. For if today's French poetry largely shares the sense of disquiet, of lost values and disillusioned hopes which also permeates much of the most deeply felt poetry written since the war both elsewhere in Europe and in the United States, the French writer yet has a singular advantage over his brothers: he is the direct heir of a tradition of visionary revolt that stretches back in an unbroken line to Rimbaud, Lautréamont, Baudelaire and Nerval. Such a tradition cannot be created *ad hoc*.

The main body of the poetry written in England and in America since the Second World War serves to illuminate, by comparison, some of the essential differences to be found in the French approach. France experienced no equivalent, for example, of the conservative reaction which took place among English and American poets in the years immediately following the war. This reaction was typified by the Movement in England, and by the 'university dandies' such as Richard Wilbur and the young Louis Simpson in the United States. From the standpoint of French poetry, there were two things of interest about the Movement. First, it was anti-modern; second, it was 'social poetry', it described social feelings and social situations in a way that reached back across the Romantics to the English Augustans. The first of these characteristics is inconceivable in a French context; the French writer, and especially the French poet, is encapsulated in modernism. He cannot stand outside it, or oppose it, because it is the only tradition he knows, and his whole language has been forged by it. Similarly, no writer who echoes Rimbaud's 'Je est un autre' could profess the interests of a poet such as Philip Larkin. Larkin is alienated, but from others, not from himself.

The American poets of the immediate post-war period were less parochial than their English colleagues, but the kind of poetry they sought for was again very different from anything that a Frenchman might have thought of producing during those years. Where France was humiliated, the United States was triumphant: American poetry, as Wilbur wrote it, was the gage of American sophistication. The French poet who attracted Wilbur was Paul Valéry – the only great poet to try to bring modern French poetry within the bounds of the academic ideal (it is for this reason, perhaps, that Valéry has been so frequently translated into English, though English versions of his work, such as Day Lewis's translation of *Le Cimetière marin*, almost always miss his lapidary concision).

Later developments have not tended to bring Anglo-American poetry closer to the French tradition or the French ideal. It is true that, with the Beats, a sudden emphasis on the 'visionary' became apparent in American verse. Allen Ginsberg and his followers attempted to set up William Blake as an equivalent to Nerval, the misunderstood rather than the forgotten founder of a new tradition of poetry. Ginsberg's *Howl* and *The Change* are perhaps the most substantial attempts to assimilate the American experience to the French concept of the *voyant*: their not infrequent accesses of confusion and sentimentalism show that the empathy is only rudimentary.

One assertion frequently made about English and American, as opposed to French, poetry is that Anglo-American verse is pragmatic in its attitudes and incapable of theoretical extension. This has a grain of truth in it, although, like most generalizations, it is unfair. Theoretical texts are not entirely lacking, and the recent history of Anglo-American poetry cannot properly be understood without reference to studies such as Donald Davie's *Purity of Diction in English Verse* (1952), or Charles Olson's *Projective Verse* (first published, in a magazine, in 1950, but not published in book form until 1959). However, an interesting aspect of these texts, particularly Olson's essay, which is perhaps the most influential thing of its kind to have been published in English since the war, is that put beside, say, the essays to be found in *Tel Quel*, *Change* or *L'Ephémère*, they seem singularly unsophisticated. Olson and the other members of the Black Mountain school, notable among them Robert Creeley and Robert Duncan, have written poetry which serves as a reminder of just how specialized and limited the modernist tradition is in America. Pound's disciples have inherited more than a touch of Pound's enduring provincialism; they are still 'village explainers' – Gertrude Stein's phrase for Pound himself.

The 'confessional poets' who are now often set up by critics as the polar opposites of and the licensed opposition to the Black

Mountaineers seem closer to these supposed rivals than they do to any French writer one can name. The *voyant* seeks the essential self by every means at his disposal; the 'confessional' writer takes the self of illusion (which is also everyday reality) and, without attempting any very systematic rearrangement of its components, projects it in the way that nineteenth-century poets such as Browning projected their fictional personages. If we compare confessionalism with surrealism, we discover that we can define both in terms of their attitudes to Freud: the confessional poet is engaged in self-analysis, while the surrealist lets the free-association process possess him entirely and lead him towards an understanding of what underpins the self.

Another opportunity for a useful and more specific comparison is supplied by some of Robert Lowell's *Imitations*, since Lowell is universally acknowledged as the chief of the confessional school. His versions of Baudelaire, Rimbaud and Mallarmé are often brilliant, but we notice a loss of subtlety, and in particular a substitution of merely kinetic for spiritual energy.

Yet the two literatures, even now, are not irrevocably divorced. One finds evidence of fruitful contact in unexpected places. It would be difficult to maintain, for example, that Jon Silkin's recent sequence of 'Flower Poems' (in *Nature with Man*, 1965) would have taken precisely the form they did without a reading of Ponge. Yet, characteristically, Silkin uses Ponge's techniques to serve very English purposes. The pathetic fallacy creeps in again by the back door: Silkin says that his aim is to 'suggest correspondences with human types and situations.'

In France, there has been considerable recent enthusiasm for the poetry of Gerard Manley Hopkins, and writers as different as Jacques Roubaud and Louis-René des Forêts have numbered themselves among Hopkins' admirers. The attraction has been partly technical: Hopkins' invention, the 'curtal-sonnet' form has received considerable theoretical attention and the flattery of a certain amount of imitation. But it seems clear that the religious rhetoric which is now the least attractive aspect of Hopkins where English readers are concerned is something which the French find perfectly acceptable. Its afflatus becomes, when translated, a variety of metaphysical baroque which seems less strained in French than in English.

Finally, though, there is one important, constant and visible difference between French poetry and that written in other languages: the idealism which is the product of France's particular history. It has a moral force allied with enduring social (and often revolutionary) aspirations which have preserved it both from the narrow parochialism which has been the besetting sin of English poetry since the war, and from the naïvety and sentimentality which have often characterized American poetry in its more determinedly experimental moments.

Poetry certainly remains vital in France, in the sense that there is a great deal of it being written, published and discussed critically. In choosing from the mass of material available* we have tried to avoid preconceptions, to the point of ignoring the hierarchical judgments that are so often imposed on modern French poets by French critics. This is not, in any case, a collection of 'modern verse' in the general sense in which that term is usually interpreted by anthologists. It is, more specifically, a book of *contemporary* verse – one reason why we have not hesitated to include relatively unestablished poets, who often provide the most interesting pointers towards the future, Our view is that even the brief period since the war cannot be treated as a unity. Though the war itself marked an important shift in the French poetic consciousness, another shift seems to have taken place, with less fanfare, around 1955, when orthodox surrealism was no longer a force to be reckoned with. We have chosen poems written and published during the last decade and a half, and therefore representative of these developing trends. As regards recent work by older more celebrated poets, featured in this volume, the reader will draw his own conclusions as to which among them have responded, and in what sense, to the new *frissons* of

* The editors' card-index files reveal that they have, between them, during a period of about two years, read over 300 volumes of poetry by 127 authors, all published since 1950.

sensibility, and which have been content to remain within their established poetic territory.

We have, in all cases, tried to represent the poets we have chosen by their most recent work; but this principle has been applied flexibly, since merit was, of course, the chief consideration within the self-imposed limits of our chosen time span. The last five years do, however, deliberately receive a fuller representation than the preceding ten.

The only other restraint on our choice has been the need to find not only poems which fitted the criteria outlined above but those which could, we judged, be adequately brought over into English. Since the aims and assumptions of modern French verse differ so radically from those pursued by British or American poets, the result must occasionally seem strange or unsatisfactory. But it is the French poet's intention which we have at all times tried to follow; and we have, wherever possible, sought the advice and respected the opinions of the poets represented here. The advantage of a bilingual presentation of poetry in translation is now generally recognized; in the present instance, it seemed more than usually essential, because of the complexity and density of many of the texts.

We hope, indeed, that our selection will be of interest to French as well as to English-speaking readers, offering, as it does, a picture of a particularly vigorous and lively phase in the long history of poetry in France.

SIMON WATSON TAYLOR
EDWARD LUCIE-SMITH
London, January 1971

34

Le poème au poète

Marc Alyn

Efface encore ! Plus loin conduis ce rythme
A capturer le nuage et le soc,
Lente est la nuit qui par tes yeux regarde.
Avec les choses, veille et te prends à leurs pièges
Comme au miroir l'oiseau des glaciers.
Epouse la page, il faut naître encore,
Jambage après jambage, mot à mot, corps à corps,
Non dans l'éclair mais dans l'ordre du songe.
Je n'existe pas où tu pèses, je suis alliance
Entre des secrets qui s'ignorent
Et des sommets d'attente.

(*Délébiles*)

The poem to the poet

Marc Alyn

Rub it all out again! Extend this rhythm
To apprehend the ploughshare and the cloud,
The night is slow that gazes through your eyes.
Keep watch with things, and fall into their snares,
Like the bird of the glaciers in the looking-glass.
Marry the paper; you must be reborn
Penstroke by penstroke, word by word, combating hand to hand,
Not in the lightning-flash, but in the dream's due course.
I don't exist where you bear down; I am what joins
Secrets that are secret even from themselves
To expectation's heights.

Trahison du fruit

Marc Alyn

Parfois, l'infini prend forme
Et s'anime au cœur d'un fruit;
Se concentrer dans l'infime
Est la ruse de l'énorme.

Par le goût (non par l'esprit),
Par la langue (non par l'âme),
L'infini peuple la pulpe
Et se mêle au périssable.

O sanglot de sucre en nous
Qu'aucun verbe ne fait naître,
A nos treilles qui te cloue,
Larron des astres, des êtres?

Le fruit préface le froid.
Nul secret ne se libère
De l'extase à son sommet
Sinon la cendre et la neige.

(*Délébiles*)

Treason of the fruit

Marc Alyn

Sometimes the Infinite takes shape
And lives within the heart of a fruit;
To concentrate within the tiny
Is the trick of the enormous.

By the taste (not by the spirit),
By the tongue (not by the soul),
The Infinite breeds in the pulp
And mingles with the perishable.

O the sob of sweetness in us,
Which no word brings to birth,
Who is it nails you to our arbours,
Thief of stars and beings?

The fruit prefaces the cold.
No secret will break loose
From ecstasy at its peak
Unless it be ash and snow.

L'homme seul

Aragon

L'homme seul est un escalier
Nulle part l'homme qui ne mène
Et lui demeurent inhumaines
Toutes les portes des palais

L'homme seul a les bras obliques
L'œil impair le souffle rayé
Il n'a qu'ailleurs pour oreiller
Son sommeil est fille publique

L'homme seul a des doigts de vent
Ce qu'on lui donne se fait cendre
Plaisir même il ne peut rien prendre
Que poussière le retrouvant

L'homme seul n'a pas de visage
Il n'est que vitre pour la pluie
Et les pleurs que l'on voit sur lui
Appartiennent au paysage

Il est une lettre égarée
Portait-il une fausse adresse
A qui disait-elle Tendresses
Quelles mains l'auraient déchiré

(from *Poètes d'aujourd'hui: Aragon*)

The man alone

Aragon

The man alone: a stair that goes
Nowhere for anyone. All the gates
Of all the palaces remain
Inhuman to his single state.

The man alone has crooked limbs,
One eye, a life which does not count;
Elsewhere is his only pillow;
His sleep a girl of easy virtue.

The man alone: fingers of air;
Whatever he's given turns to ash;
When he takes it, even pleasure
Is, so he discovers, dust.

The man alone: he has no face;
Like window glass, he takes the rain;
The tears one sees upon him are
What the countryside has wept.

He's a letter gone astray.
Did he carry a wrong address?
To whom did it say 'tenderly'?
Whose hands should have torn it open?

Neruda chante:

Le paresseux

Aragon

Continueront voyager choses
de métal entre les étoiles
des gens s'exténueront monter
pour violer la lune douce
là-bas fonder leurs pharmacies

En ce temps de vendanges pleines
le vin chez nous commence à vivre
de la mer à la Cordillère
Au Chili dansent les cerises
chantent des fillettes obscures
et dans les guitares l'eau brille

Le soleil joue á toute porte
Et fait miracles pour le blé
Le premier vin est vin rosé
Il est doux comme un enfant tendre
Le second vin est vin robuste
Comme la voix d'un marinier
Le troisième est une topaze
Incendie et coquelicot

J'ai mer et terre à la maison
Ma femme a des yeux gigantesques
Couleur des noisettes des bois
Et lorsque vient la nuit la mer
Se pare de blanc et de vert
Et puis dans l'écume la lune
Rêve en fiancée océane

Pourquoi donc changer de planète

(*Elégie à Pablo Neruda*)

Neruda sings:

The idler

Aragon

Things made of metal will go on
Travelling between the stars
Men will tire themselves to climb
And violate the gentle moon
And on it found their pharmacies

Time of the full vintages
Back home the wine begins to live
From the Andes to the sea
In Chile now the cherries dance
Humble girls are singing there
Water shines in the guitars

The sun plays round every door
Works its wonders for the wheat
The first wine is *vin rosé*
Like a tender infant sweet
The second is a robust wine
Like the voice of a mariner
And the third a topaz stone
Poppy and flame of fire

I have land and sea at home
My wife's eyes are huge, their hue
That of hazelnuts in the woods
When each nightfall comes the sea
Adorns itself in white and green
Then the moon amid the foam
Dreams it is the ocean's bride

And why therefore change one's world

L'étreinte

Aragon

L'an 1905 Pablo
          Picasso quel âge
A-t-il vingt-trois vingt
               quatre on était au printemps
Ou qui sait à l'automne Il suffit qu'ici règne
La lumière d'être jeune Une chambre pour
Les amants liés n'a besoin de rien que d'un
Lit

Il y
    avait de cela douze ans quand je vins
Boulevard Saint-Germain 202 chez Guillaume
Apollinaire On entendait au loin tousser
La Bertha

Toute chose prenait couleur de bouche close
Les étages tournaient sur moi dans l'escalier
Cela ressemblait à l'arbre de Robinson
Un œil
      brille dans l'espion de la porte
                      Et comme

Un gros oiseau vêtu d'horizon le poète
M'ouvre les pieds déchaussés là-haut dans son nid
Voilà donc l'Enchanteur Où sont les Sept Epées

Blessé à la tête trépané sous le chloroforme

Je n'ai de rien souvenir d'aucune parole
Rien que de ce cœur enfant en moi qui tremblait
J'avais une petite moustache pâle et

The embrace

Aragon

AD 1905 Pablo
                    Picasso how old
Was he then twenty-three twenty-
                              four it was spring
Or perhaps autumn What matters is that here there reigns
The light of youth A room for
Entwined lovers needs nothing but a
Bed

It was
        twelve years later that I arrived
Boulevard Saint-Germain 202 to visit Guillaume
Apollinaire From the distance came the coughing of
Big Bertha

Everything took on a tight-lipped air
The storeys spiralled about me on the staircase
It was like Robinson Crusoe's tree
An eye
        glittered in the spyhole of the door
                                        And like

A plump bird clothed in the horizon the poet
In his socks welcomed me there in his nest
So here's the Enchanter Where are the Seven Swords

Wounded in the head trepanned under chloroform

I don't remember anything not a single word
Nothing but that childish heart within me trembling
I had a little pale moustache and

Mes vingt ans qui mettaient sur tout leur doux bruit d'ailes
La patte du soleil au piège des volets
En moi le chat des vers obscurément ronronne

Je me disais Guillaume il est temps que tu viennes

Il me disait Que disait-il Et m'a conduit
En s'excusant Les Picassos sont à la cave
Excepté
           La main montre le mur où se fait

L'amour dans la pièce
                à côté

Tout le reste ô baiser baiser perpétuel
Nuit et jour jour et nuit ce long arrêt d'horloge
Et la lèvre à la lèvre et le souffle accouplé
Et la vie au-dessous Réel le lit pourtant
Bien moins réel que l'instant fixé sur la toile
N'est qu'un pléonasme à l'étreinte à la durée

La vaste vie un peu toujours le cinéma
D'alors où le piano d'un petit air pardonne
Les mots qu'on tait

De tous ses yeux la salle écoute la rengaine
Et ce bouquet des doigts pour dire Elle est jolie

Ne sommes-nous pas encore au temps du muet
Un demi-siècle après c'est la même musique
Même silence dans les squares sur les bancs

My twenty years which brushed everything with their soft
   sound of wings
The sun's paw in the shutters' trap
And within me the cat of verse obscurely purring

I said to myself Guillaume it is time you came

He said to me What did he say And showed me round
With excuses The Picassos are in the cellar
Except
         His hand indicates the wall where love

Is being made in the room
                    next door

All the rest o kiss perpetual kiss
Night and day day and night this long halt of the clock
And lip upon lip and the linked breathing
And the life beneath Real the bed yet
Much less real than the moment fixed upon the canvas
The bed is only a pleonasm to the embrace to time's continuance

Life's hugeness always a little like the cinema
Of those days where the piano with a little tune forgives
The words which are not said

The hall listens with all its eyes to the refrain
And this bouquet of fingers to say It is beautiful

Are we not still in the age of silent films
Half a century later it's still the same music
Same silence in the public gardens on the benches

Au coin des rues
Au ventre sombre des maisons
Seuls rien qu'eux seuls jamais lassés d'être enlacés
Tressaillants et pressés dans leurs bras dans leurs jambes
Les amants de 1905

Dont soit le plaisir éternel

(*from Lettres françaises*, 12 June 1968)

At the corners of the streets
                    In the dark bellies of the houses
Alone nothing but them alone never weary of their embrace
Trembling held in each other's arms and legs
                    The lovers of 1905

          May their pleasure be eternal

Quatrième

Julien Blaine

              Etoile en circuit fermé
              un courant passe par les sentiers
              mouettés, grivelés, aiglés.

Alors de ce sentier un oiseau–autre s'enfuit
autour des cables-flammes de cuivre
et l'eau trace les lèvres des barrages

                    puis
                s'écoule
          dans les ressorts de verre ...

(*W M Quinzième*)

Fourth

Julien Blaine

Star on a closed circuit
a current goes through paths
that are sea-mewed, speckled, eagled.

Then from this path an other-bird soars away
circling the copper flame-cables
and the water traces the dams' lips

before
flowing away
into the glass mainsprings. . .

Onzième

Julien Blaine

3+3
et 12+3
3+ le vent suggéré par la nuit
et le vent suggéré par la nuit+ la pluie inspirée d'une cythare,
la pluie inspirée d'une cythare+ la mouette tissée de vagues ...
Et la mouette tissée de vagues+ l'oiseau en sève de frêne???

Rappel: $3 + \text{vent} = X$
$\qquad \text{vent} + \text{pluie} = Y$
$\qquad \text{pluie} + \text{mouette} = Z$
$\qquad \text{mouette} + \text{oiseau} = ?$

(*W M Quinzième*)

Eleventh

Julien Blaine

3+3
and 12+3
3+ the wind suggested by the night
and the wind suggested by the night+ the rain inspired by a zither,
the rain inspired by a zither+ the gull woven in waves . . .
And the gull woven in waves+ the bird of ash-sap???

Memo: $3+\text{wind} = X$
     $\text{wind}+\text{rain} = Y$
     $\text{rain}+\text{gull} = Z$
     $\text{gull}+\text{bird} = ?$

Treizième

Julien Blaine

Vie à l'infini
vie glisse pour souligner une feuille blanche
vie à l'infinie des fleurs qui germent des épaules des statues
    à l'infini hérétique des oiseaux qui poussent de leur bec les
gestes des statues.

(*W M Quinzième*)

Thirteenth

Julien Blaine

Life to infinity
life skids to underline a blank leaf
life to the infinity of the flowers which sprout from the statues
   shoulders
      to the heretical infinity of the birds which with their beaks
impel the statues' gestures.

Quatorzième

Julien Blaine

      Dans un mouvement inspiré des sources de flammes
comme le fer   Dans un mouvement creusé à l'aisselle
il était   un mouvement en rouge d'automne
Pâle   comme des insectes crispés.
mâle.

Loin adossé sur les collines
il ressemblait au vol
au jeu ...

Et après ce mouvement inspiré des sources de flammes
son sang est devenu sève
et bois sa chair.

(*W M Quinzième*)

Fourteenth

Julien Blaine

      In a movement inspired by the sources of flames
such as iron   In a movement hollowed at the armpit
he was   a movement in autumn red
Pale   like curled-up insects
male.

Far off leaning back on the hills
he looked like flight
like game. . .

And after this movement inspired by the sources of flames
his blood has become sap
and wood his flesh.

Le regard

Edith Boissonnas

Du dedans je déambule et des combles
Je descends jusqu'au souterrain jadis creusé
Sous un verger et mes sentiments comblent
Comme le grain dans un grenier l'espace osé
Par le secret architecte de ma nature.
Je vois au dehors et pressens l'usure
Des collines sous la croissance des eaux.
Rien ne trouble mon bonheur mais que j'aperçoive
Me guettant depuis longtemps sans un mot
Le regard du dehors, aussitôt je m'entrave
Dans les gestes les plus courants, j'ai peur
De ma voix, j'ai honte de mon épaisseur
Le trouble passe par les fentes des portes
Mon reflet monstrueux l'escorte.

(from *Nouvelle Revue française*, no. 195, March 1969)

The look

Edith Boissonnas

From withindoors I saunter out; I go
From the attics downwards to the hollowed place
Under an orchard. My feelings fill the space
Dared by the secret architect of my nature,
As grain fills up the granary. I know
Beforehand how the growth of waters wears
Away the hills, and nothing flaws my joy
Except the way what's outside dumbly stares
Inwards at me. Each ordinary gesture
Entrammels me. My own voice wakes my fears;
My coarseness shames me. Through the cracks of doors
Misgiving comes, squired by my monstrous double.

Accalmie

Edith Boissonnas

Au creux d'une vague je me sens à l'aise
En ce moment je me laisse un peu de repos.
Je ne tourmente plus ce moi, je m'apaise
Peut-être seulement je me tourne le dos.
Il n'y a pas trois ou quatre jours, une saison
Je me pressais contre le mur toujours plus âpre.
Une mort me guettait au fil de l'abandon.
L'inextricable sentiment amer douceâtre.
Pourquoi dans une vie s'invente un double-fonds,
Deux régistres d'amour l'un grave l'autre pur.
Ne faut-il pas songer à l'étrange origine
Aux nourritures plus souples dans le futur
Et si peut-être encore un passé nous incline.

(from *Nouvelle Revue française*, no. 195, March 1969)

Becalmed

Edith Boissonnas

In the wave's hollow I am now at ease,
And, for an instant, give the self repose.
No longer troubling this, I am becalmed,
Or merely turn my back upon the 'I'.
Three or four days ago, I crushed awhile
That self against an ever rougher wall.
A death watched for me, at the letting go.
The mingled bittersweet emotion. Why
Give double footing to a single life,
Two scales for love, one burdensome, one pure?
Must not one think at the strange origin,
of easier diets in the days to come,
And if, perhaps, what's past still governs us.

Le vide

Edith Boissonnas

Je descendais, je m'accrochais à des broussailles
Cherchant quelque rocher pour assurer mes pas.
D'habitude nous avons en nous ce compas
Qui mesure vite une pente à notre taille.
On sait s'il faut continuer une voltige
Et même si le goufre est un peu en retrait.
Mais ici plusieurs fois de suite le vertige
Du vide me laissait imaginer après
La même chute encore.

(from *Nouvelle Revue française*, no. 195, March 1969)

The void

Edith Boissonnas

I gripped the brambles, and was going down,
Seeking a rock where I might safely tread.
Usually within us a compass swiftly measures
The slopes that we can manage. We can tell
If the slack-wire act is safe, if the abyss
Is somewhat further off. But fear of heights
Here time and again permits me to imagine
Hereafter the same fall.

Le dialogue d'angoisse et de désir

Yves Bonnefoy

I

J'imagine souvent, au-dessus de moi,
Un visage sacrificiel, dont les rayons
Sont comme un champ de terre labourée.
Les lèvres et les yeux sont souriants,
Le front est morne, un bruit de mer lassant et sourd.
Je lui dis: Sois ma force, et sa lumière augmente,
Il domine un pays de guerre au petit jour
Et tout un fleuve qui rassure par méandres
Cette terre saisie fertilisée.

Et je m'étonne alors qu'il ait fallu
Ce temps, et cette peine. Car les fruits
Régnaient déjà dans l'arbre. Et le soleil
Illuminait déjà le pays du soir.
Je regarde les hauts plateaux où je puis vivre,
Cette main qui retient une autre main rocheuse,
Cette respiration d'absence qui soulève
Les masses d'un labour d'automne inachevé.

II

Et je pense à Coré l'absente; qui a pris
Dans ses mains le cœur noir étincelant des fleurs
Et qui tomba, buvant le noir, l'irrévélée,
Sur le pré de lumière – et d'ombre. Je comprends
Cette faute, la mort. Asphodèles, jasmins
Sont de notre pays. Des rives d'eau
Peu profonde et limpide et verte y font frémir

The dialogue of anguish and desire

Yves Bonnefoy

I

Often I imagine, up above me,
A sacrificial face, whose rays
Are like a field of ploughed-up earth.
Its eyes and lips are smiling,
Its brow is clouded, a sea noise tiring and deep.
I say to it: Be my force, and its light increases,
It dominates a country of war at dawn
And a river which calms by meanderings
This seized and quickened earth.

And I wonder now why all this time was needed,
And all this trouble. For the fruits
Reigned already in the tree. And the sun
Lit up already the country of evening.
I see the high plateaux where I can live,
This hand which holds another hand of rock,
This respiration of absence which raises
The mass of an unfinished autumn ploughing.

II

And I think of Koré the Absent; who took
The glittering black heart of the flowers in her hands
And who, unrevealed, fell, drinking blackness,
On the meadow of light – and shadow. I understand
That sin, death. Jasmines, asphodels
Belong in our land. Shores of water
Limpid, green and not too deep make the shadow

c

L'ombre du cœur du monde … Mais oui, prends.
La faute de la fleur coupée nous est remise,
Toute l'âme se voûte autour d'un dire simple,
La grisaille se perd dans le fruit mûr.

Le fer des mots de guerre se dissipe
Dans l'heureuse matière sans retour.

III

Oui, c'est cela.
Un éblouissement dans les mots anciens.
L'étagement
De toute notre vie au loin comme une mer
Heureuse, élucidée par une arme d'eau vive.

Nous n'avons plus besoin
D'images déchirantes pour aimer.
Cet arbre nous suffit, là-bas, qui, par lumière,
Se délie de soi-même et ne sait plus
Que le nom presque dit d'un dieu presque incarné.

Et tout ce haut pays que l'Un très proche brûle,

Et ce crépi d'un mur que le temps simple touche
De ses mains sans tristesse, et qui ont mesuré.

Of the heart of the world tremble there . . . Why, yes. Take it.
The sin of the cut flower is forgiven us,
The soul is all arched round some simple words,
The grey shading is lost in the ripe fruit.

The iron of the words of war disappears
In the joyous matter of no return.

III

Yes, that is it.
A dazzle in the ancient words.
The crests
Of our whole life in the distance like a joyous
Sea, made clear by a sword of living water.

We no longer need
Agonizing images in order to love.
That tree over there suffices us, which through light,
Passes beyond itself and knows no more
Than the almost uttered name of a god almost incarnate.

And all this high country the One, rising, burns,

And this wall's rough plaster that time, simply, touches
With its hands free from sadness, that have measured.

IV

Et toi,
Et c'est là mon orgueil,
O moins à contre-jour, ô mieux aimée,
Qui ne m'es plus étrangère. Nous avons grandi, je le sais,
Dans les mêmes jardins obscurs. Nous avons bu
La même eau difficile sous les arbres.
Le même ange sévère t'a menacée.

Et nos pas sont les mêmes, se déprenant
Des ronces de l'enfance oubliable et des mêmes
Imprécations impures.

V

Imagine qu'un soir
La lumière s'attarde sur la terre,
Ouvrant ses mains d'orage et donatrices, dont
La paume est notre lieu et d'angoisse et d'espoir.
Imagine que la lumière soit victime
Pour le salut d'un lieu mortel et sous un dieu
Certes distant et noir. L'après-midi
A été pourpre et d'un trait simple. Imaginer
S'est dechiré dans le miroir, tournant vers nous
Sa face souriante d'argent clair.
Et nous avons vieilli un peu. Et le bonheur
A mûri ses fruits clairs en d'absentes ramures.
Est-ce là un pays plus proche, mon eau pure?
Ces chemins que tu vas dans d'ingrates paroles

IV

Oh you,
And this is my pride,
Who are less in your own light, Oh better-loved
And strange to me no longer. We have grown, I know,
In the same dark gardens. We have drunk
The same difficult water under the trees.
The same severe angel has menaced you.

And our steps are the same, freeing themselves
From the brambles of forgettable childhood
And from the same impure imprecations.

V

Imagine one evening
Light lingers over the land,
Opening its hands of storm that bear gifts,
Their palm our place of hope and of anguish.
Imagine that the light be sacrificed
To save a mortal place, and under a god
Far-off, no doubt, and dark. The afternoon
Has been purple and simply drawn. Imaginings
Have torn in the mirror, turning their bright
Silver smiling face towards us.
And we have grown a little older. And happiness
Has ripened its bright fruits in absent branches.
Is a nearer land there, my pure water?
These roads you go along in barren words,

Vont- ils sur une rive à jamais ta demeure
«Au loin» prendre musique, «au soir» se dénouer?

VI

O de ton aile de terre et d'ombre éveille-nous,
Ange vaste comme la terre, et porte-nous
Ici, au même endroit de la terre-mortelle,
Pour un commencement. Les fruits anciens
Soient notre faim et notre soif enfin calmées.
Le feu soit notre feu. Et l'attente se change
En ce proche destin, cette heure, ce séjour.

Le fer, blé absolu,
Ayant germé dans la jachère de nos gestes,
De nos malédictions, de nos mains pures,
Étant tombé en grains qui ont accueilli l'or
D'un temps, comme le cercle des astres proches,
Et bienveillant et nul,

Ici, où nous allons,
Où nous avons appris l'universel langage,

Ouvre-toi, parle-nous, déchire-toi,
Couronne incendiée, battement clair,
Ambre du cœur solaire.

(*Pierre écrite*)

Will they, on a shore now your home forever,
Become music 'in the distance', in the evening 'grow free'?

VI

Oh with your wing of earth and shadows wake us,
Angel vast as the earth, and bear us
Here, to the same part of the mortal earth,
For a beginning. May the ancient fruits
Be our thirst and hunger, now assuaged.
The fire be our fire. And the waiting turns
Into this imminent fate, this hour, this sojourn.

Iron, ultimate seed,
That sprang up in the fallow of our gestures,
Our curses, our pure hands,
That fell as grains which welcomed the gold
Of a time, like the circle of neighbouring stars,
Both benevolent and vain.

Here, where we are walking,
Where we learned the universal language,

Open out, speak to us, tear yourself apart,
Burning crown, luminous beating,
Amber of the sun's heart.

Art de la poésie

Yves Bonnefoy

Dragué fut le regard hors de cette nuit.
Immobilisées et séchées les mains.
On a réconcilié la fièvre. On a dit au cœur
D'être le cœur. Il y avait un démon dans ces veines
Qui s'est enfui en criant.
Il y avait dans la bouche une voix morne sanglante
Qui a été lavée et rappelée.

(*Pierre écrite*)

The art of poetry

Yves Bonnefoy

Out of that night the eyes were dredged.
The hands dried up, immobilized.
The fever has been atoned for, the heart told
To be the heart. There was a demon in those veins
Who fled weeping.
In the mouth there was a cheerless bleeding voice
Which has been bathed and summoned back to life.

Ecrit en marge du poème, *trois extraits*

Alain Bosquet

En moi, c'est la guerre civile.
Mon oranger n'aime pas mes genoux:
ma cascade se plaint de mon squelette;
je dois choisir entre mon cœur
et ma valise où ronfle une île poignardée,
mon manuel d'histoire
et ma tête remplie
de souvenirs pendus.
Verbe à muqueuses !
objet qui te voudrais humain !
En moi, c'est la guerre civile.

*

Achetez mes soupirs.
Prenez mes doutes.
Je vous donne un cornet de grimaces?
Quand j'aurai tout vendu,
j'irai renaître loin de moi,
entre une mangue fraîche,
un baiser très félin,
quelques objets sans nom.
Achetez mes espoirs.
Prenez mes certitudes.
Je vous donne un cornet de sourires?
Je suis le marchand des quatre raisons.

*

Couteau,
si par toi-même tu étais couteau,
je serais inutile
et périrais de n'avoir pas à te nommer.

Written in the poem's margin, *three extracts*

Alain Bosquet

In me, civil war.
My orange tree my knees displease;
my cascade rails against my bones;
mine between my heart to choose
and a stabbed island stertorous
in my valise, between my history book
and head crammed with throttled memories.
Mucous membraned Word!
Thing that woudst be human!
In me, civil war.

★

Fresh sighs for sale!
Prime doubts a penny!
Scowls going at a loss!
When I'm sold out I'll go
far from me and these among
be born again:
a mango warm from the bough,
a more than feline kiss,
a few objects without name.
Fresh hopes for sale!
Prime sooth a penny!
Smiles going at a loss!
Bargains, bargains, in and out of reason!

★

Knife,
unaided were you knife,
then without purpose I and soon
to perish for no need of naming you.

Couteau,
tu ne serais pas un couteau
sans mes yeux qui te lèchent,
sans ma sueur qui te couvre de rouille.
Et moi,
sans ton métal,
sans la lune qu'il griffe,
je ne serais que feuille,
écume fatiguée,
nageoire sous la porte,
quart de nèfle mordue...
Tu te sais toi par nous;
je me sais moi par moi face à toi-même.
Couteau de chair, homme d'acier:
chacun de nous survit de s'incarner dans l'autre.
Tu m'as forcé de me comprendre:
je saigne!
Tu t'es forcé d'être compris,
mais tu te brises!
O coupable recontre!
Il faut réinventer
le couteau, couteau pur,
l'homme, l'homme tout seul:
jamais ils ne se connaîtront.

★

(*Deuxième Téstament*)

Knife,
you were no knife
without my eyes to scour you,
my sweat to rust you over.
And I,
without your metal,
the moon it claws,
were but leaf,
foam that is weary,
a fin under a door,
a remnant of chewed medlar . . .
You through us know you as you,
I me as me through me before your face.
Knife of flesh, man of steel,
incarnate in each other each lives on.
Me you constrained to understand myself:
I bleed!
You to be understood yourself constrained,
and break!
Oh culpable encounter!
Knife, pure knife,
must be invented anew,
and man, sole man:
two to each other never to be known.

★

Origine

Alain Bosquet

à l'origine
il y aura trois cieux
le juste le moins juste et le frivole
à l'origine
il y aura
des soleils par douzaines
     comme des œufs dans les boutiques
     certains blancs certains noirs
     et certains habités par des vautours
à l'origine
il y aura
à chaque heure midi
à chaque heure minuit
     un équinoxe on veut dire une taupe
     et un printemps au milieu du printemps
     on veut dire une rose qui croasse
à l'origine
il y aura
un homme en cœur de ceriseir
un homme en paroles de neige
un homme en naufrage de lune
à l'origine
il y aura
le divin gaspillage

(*Quatre Téstaments*)

Beginning

Alain Bosquet

In the beginning
there'll be three heavens
the right the not-quite-right and the not-quite-serious
in the beginning
there'll be
suns by the dozen
    like eggs in shops
    some black some white
    some inhabited by vultures
in the beginning
there'll be
midday every hour
midnight every hour
    an equinox that's to say a mole
    a springtime in the midst of spring
    That's to say a rose croaking
in the beginning
there'll be
a man in heart of cherry wood
a man in words of snow
a man in moon wreck
in the beginning
there'll be
divine wastefulness

L'ami caillou

Alain Bosquet

Caillou,
au lieu de dire:
«Bonjour, caillou»,
je devrais t'admirer
si longtemps, si longtemps,
que tu acceptes
de parler à ma place.
«Bonjour, poète»,
me dirais-tu, et même
«Bonjour, caillou»,
pour me prouver
que tu n'es pas dupe des mots.
Alors, caillou moi-même,
et plus digne de toi,
j'aspirerais
à devenir un homme.
Nous serions frères,
et si jaloux
de notre nature trahie.

(*Quatre Téstaments*)

Friend stone

Alain Bosquet

Stone,
instead of saying,
'Hello, stone'
I should gaze at you admiringly
so long, so very long,
that you agree
to speak instead of me,
'Hello, poet'
is what you'd say, and even
'Hello, stone'
so as to prove to me
you're not taken in by words.
Then, a stone myself,
and worthier of you,
I'd aspire
to turn into a man.
We'd be brothers
and such jealous guardians
of our nature thus divulged.

Ajournement

André du Bouchet

J'occupe seul cette demeure
blanche

où rien ne contrarie le vent

si nous sommes ce qui a crié
et le cri

qui ouvre ce ciel
de glace

ce plafond blanc

nous nous sommes aimés sous ce plafond.

Adjournment

André du Bouchet

I am the sole occupant of this white
abode

where nothing thwarts the wind

if we are what cried out
and the cry

which opens this sky
of ice

this white ceiling

we have loved one another under this ceiling.

                        Je vois presque,
à la blancheur de l'orage, ce qui se fera sans moi.

Je ne diminue pas. Je respire au pied de la lumière aride.

                                        I can almost see,
in the storm's whiteness, what will take over without me.

        I do not dwindle. I take breath at the foot of the arid light.

S'il n'y avait pas la force
de la poussière
qui coupe jambes et bras

mais seul le blanc
qui verse

je tiendrais le ciel

profonde ornière
avec laquelle nous tournons

et qui donne contre l'air.

If there were not the power
of the dust
to paralyse arms and legs

but only the white
toppling

I would hold the sky

deep rut
with which we revolve

and which knocks against the air.

Dans cette lumière que le soleil
abandonne, toute chaleur résolue en feu, j'ai couru, cloué
à la lumière des routes, jusqu' à ce que le vent plie.

Où je déchire l'air,
                    tu as passé avec moi. Je te retrouve
dans la chaleur, Dans l'air, encore plus loin, qui s'arrache,
d'une secousse, à la chaleur.
                    La poussière illumine. La montagne,
faible lampe, apparaît.

(*Où le soleil*)

In this light which the sun
abandons, all heat resolved into fire, I have run, riveted
to the roads' light, until the wind yields.

Where I rend the air,
                    you have gone with me. I find you once more
in the heat. In the air, more distant still, which tears itself away,
with a jerk, from the heat.
                    The dust illuminates. The mountain,
faint lamp, stands out.

La lumière de la lame

André du Bouchet

Ce glacier qui grince

pour dire
la fraîcheur de la terre

sans respirer.

90

The light of the blade

André du Bouchet

This glacier which grates

to tell
the earth's freshness

without breathing.

Comme du papier, à plat sur cette terre,
ou un peu au-dessus de la terre,
comme une lame je cesse
de respirer. La nuit je me retourne, un instant, pour le dire.

A la place de l'arbre.
A la clarté des pierres.

J'ai vu, tout le long du jour,
la poutre sombre et bleue qui barre le jour se soulever
pour nous rejoindre dans la lumière immobile.

Like a piece of paper flat upon this earth,
or a little above the earth,
like a blade I cease
to breathe. At night I turn over, for a moment, to say so.

In place of the tree.
In the light of the stones.

I have seen, throughout the day,
the dark blue beam which bars the day arise
to join us in the motionless light.

Je marche dans les éclats de la poussière
qui nous réfléchit.

Dans le souffle court
et bleu
              de l'air qui claque

loin du souffle

l'air tremble et claque.

(*Où le soleil*)

I walk in the flashes of the dust
which reflects us.

In the blue
gasping
            of the wind that clatters

far from the breathing

the air trembles and clatters.

Dialogues des règnes, *extrait*

Michel Butor

*

Poussière de Saxe, pétales de dahlia, gouttes de crépuscule, cornes de chevreuil, cristal d'août, écailles de couleuvre, samedi de cuivre, terre de sommeil.

La poussière d'épines et de griffes.

Un sommeil de corne et d'écailles se répandait sur la Bavière dans le crépuscule d'émeraude, venez, belle abeille, venez enfin, dit la rose de septembre, tous les narcisses de votre enfance ont disparu depuis des mois, les tulipes aux robes de salamandres dont vous rêvez encore se sont renfermées sous la terre, tous vos lilas se sont fanés, venez, je vous attends depuis des heures, j'ai gardé pour vous seule mes plus tendres gouttes, ma centaurée d'étamines, mon pistil de lièvre, mes capillaires d'améthyste, mes resserres d'or, toute ma semaine attend en vous le messager de son dimanche, hippogriffe aux ailes de mica; si seulement vous approchiez de moi ce bourdonnement de cristal, j'enverrais à votre rencontre pour en recueillir la moindre vibration toute l'Italie de mes ombres.

La poussière d'un mardi après-midi l'été, son lait de flammes.

Ombre, nuage d'orage, déployant dans le crépuscule vos élégies, vos troupes de cerfs bramant leur Rhénanie sur des talus couverts de cumins et girolles, sur des jardins plantés d'épinards et persils, d'œillets, mufliers et crocus, vos buissons de homards aux antennes d'anthracite, vos bancs d'espadons affolés, vos flots d'étain, vos courges, vos gouttes, vos écailles de gneiss et de craie, votre septembre, vos pétales d'aubergine, vos lundis désolés d'Angleterre, pourquoi vous plaignez-vous si tristement, disait un vieux loup de la Prusse, votre exil et votre remords seraient-ils comparables aux miens, auriez-vous comme moi dévasté les forêts noires de fer et votre pelage et le cristal de vos regards dans d'interminables pèlerinages comme moi et pénitences aux pays de la brume.

The kingdoms' dialogues, *extract*

Michel Butor

★

Dust from Saxony, petals of a dahlia, drops of twilight, horns of a roe-buck, crystal of August, scales of a snake, Saturday of copper, territory of sleep.

The dust of thorns and claws.

A sleep of horn and scales spread itself over Bavaria in the emerald twilight, come, beautiful bee, come at last, says the September rose, all the daffodils of your childhood vanished months ago, the salamander-robed tulips of which you still dream have shut themselves away underground, all your lilacs have wilted, come, I have been waiting for you for hours, I have been saving for you and for you alone my tenderest dewdrops, my centaury of stamens, my hare pistil, my amethyst capillaries, my golden tool-sheds, my whole week awaits in you the messenger of its Sunday, mica-winged hippogryph; if only you would bring this crystal's buzzing closer to me I would send the whole Italy of my shadows to meet you to gather its slightest vibration.

The dust of a Tuesday afternoon in summer, its milk of flames.

Shadow, storm-cloud, displaying in the twilight your elegies, your herds of stags belling their Rhineland over slopes covered with cummins and chanterelles, over gardens planted with spinach and parsley, sweet-williams, snapdragons and crocuses, your thickets of lobsters with anthracite antennae, your shoals of frantic sword-fish, your waves of tin, your pumpkins, your dew-drops, your flakes of gneiss and chalk, your September, your aubergine petals, your dreary English Mondays, why do you complain so sadly, said an old Prussian wolf, could your exile and your remorse be comparable to mine, have you perhaps like myself devastated the black forests of France and Spain in a great adolescence of carnage? But you cannot have lost your iron teeth and your fur and the crystal of your gaze in endless pilgrimages as I have done and in penitences in the land of mist.

D

Ou bien:

Brume de feu, œil de griffon, nuit de myrtes, centaurée d'octobre, bulbe de saphir, mardi de lézards, facettes de lilas, sang de salamandre, griffe de renard, Cornouaille d'ombre.

La brume, vous ne pouvez comprendre.

L'ombre des séquoias, des eucalyptus, des araucarias, des magnolias, des catalpas, dans un jardin botanique du Yorkshire, s'allongeait, la lune étant très basse, jusqu'aux carrés de courges et d'épinards de France, aux choux du Kent, aux roses et aux lilas du Somerset; venez, bel œil de la nuit d'octobre, disait un bulbe de feu, illuminez les plus profonds recoins de cette serre que j'échauffe, pénétrez toutes ses facettes, faites glisser vos bénédictions dans les galeries de notre musée, sur nos échantillons de craie et de gneiss, sur nos minerais d'étain et de cuivre, sur nos spécimens d'Allemagne, dans les galeries de notre aquarium sur nos algues et nos méduses, lavez de votre argent le sang de nos vives couleuvres, les regards de nos cerfs, de nos chevreuils et de nos lièvres, laquez les griffes de nos renards, mais tandis que je vous supplie, en ces premiers balbutiements de mercredi, pourquoi vous plaignez-vous si tristement, lune, ah, votre plainte est devenue la mienne, et c'est de tous vos rayons que je brûle en en consumant toute la tristesse alors que le jardin entier nous remercie dans son sommeil.

Ou bien:

Sommeil de boue avec souffles d'hélium, dent de tarasque parmi les tiges de thym, lait de Provence sur des poils de renard, jeudi de gneiss orné de cerfs de novembre, nuit de murmures.

L'ombre.

Murmure de lézards, souffle de minuit sur la boue des Flandres,

Or again:

Mist of flames, gryphon's eye, night of myrtles, October centaury, sapphire corm, Tuesday of lizards, facets of lilacs, salamander blood, fox's claw, Cornwall of shadow.

The mist, you cannot understand.

The shadow of sequoias, of eucalyptuses, of monkey-puzzles, of magnolias, of catalpas, in a botanical garden in Yorkshire, lengthened, the moon being very low, at the level of the plots of pumpkins and spinach of France, the cabbages of Kent, the roses and lilacs of Somerset; come, beautiful eye of the October night, said a corm of flame, light up the deepest recesses of this glasshouse that I am turning into a hothouse, penetrate all its facets, make your blessings glide through the galleries of an art museum, over our samples of chalk and gneiss, over our tin and copper ores, over our specimens from Germany, in the galleries of our aquarium over our seaweeds and our jelly-fish, wash with your silver the blood of our mercurial snakes, the gaze of our stags, of our roe-deer and our hares, lacquer the claws of our foxes, but while I plead with you, in these first stammerings of Wednesday, why do you complain so sadly, moon, ah, your complaint has become mine too, and I burn from all your beams as I consume all their sadness while the whole garden thanks us in its sleep.

Or again:

Sleep of mud with breaths of helium, tooth of a carved monster among the stems of thyme, Provençal milk on fox's hairs, Thursdays of gneiss adorned with November stags, night of murmurs.

The shadow.

Murmur of lizards, breath of midnight on Flanders mud, stem

tige d'un œillet au milieu de dents de saphir, poils de jeunes chevreuils abreuvés du lait de novembre, granit de Bretagne dans un vendredi de poussière.

Le sommeil.

La poussière de l'Allemagne recouvrait la plaine et sa boue, venez, beau minuit de l'Alsace, dit un loup d'argent, venez me rendre enfin ma forme humaine; ce crime antérieur ignoré qui m'a valu un si affreux destin, ne pouvant subsister que par meurtres, mais ne pouvant me supprimer, dévorant, hurleur, ravisseur, frémissant d'aise quand je sentais frémir d'effroi les bergeries ou même les nurseries de l'Aquitaine, de l'Espagne, de l'Angleterre, car sous quels cieux ne m'a mené ma course errante? Dans le fond de l'Italie même je me suis plu à tacher de sangs divers le porphyre des monuments, les roses, les bois de myrtes, les plus risibles potagers de choux, de laitues, d'épinards... Ce crime, tige de mes crimes, n'est-il point assez expié? Je reviens pour vous supplier tous les samedis de décembre; quand me sera enfin rendu le lait de la tendresse, quand serai-je enfin délivré de ces dents de diamant, de ce fer en moi, de ces poils qui se décolorent, de ce goût cruel qui me tient? Venez, absolvez-moi de votre brume.

Le murmure.

Brume, boue de bore de brume, souffle de minuit dans la brume de titane, lichens de brume, méduses, diatomées d'un dimanche de brume, dents des couleuvres de la brume, tiges des lilas de la brume de décembre, lait des glaïeuls de brume, la brume de cadmium et de cuivre disait à la brume de cobalt et d'or: pourquoi vous plaignez-voux si tristement? Ah, c'est que je ressens le poignant appel d'une autre brume et que je me sens impuissante à la délivrer de son ombre.

(*Illustrations II*)

of a sweet-william in the centre of sapphire teeth, hairs of young roe-deer nourished by the milk of November, Breton granite in a Friday of dust.

Sleep.

The dust of Germany will cover the plain and its mud, come, beautiful midnight of Alsace, says a wolf made of silver, come and give back to me my human form once more; this previous crime about which I knew nothing but which condemned me to so dreadful a fate, being no longer able to survive except by murders, yet powerless to do away with myself, devouring, howling, plunderer, shivering with pleasure when I felt a shiver of fear pass through the sheep-folds or even the nurseries of Aquitania, Spain, England, for my wandering path has led me under these and so many other skies. In the depths of Italy itself I took pleasure in staining with various bloods the porphyry of monuments, the roses, the myrtle woods, the most ridiculous vegetable gardens of cabbages, lettuces, spinach. . . Has not this crime, stem of my crimes, been sufficiently expiated yet? I return to plead with you each Saturday of December; when will the milk of tenderness be yielded to me at last, when shall I at last be released from these diamond teeth, from this iron within me, from these fading hairs, from this cruel taste which has me in its grip? Come, absolve me from your mist.

The murmur.

Mist, mud of boron of mist, breath of midnight in the mist of titanium, lichens of mist, jelly-fish, diatoms of a Sunday of mist, teeth of the mist's snakes, stems of the lilacs of the December mist, milk of the mist's gladioli, the mist of cadmium and copper said to the mist of cobalt and gold: why do you complain so sadly? Ah, it is because I feel the poignant appeal of another mist and I fear I am powerless to deliver it from its shadow.

Complainte du lézard amoureux

René Char

N'égraine pas le tournesol,
Tes cyprès auraient de la peine,
Chardonneret, reprends ton vol
Et reviens à ton nid de laine.

Tu n'es pas un caillou du ciel
Pour que le vent te tienne quitte,
Oiseau rural; l'arc-en-ciel
S'unifie dans la marguerite.

L'homme fusille, cache-toi;
Le tournesol est son complice.
Seules les herbes sont pour toi,
Les herbes des champs qui se plissent.

Le serpent ne te connaît pas,
Et la sauterelle est bougonne;
La taupe, elle, n'y voit pas;
Le papillon ne hait personne.

Il est midi, chardonneret.
Le séneçon est là qui brille.
Attarde-toi, va, sans danger:
L'homme est rentré dans sa famille !

L'écho de ce pays est sûr.
J'observe, je suis bon prophète;
Je vois tout de mon petit mur,
Même tituber la chouette.

Complaint of the amorous lizard

René Char

Do not pick the seed from the sunflower,
Your cypress trees will grieve for it,
Goldfinch take flight again
Back to your nest of wool.

You are not a stone from the sky
For the wind to forgive you,
Country bird; the rainbow
Blends into the daisy.

Man has a gun, so hide;
The sunflower abets him.
Just the grasses are yours,
The field grasses, bending.

The snake does not know you,
And the grasshopper grumbles;
The mole minds her business;
The butterfly hates no one.

Goldfinch, it is noon now,
And there shines the groundsel.
Wait. Go. No danger;
The man is at home now!

The echo of this land rings out clear.
I am the observer, an excellent prophet;
I see all from my little wall,
Even the owl swaying.

Qui, mieux qu'un lézard amoureux,
Peut dire les secrets terrestres?
O léger gentil roi des cieux,
Que n'as-tu ton nid dans ma pierre!

(from *Lettres françaises*, December 1966)

Who, better than a lizard in love,
To tell earthly secrets?
O light sweet king of the skies,
Would that you nested in my stone!

Tradition du météore

René Char

Espoir que je tente
La chute me boit.

Où la prairie chante
Je suis, ne suis pas.

Les étoiles mentent
Aux cieux qui m'inventent.

Nul autre que moi
Ne passe par là,

Sauf l'oiseau de nuit
Aux ailes traçantes.

(*Dans la pluie giboyeuse*)

Tradition of the meteor

René Char

Hope that I tempt
The fall drinks me.

Where the meadow sings
I am, am not

The stars lie
To the heavens that invent me.

None other but me
Passes that way,

Save the night bird
With tracing wings.

Le ramier

René Char

Il gît, plumes contre terre et bec dans le mur.
Père et mère
Le poussèrent hors du nid quadrillé,
L'offrirent au chat de la mort.

J'ai tant haï les monstres véloces
Que de toi j'ai fait mon conscrit à l'œil nu
Jeune ramier, misérable oiseau.
Deux fois l'an nous chantons la forêt partenaire,
La herse du soleil, la tuile entretenue.

Nous ne sommes plus souffre-douleur des antipodes.
Nous rallions nos pareils
Pour éteindre la dette
D'un volet qui battait
Généreux, généreux.

(*Dans la pluie giboyeuse*)

The wood pigeon

René Char

He lies, feathers to the earth and beak against the wall.
Father and mother
Pushed him from the chequered nest,
Gave him to the cat of death.

I have so much loathed the swift monsters
That I made of you my conscript to the naked eye
Young wood-pigeon, miserable bird.
Twice a year we sing the associate forest,
The harrow of the sun, the tile kept in repair.

We are no longer scapegoats of the antipodes.
We win over our kindred
To wipe out the debt
Of a shutter beating
So generous, generous.

Prose

Michel Deguy

Tu me manques mais maintenant
Pas plus que ceux que je ne connais pas
Je les invente criblant de tes faces
La terre qui fut riche en mondes
(Quand chaque roi guidait une île
A l'estime de ses biens (cendre d'
Oiseaux, manganèse et salamandre)
Et que des naufragés fédéraient les bords)

Maintenant tu me manques mais
Comme ceux que je ne connais pas
Dont j'imagine avec ton visage l'impatience
J'ai jeté tes dents aux rêveries
Je t'ai traité par-dessus l'épaule

(Il y a des vestales qui reconduisent au Pacifique
Son eau fume C'est après le départ des fidèles
L'océan bave comme un mongol aux oreillers du lit
Charogne en boule et poils au caniveau de sel
Un éléphant blasphème Poséidon)

Tu ne me manques pas plus que ceux
Que je ne connais pas maintenant
Orphique tu l'es devenu j'ai jeté
Ton absence démembrée en plusieurs vals
Tu m'as changé en hôte je sais
Ou j'invente

(*Figurations*)

Prose

Michel Deguy

I miss you but now
No more than those I do not know
I invent them using your many faces to riddle
The earth once so rich in worlds
(When each king steered an island
Dead-reckoning his goods (ash of
Birds, manganese and salamander)
And when castaways federalized the shores)

Now I miss you but
Like those I do not know
Whose impatience I with your face imagine
I have thrown your teeth to daydreams
I have dealt with you over my shoulder

(There are vestals leading back to the Pacific
Its water smokes The faithful have departed
The ocean slavers like a mongoloid on the bed's pillows
Carrion curled up and bristling in the salt gutter
A sea-elephant blasphemes Poseidon)

I do not miss you more than those
I do not know at present
Orphic you became I have thrown
Your quartered absence into several valleys
You have changed me into a welcome host I am aware
Or I invent

L'été l'hiver la nuit la nuit

Michel Deguy

L'ÉTÉ

La terre tombe en parachute
Les deltas du sang se jettent à l'air
Auréoles éperonnent les têtes
Et les empreintes digitales de la mer sont respectées

L'HIVER

L'hiver n'intéressait personne
Les livres gonflés de défiance
Recueillent seuls *les anges de nos campagnes*
Nous lapidant le soleil affaibli
Refîmes apaisés les gestes du déluge
(charge d'enfant sur l'humérus)

LA NUIT

Né à né dans le lit
La main reconnaît la carte d'un corps
Se chiffrent en nous les ondes d'une eau vicinale
Cette boue héritée
Ce fut un seul jour par monts et vals

LA NUIT

Lumière sous l'horizon du monde voisin qui passe
Remonte vers l'actrice de nuit cernée Vega
Comme Yvette Guilbert ou les cils d'un Degas

Figurations

The summer the winter the night the night

Michel Deguy

THE SUMMER

The earth falls by parachute
The blood's deltas leap into the air
Haloes spur the heads
And the sea's fingerprints remain inviolate

THE WINTER

The winter interested no one
The books swollen with defiance
Are the only ones to receive *the herald angels*
We stoning the weakened sun
Repeated mollified the gestures of the flood
(child a charge upon the humerus)

THE NIGHT

Berthed side by side at birth
The hand recognizes the map of a body
The waves of a local water this inherited mud
Decode us
It was a single restless day up hill down dale

THE NIGHT

Brightness beneath the horizon filtering through from the
next-door world
Flows up towards the haloed night actress Vega
Like Yvette Guilbert or the eyelashes of a Degas

La soif

Jacques Dupin

J'appelle l'éboulement
(Dans sa clarté tu es nue)
Et la dislocation du livre
Parmi l'arrachement des pierres.

Je dors pour que le sang qui manque à ton supplice,
Lutte avec les aromes, les genêts, le torrent
De ma montagne ennemie.

Je marche interminablement.

Je marche pour altérer quelque chose de pur,
Cet oiseau aveugle à mon poing
Ou ce trop clair visage entrevu
A distance d'un jet de pierres.

J'écris pour enfouir mon or,
Pour fermer tes yeux.

(*L'Epervier*)

Thirst

Jacques Dupin

I call the landslide
(Its light reveals you naked)
And the book's dislocation
Among the uprooting of stones.

I sleep so that the blood your torment lacks
May battle with the fragrance, gorse and stream
Of my enemy mountain.

I walk interminably.

I walk to taint something pure,
This blind bird at my wrist
Or this pellucid face glimpsed
Just a stone's throw away.

I write to bury my gold,
To close your eyes.

Saccade

Jacques Dupin

Ta nuque, plus bas que la pierre,
Ton corps plus nu
Que cette table de granit ...

Sans le tonnerre d'un seul de tes cils,
Serais-tu devenue la même
Lisse et insaisissable ennemie
Dans la poussière de la route
Et la mémoire du glacier?

Amours anfractueuses, revenez,
Déchirez le corps clairvoyant.

(*Saccades*)

Staccato

Jacques Dupin

The nape of your neck, lower than the stone,
Your body more naked
Than this granite table . . .

Could you, without the thunder of a single eyelash,
Have become the same
Sleek and ungraspable enemy
In the dust of the roadway
And the glacier's memory?

Anfractuous loves, come back,
Rip up the clairvoyant body.

L'issue dérobée, *extrait*

Jacques Dupin

10

Le soleil le dos tourné

une ligne nous absoud

ta mort donne le signal :
l'évulsion la trajectoire
derrière une vitre sanglante,
et la grande retombée planeuse
des éclats emblématiques

débris de soleil sur le remblai

toi, cru mort, seulement dévoyé
vers une cible inverse
un chemin de ronde avec
la salive sèche du renégat

scrute ta comptabilité stellaire
elle atteint l'obscénité

The secret exit, *extract*

Jacques Dupin

10

The sun its back turned

a line absolves us

your death gives the signal:
the evulsion the trajectory
behind a pane that oozes blood,
and the great gliding fall
of emblematic fragments

sun's debris on the earth-mound

you, thought dead, simply strayed
towards an inverted target
a circular rampart-walk with
the renegade's dry saliva

scrutinize your stellar accountancy
it verges on the obscene

11

De ce qui, hors du temps, s'accumule
osselets plutôt qu'ossements
l'inscription
                    se retire
erre dans la forêt comme une bête
une borne qu'on déplace

restreinte puis scindée
par la banalité d'un mort
sans griefs
et replongée dans son identité violente
pour en ressurgir

non moins ruineuse que le texte dilacéré
du soleil

12

Qui ravaude l'aigre tranchée
manteau fendu dans sa longueur
contre l'accolade

la boue enfante un oiseau

et la conspiration de l'air maternel
bien que réprouvé, bien qu'éblouissant

dur horizon rapproché

d'un cristal intelligible
il résume le voyage

11

From what accumulates outside of time
Knucklebones rather than cemetery bones
the inscription
                         withdraws itself
roams the forest like a wild animal
a displaced boundary-mark

diminished then divided
by the banality of a death
without grievances
and plunged again into its violent identity
to rearise from it

no less ruinous than the sun's
dilacerated text

12

Which botches the acrid cutting
cloak ripped lengthwise
against the accolade

the mud begets a bird

and the maternal air's conspiracy
although outlawed, although quite dazzling

harsh horizon brought nearer

it sums up the voyage
of an intelligible crystal

la piqûre du serpent

a déposé sur nos langues
un immense oiseau entravé

13

Nos mains broyées
par les outils insaisissables

et la lumière s'éloigne de la plaie

nos mains énigmatiques
à force de froisser le plan du temple de Louqsor

qui bifurque et bourgeonne
à chaque dynastie
jusqu'à nous

le soleil

au delà
l'insoutenable

entre chaque vertèbre explosant

vivants irréductibles
— et la lumière s'éloigne de la plaie

(*L'Embrasure*)

122

the snake's bite

has deposited on our tongues
a huge trammelled bird

13

Our hands crushed
by the ungraspable tools

and the light recedes from the wound

our hands enigmatic
through dint of crumpling the plan of Luxor temple

which branches off and blossoms
from dynasty to dynasty
down to our own days

the sun

beyond
the unendurable

exploding between each vertebra

indomitable living beings
– and the light recedes from the wound

3e jour

Jean-Pierre Duprey

Dans ma tête, dans ma tête est la personne
Qui répond le plus au silence;
Les mots viennent quand elle sonne
Sans que jamais bouge la balance.

Dans mon ciel est un corbeau
Aux ailes ouvertes de chaleur,
Derrière lui l'espace d'un caveau
Ferme une porte de voleur.

Et la caverne s'agrandit
Dans mes mains d'un peu d'une mer
Qui, penchée par-dessus bord, fuit,
Fuira toujours son vaisseau de terre.

Une main de verre la rejoint,
Dans ma fenêtre, lancée au galop
De toutes les plumes de son corbeau
Noirci de tout un pouvoir de chagrin.

(*La Fin et la Manière*)

Third day

Jean-Pierre Duprey

In my head, in my head is the person
Who responds to silence most easily;
Words come when that person rings
Yet the balance is never upset.

In my sky is a raven
With heat's outstretched wings,
Behind it a cellar's space
Closes a thief's door.

And the cellar is swollen
In my hands by a small piece of a sea
Which, leaning overboard, flees,
Will always flee its earthen vessel.

A glass hand keeps it company
In my window, launched at the full speed
Of all the feathers of its raven
Blackened with a whole power of grief.

Cri

Jean-Pierre Duprey

Un cri barré de foudre en jet enlumineur,
Appel happé sur un fil d'aiguille ...
Au tranchant mouillé d'ombre,
Contre quoi s'est troquée
La tête mouillée noire,
L'oiseau de mal-passage
S'est barré les ailes en croix.

Armé de foudre sèche, un cri
Arrache la voix et crache la bouche ...
Muet, creusé de sang, taillé
En pointes vives,
La mort a desserré sa voix et morcelé
Son rire
En glaçons épousant les regards bleu-noyé.

Le glas fait pierrement au coulement du froid.

Au tranchant rouillé d'ombre,
Contre quoi s'est troquée
La tête mouillée noire,
Le cri file un ciseau de deux pointes fermées,
L'oiseau d'ombre-passage,
S'ouvrant le corps au souffle bas,
A labouré la houle sourde.

Puis
Retenu, griffé, forcé
S'est encastré aux griffes basses.

(*La Fin et la manière*)

Cry

Jean-Pierre Duprey

A cry crossed out by a bright flash of lightning,
Call trapped on a length of needle-thread. . .
With cutting-edge moist with darkness,
For which the head moist with blackness
Has swopped itself,
The bird of ill-passage
Has crossed itself out with the cross of its wings.

Armed with dry lightning, a cry
Tears out the voice spits out the mouth. . . .
Mute, furrowed with blood, sharpened
Into living points,
Death has unclenched its voice and chopped up
Its laughter
Into icicles exactly matching the saturated blue glances.

The knell becomes a stoniness to the cold's flowingness.

With cutting-edge rusty with darkness,
For which the head moist with blackness
Has swopped itself,
The cry threads a scissor of two closed points,
The bird of darkness-passage,
Opening its body to low breathing
Has grazed the muffled sea-swell.

Then
Curbed, clawed, compelled
Has embedded itself in base claws.

De derrière les loups

Jean-Pierre Duprey

Comme les loups hurlent la nuit resserre l'écrou,
La terre s'arrête de tourner
Pour que le ciel se mette debout.
Ce soir, la terre est transparente
Au soleil-deux, sang noir, vent glissant
Déployé dans le sens
Du plus profond qui s'ouvre sur lui-même
En ses tours de cent visages.

Visage de derrière les loups
Où la nuit trépasse, passe
Un bras d'épouvante.
... Lisse comme un miroir
Où l'on se glace à la vague des yeux.

Le visage de derrière les loups,
Comme un silence vient à peine de maudire,
Sa vie d'espace
Dépasse déjà la cordillère des sens.

Frappe le visage, frappe
Le visage lisse comme une glace;
Passe le couteau sur ton visage,
Prends ta vie par les deux bouts
Et fais la roue,
Fais la roue ...

(*La Fin et le manière*)

From behind the wolf-masks

Jean-Pierre Duprey

As the wolves howl the night tightens the screw-shut,
The earth stops turning
So that the sky may right itself.
This evening, the earth is transparent
To the two-sun, black blood, slippery wind,
Unfurled towards
The deepest depth which opens upon itself
In its towers of a hundred faces.

Face from behind the wolf-masks
Where the night sinks, raises
An arm of horror.
. . . Smooth as a mirror
Where one is frozen by the glassy-eyed stare.

The face from behind the wolf-masks
Has like a silence just pronounced a curse,
Its spatial life
Has already overtaken the senses' cordillera.

Strike the face, strike
The face smooth as a looking-glass;
Pass the knife across your face,
Take your life by both its ends
And strut around,
Strut around. . .

E

La tour

Pierre Emmanuel

Le son se meurt. Passé le plus haut des nuages
Nulle buée n'atteint le silence. La Tour
N'est plus qu'esprit. L'air et les pierres se pénètrent,
Toute matière a disparu. Mais tout se tait.

Des hommes prisonniers de leur raison de verre
Travaillent sans se voir ni s'entendre, ajustés
Par l'aveugle folie d'une pensée trop claire:
Et quand l'excès de sa clarté dissout la Tour
Ils restent suspendus, à quoi? Mais ces fébriles
N'en poursuivent pas moins leur rêve machinal.

O conscience par saccades, ô grenouille
Triste à mourir dans ton bocal où manque l'eau,
Tu ne sais pas que tu es triste! Sais-tu même
Qu'il fut jadis des hommes libres et foulant
Avec des enjambées à rendre fous les arbres,
Le sol, le sol puissant qui vous monte au poitrail
Et vous assaille d'herbe humide, vous inonde
D'immensité vague après vague contre vous?

Tu sais tout, l'œil vissé à l'apparence. Il vente
Des forêts, des moissons autour de soi. Tu sais
Tout? Ce courroux splendide au large de l'histoire,
Qui va creuser la Terre au-dessous de Babel,
Cette force qu'un seul brin d'herbe contient toute
Et que la mer ne suffit pas à contenir,
Tu l'oublies donc, ô rachitique? Le mystère
Va se venger non point d'en-haut, car l'Éternel
Se fie au cours parfait des fatales étoiles,

The tower

Pierre Emmanuel

The sound dies away. Silence rises above the tallest cloud
So that no wisp reaches it. The Tower
Is solely spirit now. Air and stones intermingle,
All matter dissipated. But all is hushed.

Men, prisoners of glassy reason,
Labour without seeing or hearing each other, tuned
To the blind folly of too lucid thought:
And when its too great lucidity dissolves the Tower
They remain suspended, from what? But their feverish souls
Still pursue doggedly their mechanical dreams.

Fitful awareness, you are a frog
So sad in your waterless jar that you could die
Yet unaware that you are sad! Do you even know
That in times past there were free men who walked
With so huge a stride that the trees shook, trampling
The same ground which rises inexorably up to your waist,
Besetting you with humid vegetation, drowning you
With vastness wave after wave beating against you?

You know everything, eye glued to appearances. Forests,
Harvests are blowing around our ears. You know
Everything? Have you forgotten, rickety creature,
The splendid wrath abroad in history
That will hollow out the Earth beneath Babel,
The force encompassed in a single blade of grass
Yet which the vastest ocean could not hold? Mystery
Will avenge itself. But not from on high, for the Eternal
Commands the fateful stars' predestined course.

Mais du fond du chaos enseveli, du noir
Besoin d'amour de la matière. Rien ne bouge
Encore: mais les eaux se ramassent. J'ai peur.

(*Babel*)

Rather, from the depths of buried chaos, from matter's
Black need for love. Nothing is moving
Yet: but the waters gather. I am afraid.

Le vent

Pierre Emmanuel

Laisse aller la parole
Avec le vent
Ne souffle pas dans le vent
Ce n'est pas toi qui le portes
Il vient de plus loin que toi
Le temps qu'il frôle ton épaule
Il est déjà loin de toi

Ce n'est pas toi qui plantes la graine
— La planterais-tu dans la mer?
La planterais-tu dans le nuage?
La planterais-tu dans le vent?
Ne dis pas: «Je te parle, écoute»
Cet autre n'est pas ton champ
Le vent laboure où il veut
Peut-être en l'autre
Peut-être en toi
Ni toi ni l'autre ne savez
Qui parle qui écoute l'autre

Seul circule entre vous le vent

(*Visage nuage*)

The wind

Pierre Emmanuel

Let the word float
With the wind
Don't breathe a word into it
It isn't you bears the wind aloft
It has come a longer way than you
By the time it has caressed your shoulder
It is already far ahead

It isn't you who plants the seed
– Would you plant it in the sea?
Would you plant it in the cloud?
Would you plant it in the wind?
Don't say: 'I am speaking to you, listen'
This other is not your field
The wind tills and reaps where it wishes
Perhaps within the other
Perhaps within you
Neither you nor the other knows
Who speaks who listens to the other

Only the wind moves between you both

Prière athée

Pierre Emmanuel

Mes yeux mes mains c'est là tout mon royaume
Mes yeux ma bouche et le creux de mes mains
J'y vois la nuit Le jour m'est un fantôme
Je parle au vent Je me tais chez les miens
Moi qui pourrais boire un ciel dans ma paume
Ce n'est que lie en moi que je retiens

Je ne sais plus crisper les doigts sur rien
Mes yeux ouverts ont brûlé leurs paupières
Ce qui me fuit est mon unique bien
Déjà perdu quand je m'y désaltère
Ma langue est sèche et je l'humecte en vain
A peine dit le mot fond en lumière

Que suis-je donc L'oblat d'une misère
Que l'être affame en lui donnant le sein
Je meurs sans cesse aux choses que j'espère
Mais cette mort de mourir me retient
O mon énigme O néant qui m'éclaires
C'est être Dieu qu'être pauvre à ce point

(*Evangéliaire*)

Atheist prayer

Pierre Emmanuel

My eyes my hands these are my whole kingdom
In my eyes my mouth and the hollow of my hands
I see the night The day is ghostlike to me
I talk to empty space keep silent among my fellows
I who could gulp a heaven from my palm
Can keep down nothing but dregs

I no longer know how to grip hold of nothingness
My open eyes have burned away their lids
What flees me is my one and only good
Already lost to me as I slake my thirst with it
My tongue is dry and I moisten it in vain
Scarcely uttered the word dissolves into light

What am I then An affliction's lay brother
Starved by the very being who proffers her breast
I die each time I lose the thing I yearn for
But this repeated death prevents me from dying
O my enigma O nothingness which lights me
To be so very poor is to be God

Le change, *extrait*

Jean Pierre Faye

15   15

ce qui compte se dessine
au plus vite, ce qui dès
maintenant se conte
ici : : au travers du
carré des quatre verres, et du haut
de qui voit, cela prend
tout autour : : ce que les
sons redonnent en l'effaçant
métal, bête, insecte
produits par le son, et rendus
ici : : fichés par le son, ou
piqués sur le noir de nuit
bêtes piquées sur la nuit par le son
seul entendu sur le fond du noir
plantées ou bougeant dans la chaleur
              et qui se comptent
par le son, dans le noir se content par
noms et par mains, s'agrafent
au son de métal, se griffent
au plus chaud du noir
ici : la bête : : le son : là

le sait
qui descend du carré
des verres, pour voir

The change, *extract*

Jean Pierre Faye

15   15

what counts traces itself
speedily, what from
now on is related
here : : through the
square of the four glass panes, and from the height
of whoever sees, this catches on
all round : : what the
sounds re-echo in erasing it
metal, animal, insect
produced by the sound, and rendered
here : : fixed by the sound, or
stitched to the blackness of night
animals stitched to the night by the sound
heard only against the black depth
transfixed or stirring in the heat
        and which are counted
by sound, in the blackness are related by
names and by hands, cling
to the sound of metal, fasten their claws
round the hottest of the blackness
here : the animal : : the sound : there

aware of it
whoever descends from the square
of the glass panes, to see

                    car juste
              ici : cela
          commence à se
        voir et se savoir
      se déplaçant et bougeant, à
    rebours, en faisant se retour-
  ner qui entend, et qui
dessine en tendant

là : écoutant et
ici : agrafant ou
gravant, sur-
plomb, sur l'
à pic

18   18

même lorsque l'air jette
sur la figure toute la surface
et même blanchie, chaux et lave
mouches contre cryptoméria, ou même
quand la figure de façon
brusque s'enchevêtre sur
le froid, le plus blanc

for just
here : this
begins to see
itself and to know itself
to be shifting and stirring, in
reverse, forcing an about-
turn on whoever hears, and whoever
traces while tending

there : listening and
here : clawing or
engraving, over–
hang, over the sheer preci-
pice

even when the air blasts
on to the figure the whole surface
and even whitewashed, lime and lava
winged insects against cryptomeria, or even
when the figure abruptly
trips up over
the cold, the whitest

19   19

et si bouge un peu la figure, poulpe ou lave
et noirceur du sable,   cela va se mettre
à conter, cela va   même commencer
à cela va se   mettre à compter
non sans le   sang, non sans
tourner les   rochers ou
crever la   boue ici
                    là bouge
                l'eau chaude
            et sonore, la percée
        non sans histoire et non
    sans chaleur et encore sans
    nom, mais non sans histoire et sang
mais non   sans   encore

20   20

bougeant le sillage de
cri, et vol, sur la mousse noire et le jaune
et le cercle d'eau sur
le fond éteint, ceint de terre, elle-
même ceinte de mer, et
d'être venu jusqu'ici l'on
commence déjà ne serait-ce qu'en
dessinant sur la mer
et déjà contre le fond
maintenant plan, et l'eau
sans bord, la surface tracée pour

142

19

19

and if the figure, octopus or lava stirs slightly
and the sand's sable blackness,   this will start
to relate, this will   even begin
to, this will   start to count
not without the   blood, not without
turning over the   rocks or
bursting the   mud here
               there stirs
            the water hot
         and resonant, the opening
       not without history and not
      without heat and still without
   name, but not without history and blood
but not   without   still

20

20

stirring the wake of
cry, and flight, on the black foam and the yellowness
and the circle of water against
the dim depths, circled with earth, it-
self circled with sea, and
to have come as far as this, already
a beginning has been made if only by
tracing on the sea
and already against the depths
now flat, and the rimless
water, the surface outlined to

effacer, en l'écoutant au ras
ou bien se levant et par la seule
montée, pinçant le cercle entre les masses
et nouant les volumes par dessus, voyant
que les dessins changent

du plus haut, l'on a
la prise, sur l'agrafe
qui tient la mer, là-
dessus, et cerclant

inscrivant les arcs de
bois, en tonneau, arquant
les lignes de bois, les entrant
dans le cercle, et le trait

et cela ne cesse
plus de tirer, sur
ce qui s'égratigne ou écorche
en gravant, ce qui par

en haut commence à battre
les figures, pierre rouge sur le jaune
et pierre grattée pierre ponce
pointe : ici : : la bête : là

erase, listening to it at its level
or else getting up and by the single
step upwards, gripping the circle between the masses
and knitting the volumes from above, seeing
that the patterns change

from highest up, one has
control over the clasp
that holds the sea, on
top of it, and circling

inscribing the arched
bows, barrelled, arching
the wooden lines, inserting them
into the circle, and the arrow-line

which never stops now
stretching and letting fly, upon
whatever scratches itself or rasps
while engraving, whatever from

above begins to beat
the figures, red stone on the yellow
and scraped stone pumice-stone
point : here : : the animal : there

or vin et feu, ou   n'importe quelle
    tout autre rouge   forme commence
       vivace, renversé   en enfant, n'importe
          n'importe où par   quelle fissure ou
              saccade et   femme va
                 chassant la mer
              et nageant   du plus haut des
           au profond des   points et voyant
       écarts et plongeant à   l'écaille des bords
    l'écart en comptant   coupante à plat ou
  sur l'offre de   vertement lisse et
 l'eau et, non   herbeuse à conte
sans histoire ou   perdu, à perte de
sang   navire, à vue

(from *Change*, no. 1, November 1968)

gold, wine and fire, or
any other lively
red, upset
no matter where by
fits and starts and
chasing the sea
and swimming
in the depths of gaping
distances and diving at a
distance while counting
on the offer of
the water and, not
without history or
blood

no matter what
shape begins
a child, no matter
what cleft of
woman goes

from the highest of the
points and seeing
the rim's cutting
scale flat or
sharp-lined smooth and
grassy its tale
vanishing, out of
ship, of sight

Le cri

Jean Follain

Dans la cité fortifiée
des quartiers s'abîment
un homme s'arrête étonné
d'une voix qui mue
une à une à l'asile
il faut laver les folles
une restant belle s'y prête
malgré des larmes silencieuses.
Des chiens s'acharnent
autour d'os à lambeaux
quelqu'un vainement crie: assez.

(D'après tout)

The cry

Jean Follain

In the fortified city
whole districts crumble
a man stops astonished
by the sound of a voice breaking
one by one at the madhouse
the madwomen must be washed
one of them still lovely agrees to do it
despite silent tears.
Dogs wax furious
around scraps of bone
someone vainly shouts: enough.

Symboles du temps

Jean Follain

En cet univers de fuite, ils vont
hommes et femmes cheveux dans le vent
un seul reste à chanter
sous le porche d'église
on voit sur l'étendue
l'emplacement des fiefs
et restées sur la table
les cuillers d'étain
des gouttes d'eau suintent.
Les croix de pierre
de bois ou feuillage
demeurent : symboles du temps.

(D'après tout)

Symbols of time

Jean Follain

In this world of flight, they go
men and women hair streaming in the wind
one alone remains to sing
under the church porch
the wide plain shows
the sites of all the fiefs
and there still on the table
the tin spoons
ooze waterdrops.
The crosses made of stone
of wood or greenery
remain: symbols of time.

Art de la guerre

Jean Follain

A la fenêtre une rose a les couleurs
d'un jeune mamelon de blonde
une taupe marche sous terre.
Paix dit-on au chien
à l'existence brève.
L'air reste ensoleillé.
De jeunes hommes
apprennent á faire la guerre
pour racheter leur dit-on tout un monde
mais le livre de la théorie
leur reste illisible.

(D'après tout)

Art of war

Jean Follain

At the window a rose has the hues
of a blonde's young nipple
a mole slow-marches underground.
Leave us in peace! people say to the dog
whose days are numbered.
There is still sunshine in the air.
Young men
learn to make war
to save so they're told a whole world
but the drill-book's instructions
will never make sense to them.

Dans les lointains parages

André Frénaud

Dans les lointains parages
vers lesquels j'avançais
peut-être m'écartant
gardé en un pays
où rien ne me concerne

Montant et remontant
l'environ l'épaisseur
sans poids non sans feintise
quelque éclat pour me plaire
et m'aider à durer

Cerné m'exténuant
l'interminable haleine
marche à marche après moi
comme une bête obscure

Pas à pas des figures
disparues aux lanternes
les apprêts se déroulent
d'une fête advenue

Et toujours je me leurre
Et toujours le froid pier
Par qui est interdit
le chemin désigné

Dans la foule éclatante
les sourires déserts
Dans ma bouche du sable
Le temps ferme ses trappes
Dans l'âtre un oiseau blanc
les yeux gros se renverse

In the distances

André Frénaud

In the distances
that were my destination
straying perhaps
detained in a country
where nothing affects me

Ascending and reascending
the outskirt, the thickness
weightless not deceitless
some radiance to please me
and help me endure

Hemmed in exhausting myself
the interminable breath
tread by tread following me
like a shadowy creature

Step by step forms
swallowed up by the lanterns
the preparations are under way
for some festival already celebrated

And always I delude myself
And always the bitterest cold.
By whom is the appointed
path forbidden?

In the brilliant crowd
the smiles that are deserts
Sand closes my mouth
Time shuts its trapdoors
On the hearth a white bird
glaring stretches out

Égaré qui m'entête
allant et revenant
vers les lointains parages
où je vais accéder
quand tout sera obscur.

19–20 juin 1959

(*Il n'y a pas de paradis*)

Lost but stubbornly
going and returning
towards the distances
which I shall reach
when all is dark.

Prise à partie

André Frénaud

Porc, que fais-tu?
Je m'essuie à ma bauge.

Porc, que fais-tu?
Je rêve aux dieux qui m'aiment.

Porc, ne mens pas.
Hé! Je pense à la truie.

Porc, dis encore.
Je veux mourir ailleurs

Porc, tu te moques.
Hélas, je plaisantais.

Porc, c'est assez. Avoue.
Je manque d'un je ne sais quoi, j'avale.

25 septembre 1963

(*La Sainte Face*)

Indictment

André Frénaud

What are you up to, pig?
Scraping myself in my sty.

What are you up to, pig?
Dreaming of the gods who love me.

Don't lie, pig.
Well – thinking of the sow.

Go on, pig.
I want to die elsewhere.

You're poking fun, pig.
Joking, I'm afraid.

Enough, pig. Own up.
Something is lacking in me, I gobble.

Linge propre ou l'héritier

André Frénaud

Prendras-tu la canne du mort
pour te rendre aux obsèques?

Mettras-tu le linge du mort
pour aller au plaisir?

Oui, c'est moi désormais
le défunt, justement.

25 février 1965

(*La Sainte Face*)

Clean linen or the heir

André Frenaud

Will you take the dead man's stick
to go to the funeral?

Will you wear the dead man's linen
to go and have fun?

Yes, that's just it –
from now on I'm the deceased

Jours hirsutes, temps incertains, moments furtifs . . .

Jean Grosjean

Jours hirsutes, temps incertains, moments furtifs,
c'en est fini des hasards, voici votre maître.
L'amour déploie tous ses mois de septembre à juin
sur de vastes déclivités catalauniques.

C'en est fini du blasphème quand les saisons
se rangent en bataille à travers l'étendue.
Aux armes, boues de novembre et pommiers en fleur.
Hirondelles des deux équinoxes, cernez
l'été rétif dans son fort qui se démantèle.

Chargez, vents grêleux de ventôse et pluies d'automne,
pluies lorraines cuirassées de flambants feuillages
sur vos lourds chevaux ombrageux comme ces filles
qui font courir leur bétail à travers la rue
avec de la paille aux cheveux et des cris rauques.

A mort l'été ! Nous tenons la neige en réserve
pour enfouir le corps du vaincu quand les frimas
l'auront étranglé dans sa geôle. A mort l'été !

L'amour accueille au seuil d'un hameau sa victoire.
Il ne dit rien, il la prend dans ses bras, il rit.
Alors devant lui passe, ardente et lente et sombre,
sa garde, les nues austères de février
dont on voit luire les pertuisanes d'averse
contre les toits et sur les bourbiers des chemins.

(*Hiver*, V.)

162

Unkempt days, uncertain weather, furtive moments . . .

Jean Grosjean

Unkempt days, uncertain weather, furtive moments,
what's chancy is done with, here comes your master.
Love deploys all its months from September to June
upon vast Catalaunian slopes.

Blasphemy's done with when the seasons
range themselves for battle along the whole front.
To arms, November mud, apple trees in bloom.
Swallows of the two equinoxes, encircle
stubborn Summer in his crumbling fortress.

Charge, hailstorm winds of March and autumn downpours,
downpours of Lorraine armoured in flaming leafage
on your heavy horses, skittish as those girls
who drive their cattle through the street
with straws in their hair and raucous outcries.

Death to summer! we will keep the snow in reserve
to bury the corpse of the vanquished when the hoar-frosts
have strangled him in his prison. Death to summer!

Love welcomes his victory at the entry to a hamlet.
He says nothing, he takes her in his arms, he is laughing.
Then there passes before him, ardent and slow and sombre,
his guard, the austere clouds of February
whose halberds of rain are seen shining
against the roofs and upon the mire of the roads.

Je ne suis plus qu'avec toi depuis si longtemps . . .

Jean Grosjean

Je ne suis plus qu'avec toi depuis si longtemps.
Les basses forêts de l'hiver sur l'horizon
assiègent depuis si longtemps notre royaume.

Tes regards sont les matins fragiles du ciel.
Ton geste a la gravité du nuage errant.
Si tu rêves le jour s'arrête sur les flaques.
Une ombre s'assied près de nous si tu t'endors.

Plus en fruit, pas de fleurs encore, aucun tapage,
aucun feuillage à part d'erratiques genièvres,
point de passant sinon la corneille ou la pie
ou l'heure avec son pas tranquille à travers champ.

Les dieux? quels dieux? à moins de ton rire insolite
à la croisée des chemins vicinaux, ton rire
avec pour temple un silence énorme au-dessus.

(*Hiver*, VI)

For so long now I have been with you alone . . .

Jean Grosjean

For so long now I have been with you alone.
The low woods of the winter upon the horizon
have so long put our kingdom under siege.

Your glances are the frail mornings of the heavens.
Your gesture is as grave as a wandering cloud.
If you dream the day hovers over the puddles.
A shadow sits down by us if you fall asleep.

No more fruit, no flowers left, no noise,
no leaves apart from erratic junipers,
no passers-by save the crow or the magpie
or the hour patiently plodding across the fields.

The gods? what gods? save your strange laughter
at the crossing of the by-roads, your laughter
with, for its temple, an enormous silence above.

Paliers

Guillevic

Alors il y avait la convergence
De la mésange et du beau temps.

L'air vers le soir
Prenait le frais.

Ses regards avaient des pouvoirs
Sur les chemins, les interdits.

Même chercher au-delà d'elle
C'était aller selon sa loi,

La promener
Dans son royaume.

★

Nuages, feuillages,
Bouts de cailloux, bouts de brindilles,

Cheminées, graminées,
Le vent, le temps, et quoi?

De ce qui passe,
De ce qui reste
Dessus, dessous,

De ce qui vient,
Qui ne vient pas,
Ne viendra pas,

Fleurs de granit,
Œil de zénith,

Levels

Guillevic

Then there converged
The tomtit and the fine weather.

The air enjoyed
The cool of the evening.

The bird's glances carried powers
Over paths, over prohibitions.

Even to seek beyond it
Was to follow its law,

To show it around
Its own kingdom.

*

Clouds, foliage
Bits of pebbles, bits of twigs,

Chimney-stalks and grass-stalks,
The wind, the weather, and what else?

From what slips by,
From what remains,
Above, below,

From what arrives,
Does not arrive,
Will not arrive,

Flowers of granite,
Eye of the zenith,

Eau mal tendue,
Herbe dodue.

Je suis présent, je vous attends.
Je n'ai pas mal.

★

J'ai entendu:
Je crois que c'était un oiseau
Et qu'il chantait.

J'ai entendu:
Bien sûr qu'il chantait,
Que je passais par là.

Je crois qu'il savait
Que j'allais passer.

C'était admis par les halliers,
Par tous les champs,
Par les chemins, le bas du ciel.

Je savais que j'étais un peu
De tout cela, de la confiance
Que tout cela se donne
En de tels jours.

Et l'oiseau,
Est-ce que ce n'était pas
Mon pareil, mon écho, mon autre,
Peut-être moi tout simplement?

Unkempt water,
Plump grass.

I am here, I await you.
I am all right.

★

I heard:
I think it was a bird
And that it was singing.

I heard:
Of course it was singing,
As I went by.

I think it knew
I was going to pass by.

The thickets admitted it,
And all the fields,
The paths, the skyline.

I knew I had a small share
In all these things, in the confidence
That all these things inspire
On days like this.

As for the bird,
Was it not
My equal, my echo, my other,
Perhaps simply myself?

Ce qui de moi n'est plus à moi,
Qui s'est donné?

★

Dans tout cet arbre
Il n'y a pas de feuille

Qui serait de toi plus parente
Qu'une autre feuille.

Toutes sont feuilles,
Vivent l'air, la terre et la forme.

Toutes vivront
Ce que tu peux leur apporter.

★

Ce n'est pas moi
Qui creuse l'eau de la fontaine
Ou qui lui donne plénitude.

Je suis près d'elle,
Rien que près d'elle.
Je veux y boire.
Je voudrais plus.

Etre le soir qu'elle sera,
Son épaisseur,
Tout son silence.
Plus que cela.

170

Something of me which is no longer mine,
Which has given itself elsewhere?

★

In this whole tree
There is not a single leaf

Which would be more akin to you
Than any other leaf.

They are all leaves,
Consummating air, earth and form.

All will consummate
What you can bring them.

★

It is not I
Who digs down for the fountain's water
Or makes it abundant.

I am close to the fountain,
Not so very close.
I want to drink from it.
Or perhaps not.

To be the evening that it will become,
Its depth,
Its whole silence.
More than that.

171

Je voudrais te dormir,
A toi-même t'offrir
Quand la nuit sera noire,

Te redonner à toi
Quand viendront les regards
Qui croient avoir des droits.

★

Assis dans la barque,
J'ai plongé mes mains dans les eaux du lac.

Je voyais mes mains,
Tu n'étais pas là.

Je n'avançais pas,
Tu n'étais pas lá.

★

Sur les paliers du vent,
Se rire du dernier
Que l'on vient de quitter
Pour plus de ciel offert.

★

Il y avait de la lumière dans cette nuit,
Si c'était la nuit.

C'était peut-être le jour, et la lumière
Etait celle du soleil.

Ou bien la lumière
Venait d'ailleurs,
Du ciel ou d'un coin de la terre.

172

I would like to put you to sleep,
Offer you to yourself
When the night is pitch-black,

Give you back to yourself
When the glances arrive
Thinking they have rights.

★

So sitting in the boat
I plunged my hands into the lake's waters.

I saw my hands,
You were not there.

I stayed where I was,
You were not there.

★

       At the wind's levels,
       To mock the summit
       From which one has just stepped
       To attain the generous sky.

★

There was light abroad in this night,
If it was the night.

Perhaps it was the day, and the light
Was that of the sun.

Or maybe the light
Came from elsewhere,
From the sky or some corner of the earth.

Peut-être même
De quelqu'un qui serait moi.

★

    Par la rose trémière
    Que le vent a couchée

    Et dont le rose blanc
    Invoque ce qui passe,

    Par la rose trémière
    Qui demeure debout

    Et tend contre le jour
    Du rouge mal reçu,

    Avance encore un peu.

★

Je maugréais la plaine,
Le nuage et le ciel,

Ce qui laisse voir
Du passage du vent,

Tant de choses montrées
Que j'approchais de moi.

Qu'est-ce que je profère
Lorsque tout veut se taire?

Qu'est-ce qui se profère
Alors que je me tais?

★

Perhaps even
From someone who turned out to be myself.

★

   By the hollyhock
   That the wind has bent over

   And whose white bloom
   Conjures the moment

   By the hollyhock
   That remains upright

   And confronts the day
   With unwanted red,

   Come a little closer.

★

I cursed the plain,
The cloud and the sky,

The glimpse that let me see
The way the wind went,

So many things on show
Which I drew towards me.

What word do I utter
When all is vowed to silence?

What word is uttered
While I keep silence?

★

L'oiseau vient, on dirait,
En survolant la grange,
De franchir quelque chose

Qui pourrait être une frontière,
Un règlement.

De sortir d'un espace
Où crier se condamne.

Il reste oiseau.
Il vient vers toi.

★

On entre dans des chambres. C'est facile.
Chacun le fait.

Dans des cours, dans un lit,
Dans un bois, dans la grange.

Il suffit de venir d'un endroit plus ouvert,
D'avancer, de pousser
La porte quelquefois, de se glisser.

Mais entrer dans l'espace ouvert
Quand il fait clair

Et se sentir enveloppé par un volume
Qui n'est pas dit.

(from *Nouvelle Revue française*, no. 166, October 1966)

It would seem that the bird,
In flying over the barn,
Has broken through something

That might be a frontier,
A regulation.

To emerge from a space
Where weeping condemns itself.

It remains a bird,
It is coming towards you.

*

One enters rooms. It's easy,
Everyone does it.

Enters courtyards, a bed,
Enters a wood, a barn.

It is enough to come from somewhere more open,
To step forward, to push
The door sometimes, to slip through.

But to enter the open space
When it is broad daylight

And to feel oneself enveloped by a volume
Which is unspoken.

Dans un tourbillon de neige

Philippe Jaccottet

Ils chevauchent encore dans les espaces glacés,
les quelques cavaliers que la mort n'a pas pu lasser.

Ils allument des feux dans la neige de loin en loin,
à chaque coup de vent il en flambe au moins un de moins.

Ils sont incroyablement petits, sombres, pressés,
devant l'immense, blanc et lent malheur à terrasser.

Certes, ils n'amassent plus dans leurs greniers ni or ni foin,
mais y cachent l'espoir fourbi avec le plus grand soin.

Ils courent les chemins par le pesant monstre effacés,
peut-être se font-ils si petits pour le mieux chasser?

Finalement, c'est bien toujours avec le même poing
qu'on se défend contre le souffle de l'immonde groin.

(*L'Ignorant*)

In a snow storm

Philippe Jaccottet

They still ride through the frozen spaces,
Death could not tire them, these few on horses.

They light fires in the snow far apart,
at each gust of wind at least one flickers out.

They're incredibly little, sombre and harassed,
facing the huge, white, gradual misery to be crushed.

Of course they've no gold and no hay in their store,
but hide there the hope that's polished with such care.

They travel paths worn smooth by the monster's plodding paws,
perhaps they've made themselves so tiny the better to give chase?

In the end it's always with the same fist
that we ward off the breath of the foul beast.

Tout fleur n'est que de la nuit …

Philippe Jaccottet

Toute fleur n'est que de la nuit
qui feint de s'être rapprochée

Mais là d'où son parfum s'élève
je ne puis espérer entrer
c'est pourquoi tant il me trouble
et me fait si longtemps veiller
devant cette porte fermée

Toute couleur, toute vie
naît d'où le regard s'arrête

Ce monde n'est que la crête
d'un invisible incendie

(*Airs*)

Each flower is just a little night . . .

Philippe Jaccottet

Each flower is just a little night
pretending to have drawn near.

But whence its perfume rises
I cannot hope to enter
good reason why it stirs me
and makes me watch so long
in front of that shut door

Each colour and all life
is born where the glance halts

This world is just the crest
of an invisible fire

Dans l'herbe à l'hiver survivant...

Philippe Jaccottet

Dans l'herbe à l'hiver survivant
ces ombres moins pesantes qu'elle,
des timides bois patients
sont la discrète, la fidèle,

l'encore imperceptible mort

Toujours dans le jour tournant
ce vol autour de nos corps
Toujours dans le champ du jour
ces tombes d'ardoise bleue.

(*Airs*)

In the grass that's survived the winter . . .

Philippe Jaccottet

In the grass that's survived the winter,
these shadows, lighter than it is,
of woods, timid, patient;
they are the discreet, the faithful,

the as yet imperceptible death

Always in the day whose flight
circles our bodies
Always in the day's field
these tombs of blue slate.

Sur les pas de la lune

Philippe Jaccottet

M'étant penché en cette nuit à la fenêtre,
je vis que le monde était devenu léger
et qu'il n'y avait plus d'obstacles. Tout ce qui
nous retient dans le jour semblait plutôt devoir
me porter maintenant d'une ouverture à l'autre
à l'intérieur d'une demeure d'eau vers quelque chose
de très faible et de très lumineux comme l'herbe:
j'allais entrer dans l'herbe sans aucune peur,
j'allais rendre grâce à la fraîcheur de la terre,
sur les pas de la lune je dis oui et je m'en fus...

(*Airs*)

In the steps of the moon

Philippe Jaccottet

Tonight, leaning at the window,
I saw that the world was weightless,
and its obstacles were gone.
All that holds us back in the daytime
seemed bound to carry me now
from one opening to the other,
from within a house of water
towards something weak and bright
as the grass I was about to enter,
fearless, giving thanks for earth's freshness,
in the steps of the moon I said
yes and then off I went. . .

Adrianopol, *extrait*

Alain Jouffroy

Tu as entendu demain
          J'ai entendu demain
                    Avoir entendu demain

Mais par-dessus tout Adriana a un coeur, un coeur en puits à
pétrole au bout de la grande plaine où l'on roule en silence, en
silence pendant des heures où l'on ne voit que poteaux poteaux
poteaux poteaux poteaux poteaux poteaux poteaux poteaux
terre terre terre terre terre terre terre terre terre terre.

```
t  |           ABC
é  |        DEF
l  |     GHI
é  |   JK      cadran
p  |   LMN
h  |       OPQ
o  |          RST
ne+fil
```
                    : avoir attendu la main de quelqu'un

Mais par-dessus tout Adriana a un coeur, un coeur en forme de
téléphone en forme de fil de téléphone en forme de cadran de
téléphone en forme de cabine de téléphone:
                                        pare-chocs.

                    ✶

Adrianopolis, *extract*

Alain Jouffroy

You have heard tomorrow
>   *I have heard tomorrow*
>   *To have heard tomorrow*

But above all Adriana has a heart, a heart of petroleum well at
the end of the great plain through which we are driving in
silence, a silence lasting hours during which we see nothing but
poles poles poles poles poles poles poles poles poles ground ground
ground ground ground ground ground ground ground ground.

```
t   |            ABC
e   |        DEF
l   |    GHI
e   |    JK      dial
p   |    LMN
h   |        OPQ
o   |            RST
ne + wire
                : to have awaited someone's hand
```

But above all Adriana has a heart, a heart in the form of a
telephone in the form of a telephone wire in the form of a
telephone dial in the form of a telephone booth:

>   *fenders.*

★

mer

portière

ouverte

stop

avoir jeté l'eau de sa baignoire / avoir enlevé le bouchon / avoir
laissé couler l'eau / avoir laissé couler son corps avec l'eau / — /
avoir écouté pendant des après-midi entières, quand le jour meurt,
quand les oiseaux pleurent vraiment de désespoir / — / *avoir des
seins en viande très tendre, dont la pression donne la folie* / — avoir
écouté avec les poils du visage / avoir écouté à travers le Son /
avoir écouté à travers le sourire / avoir écouté le ventre d'un
autre / avoir un con comme une route où l'on roule décapoté au
bord de la mer où la nuit tombe.

★

île   *île*   *île*

enfants

rocher

enfants

sea

door

open

$$\begin{array}{ccc} r & & t \\ e & & o \\ & a & o \\ & r\ b & \end{array}$$

    stop

to have thrown the water out of one's bath-tub / to have pulled out the plug / to have let the water run out / to have let one's body run out with the water / — / to have listened through whole afternoons, when the day is dying, when birds really weep in despair / — / *to have breasts of very tender meat, which would drive mad anyone who squeezed them* / to have listened with the hairs of the face / to have listened across sound / to have listened across smiles / to have listened to another's belly / to have a cunt like a road along which one is driving with the hood down by the edge of the sea as night falls.

★

island   *island*   *island*

                     children

                  rock

                     children

«Nous avons une âme. Nous avons une âme où l'on se deshabile comme
«sur la plage. Nous avons une âme comme un seul livre lu à deux.
«Nous avons une âme comme l'espace qui sépare les enfants des îles.
«Nous avons une âme comme les lieux où nous ne sommes pas encore
«allés. Nous avons une âme comme un seul oiseau de mer se posant sur
«le rocher entre trois garçons et trois filles. Nous avons une âme. Nous
«avons deux âmes. Nous avons trois âmes. Nous avons quatre âmes.
«Nous avons mille âmes. Nous avons sept mille années.»

A. et A.

★

```
            u                    l   o
     e   a                   f         t
 d              q u i                    t
  i                                        e        e
 r                                                r t ê
                                                  n
             b                                    e f
             o                                        la
             r
             d
             de
```

Tu as rattrapé tous mes frissons. J'ai rattrapé tous tes frissons.
Tu m'as montré tes pieds. Je t'ai montré mes pieds. Tu as brûlé
de petites souris. J'ai brûlé de petits citrons. Par cette fenêtre ou
tu as (où j'ai) voulu te (me) jeter, tu as rattrapé la lune avec tes
dents. Nous en sommes arrivés à jouir de tous les moments où
ton cerveau s'envole dans le mien par cette fenêtre où nous ne
nous sommes pas jetés.

Nous en sommes là

(*Libertés de la liberté*)

190

'*We have a soul. We have a soul in which we undress as though on the beach. We have a soul like a single book read by two people together. We have a soul like the space which separates the children from the islands. We have a soul like the places we have not yet visited. We have a soul like a single seabird alighting on the rock between three boys and three girls. We have a soul. We have two souls. We have three souls. We have four souls. We have a thousand souls. We have seven thousand years.*'

*

A. and A.

```
              n                    l  o
      t   a i                           f    a
  r                                           t
u                    w  h  i  c  h             s      w
c                                                     o
                                                      d
                         e                            n
                         d                            i
                         g                            w
                         e
                         of                          the
```

You have recaptured all my frissons. I have recaptured all your frissons. You have shown me your feet. I have shown you my feet. You have burned some little mice. I have burned some little lemons. Through this window from which you (I) wanted to throw yourself (myself), you have reached for the moon and recaptured it. We have reached the point of enjoying all the moments when your brain flies into my own through this window from which we have not thrown ourselves.

We have reached that point.

191

Ces livres

Pierre Jean Jouve

CES LIVRES, portant papier fin, initiales, et figures
de sphinx mêlés, ces grands livres ont été entassés par
chagrin sur une image de femme perdue, sur une douleur
inavouable, sur une misère de voies à suivre, sur un doute
premier né, et sur l'oubli,
   la mémoire des endroits, des tournants, des yeux et
des nez, la mémoire des pistes, et la mémoire des erreurs
et des offenses,
   l'oubli des états sacrés, des transports, quand les
mots noircissent difficilement la ligne et que les signes
ou lettres se déforment par la méchanceté exprès;
   l'oubli du radieux chassé et pourchassé et saisi et
peut-être né, dans ces livres, qui regardent à l'extérieur
avec les yeux crevés.

(*Langue*)

These books

Pierre Jean Jouve

THESE BOOKS, WEARING fine paper, initials and mixed
sphinx faces, these great books have been piled up through
grief on the image of a lost woman, on a sorrow too shameful
to be told, on a wretchedness of ways to be followed, on a
firstborn doubt, and on forgetting,

memory of places, turnings, eyes and noses, memory of
trails, and memory of mistakes and offences,

forgetting of sacred states, ecstasies, when words find
it hard to blacken the line and signs or letters lose their
shape through wickedness on purpose;

forgetting of the radiant – hunted and hounded and
seized and maybe born, in these books, which stare outward
with pierced eyes.

Vaisseau

Pierre Jean Jouve

Depuis longtemps sur l'étrange vaisseau
Qui me porte à travers les terres les plus sèches
Les visages sont tourmentés, les paroles sans écho,
L'insomnie est pénétrante, énorme et verte la tempête,

Depuis longtemps j'ai douté de mes sondes,
Je fus sûr des débauches de l'adversité,
Je manquai le chenal ou le seuil de ce monde
Je me glisse comme au travers, un œil fermé,

Depuis longtemps le pays traversé se meurt
Et le féroce gouvernail reste conduit
Depuis longtemps et contre tout espoir j'espère

Un port; et je connais que hors ma nuit
A l'étoile restée unique il faut douleurs
Energie et tressaillement de chair amère.

(*Mélodrame*)

Vessel

Pierre Jean Jouve

On the strange vessel that long since
Has carried me across the driest land
Faces have been twisted, words without resonance,
Sleeplessness sharp and deep, storms green and unconfined,

My soundings have been long in doubt,
I trusted to misfortune's running wild,
I missed the fairway or this world's threshold
I slip as though broadside, with one eye shut,

The country I have crossed has long been dying
And the fierce helm has guessed which way to go
Long since and hopeless is my wish

For harbour; and outside my night, I know,
With the sole star left to me there is crying
Energy and the jolt of bitter flesh.

Cheveux et miroirs

Pierre Jean Jouve

Dans ma pauvre maison coulent toujours des larmes
Anciennes répétant les reflets aux miroirs
Des songes, des cheveux de mortes, rideaux noirs
Du temps plein de soupirs et d'amertume;
Et que des formes nues
S'ouvrant augmentent brusque un animal mystère
Ne guérit pas de n'avoir plus chose d'amour
N'assèche pas mes yeux de voyageur
Devant tant de cheveux de mortes aux miroirs.

(*Mélodrame*)

Hair and mirrors

Pierre Jean Jouve

In my poor house a steady flow of old
Tears reiterates mirror images
Of dreams, dead women's hair, and curtains black
With seasons full of tears and bitterness;
And naked forms
Opening full on a brute mystery
Leave me unhealed with no love object left
My traveller's eyes undrained before
Images of so much dead women's hair.

Un jour sera connu ...

Pierre Jean Jouve

UN JOUR SERA CONNU par pensée ou par foudre
Ce mélodrame qu'en des lignes de noirceur
Je chantai: quand mes yeux seront poudre en la poudre
Ma force mâle absente et ma main sans auteur,

Ce que j'ai maintenu par la force du mot
La passe très secrète
Vers l'autre mot ou membre informé et nouveau
De passion fureur et douleur et sagesse;

Alors votre folie aura changé de sens
Vous aurez le rachat l'invention des sens
Abordant après moi aux amours éternelles.

(*Mélodrame*)

One day the world...

Pierre Jean Jouve

ONE DAY THE world by thought or lightning blast
Will know this melodrama which in black
Lines I sang: when my eyes are dust in dust
My maleness gone, my writing hand gone slack,

What I have upheld with a word's sinew
The secret pass
To the other word or member informed and new
With passion fury wisdom and distress;

And then your folly will have swivelled round
Your senses will have been redeemed and found
Following me to everlasting loves.

Beauté

Pierre Jean Jouve

Que Dieu me donne encore le pouvoir d'écrire
La proportion merveilleuse de beauté
Libre des tenailles de chair où sexe et larmes
Se mélangent pour enfanter le mélancolique passé;

Que Dieu m'accorde encor le secret de beaux vers
Qui soient le pain le vin contre le diable triste
O belle souviens-toi, la morte, reviens vers
Ton pauvre messager guéri de sa misère;

O Beauté toujours seule au milieu de l'esprit
Que nul dessein ne peut posséder ni atteindre
Tu connais mon soupir
                            l'ignorance m'a pris
Le jour où par hasard je te rendis mes armes,
Et depuis à t'aimer je me suis épuisé.

(*Moires*)

Beauty

Pierre Jean Jouve

May God give me the power still to write
Beauty as she is wonderfully cast
Free from the tongs of flesh where sex and tears
Mix to beget the melancholy past;

May God still grant the secret of fine verse
For bread and wine against the sorry devil
O fair, dead one, remember, come back to
Your poor envoy cured of his wretchedness;

Beauty ever alone amid the mind
That no ruse can possess or reach, you know
My sigh
       I was imprisoned in unknowing
The day by chance I tendered you my arms
Since when I have drained myself for love of you.

201

Je suis encore ému ...

Pierre Jean Jouve

JE SUIS ENCORE ÉMU mais je suis effrayé
D'elles toutes. Je les vois rangées confondues
Brillantes de chagrin sinon dans les enfers
Même touffe du pli du marbre de la hanche
Infirmes ou vieillies, belles au carrefour,
Je mélange leurs seins crinières et fortunes
Et tant de voluptés du savoir des amours,
Quand je croyais les perdre je m'engloutissais
Au seuil du paradis leur étroite Nature:
Mais l'ombre alors prenait l'esprit! La mort tournait
Les pages folles de l'illusion luxure.

(*Moires*)

I am still stirred . . .

Pierre Jean Jouve

I AM STILL stirred but I am frightened now
By all those women. I see them lined up, blurred
Brilliant in their grief if not in hell
The same tuft in the fold of marble hip
Ill or grown old, beauties at the crossroads,
I mix their breasts their manes and fates together
So many pleasures of love's scholarship,
When I thought I was losing them I sank
At Eden's gate the straits of their Nature:
But shadow gripped my mind then! Death was turning
The crazed and foolish pages of my burning.

Promenade

Pierre Jean Jouve

Je suis dans ces chemins de douceur rude
Où l'on va lentement
A cause de la hauteur où le cœur respire,
Les grands arbres plaintifs
Hier encor sous la neige
M'escortent dans l'odeur parfumante du vent;

Je sens les pas dans les pas
Devenir plus sûrs de lumière belle
A la fois comme monte énorme entre les troncs
La muraille affirmant que la fin est mortelle.

(*Moires*)

A walk

Pierre Jean Jouve

I am among those ways of harsh sweetness
Where the going is slow
Because of the height where the heart takes breath,
The great grieving trees
Yesterday still under snow
Escort me in the fragrance of the wind;

I feel steps in my steps
Growing more confident of lovely light,
Meanwhile immense between the treetrunks looms
The wall asserting that the end is death.

Vendange

Olivier Larronde

La fleur déclose me prive de tout comme elle s'abandonne
en fruit. Mon sang charrie des glaçons, fleur de la récolte quand
le cortège de ce soir m'ouvrira les veines.

Meuniers, ramoneurs et ceux que le sel a déteints, mes démons
se laissent apparaître, vêtus de soufre et plus près des papillons
pour cette race légère que saura fixer une pointe dans l'aile. A des
fleurs les papillons font l'amour, eux vont aux baisers des fruits.

Délaissant ces bouches entr'ouvertes qui pendent aux branches,
d'un galop les vendangeurs passeront fouler mon corps
une grappe de leur vigne.

(*Rien voilà l'ordre*)

Vintage

Olivier Larronde

The opened flower robs me of everything as it gives itself over to fruiting. My blood drifts with ice, flower of the harvest when this evening's pageant will open my veins.

Millers, chimney sweeps and those whom the salt has imprisoned, my demons let themselves appear, clothed in sulphur and more like butterflies for that light race whom the pin in the wing will know how to transfix. The butterflies make love to the flowers, while they, in their turn, come to the fruits with kisses.

Forsaking these half-open mouths which hang from the branches, the vintagers pass by at a gallop to tread my body
a grape-cluster upon their vine.

L'éhontée

Olivier Larronde

Solitude éhontée répondant sans répondre
«C'est moi qui m'offre à tous pour m'y cacher des autres!
Écorche-toi, veux-tu? je vais être encor là.
Si tu veux m'étrangler, c'est moi qui nous sépare.

Mon tonnerre est sans bruit! Silence en fait l'écho
Par ta voix étonnée quand rien ne lui arrive
D'un visage passable aux immobiles rives;
Où mon seul coup de foudre y fait ton cœur mordant.

Tu n'es pas plus qu'un bois si j'en suis la Druidesse,
Ou la cultivatrice à l'intime jardin
Aux regards en allées, vides vers chaque objet

Car le moindre ustensile y met un monument.»
Le signe que je fais dans toutes les bouteilles
Nous ramène, humble bête en chœur des basses-cours

«Partageons … Sans rancune. A la prochaine fois!»

(*L'Arbre à lettres*)

The shameless one

Olivier Larronde

Shameless solitude replying without reply
'It is I who offer myself to all to hide thus from the others!
Flay yourself, will you? I shall still be there.
If you try to strangle me, it is I who keep us apart.

My thunder is soundless! Silence makes the echo
Through your astonished voice when nothing is altered
By a tolerable face on the motionless shores;
Where my single lightning flash makes your heart corrosive.

You are no more than a wood if I am its Druidess,
Or the cultivator of an intimate garden,
With glances in avenues, going emptily towards each object,

For the most trivial utensil makes a monument there.'
The sign that I make within all the bottles
Brings us back, humble beast in the farmyard chorus

'Let us share things between us. . No hard feelings.
  Until the next time!'

Compte tu

Olivier Larronde

Que ne pas dire tout est là
Pour chacun depuis que l'on parle.
Il faut bien deux silences pour faire un mot
Deux grands silences pour la phrase, un nuancé pour la virgule
Une légère absence et c'est le paragraphe
Ce clin d'œil à la parenthèse
Un brin d'hystérie l'interrogation
Des guillemets ça ne se dit pas
Un grain d'épilepsie point d'exclamation
Deux grains tout seuls c'est concluant
Et le discontinue pour le trois points final.

(*L'Arbre à lettres*)

Just consider

Olivier Larronde

Why not say it is all there
For everyone since speech began
Two silences needed for a word
Two big silences for the phrase, one with a nuance for the
    comma
A small absence that's the paragraph
This wink at the parenthesis
A bit of hysteria the question mark
Quotation marks one doesn't say that
A grain of epilepsy exclamation mark
Two grains by themselves it is conclusive
And the discontinuous for the three final dots

Menu ou la quinte

Olivier Larronde

Des chants liquides
Et de ces vins coulants
Quel combustible pur
Veux-tu comme aliment
Pour ta flamme

Capter sa danse,
Quel étrange alambic
Dis quelle était l'allure
Où des fines musiques
A son âme

L'essence triste
Consommera ton cœur
Et la flamme si bleue
Se nourrit des vapeurs
Pour ta mort.

(*L'Arbre à lettres*)

Minor or the fifth

Olivier Larronde

From the liquid songs
And these wines flowing
What pure combustible
Do you require
For your flame's feeding

To capture its dance
What a strange alembic
Say what was its outline
Where delicate musics
Possess its soul

The sad essence
Will eat up your heart
While the bright blue flame
Feeds on the vapours
Destined for your death

Le prospecteur

Patrice de La Tour du Pin

Chercheur d'or? Aux veines profondes
De tout homme au temps gravitant,
L'or qui dépasse en prix le monde,
Je l'écoute en fusion qui rend
Malgré l'épaisseur de sa gangue
Témoignage qu'il est de Dieu!
Je le goûte presqu'à la langue,
Je le devine au fond des yeux,
Ce fruit tombé dans les ténèbres
Que nul prospecteur n'a pu voir
Malgré ses subtiles algèbres
Ou ses extrêmes laminoirs.
Je ne veux pas sa découverte
Sans qu'il me découvre d'autant:
Il lève douloureusement
A travers mes couches inertes
Ou vives, en les traversant.
Quand je l'approche, aussitôt change
La teneur du corps ou du temps.
Je suis pris au rayonnement
D'un or qui passe en prix tout ange,
Je hume son signe d'échange
Rien qu'à me pencher sur mon sang
Où vacille l'intolérable ...
Épiphanie! Dieu de tous ors
Même en nos nuits abominables,
Si tu ne levais de la mort,
J'en serais encor aux mirages
De l'homme figeant ses accords
Dans un sein qui n'est que passage ...

(*Une Somme de poésie: petit théâtre crépusculaire*)

The prospector

Patrice de La Tour du Pin

Seeker for gold? In the deep veins
Of every man who feels time's pull
Lies gold worth more than all the world;
I hear it fusing, rendering,
Despite the thickness of the matrix,
Its witness that it comes from God!
I almost taste it on my tongue,
I find it in the depths of eyes,
This fruit fallen in the dark
Which no prospector can have seen
Despite his subtle algebras,
And though his mills can grind so fine.
This gold I do not wish to find
Unless it too discovers me.
Painfully it rises, through my inert
Or living strata, passing through.
When I come near it, forthwith changes
The quality of the flesh or time.
I'm taken captive by the shining
Of gold more precious than an angel,
I can inhale its sign of worth
Simply by stooping towards my blood
In which there lurks the intolerable . . .
Epiphany! God of all golds,
Even in our most hideous nights,
If you do not raise from the dead,
I am deceived, my concord fixed
Upon a transitory breast. . .

Promesse

Patrice de La Tour du Pin

Et tous les soirs de ces matins de dure enquête,
J'allais rêver aux bords des vallées de chair douce,
Très loin des plateaux gris et mornes de ma tête,
Et comme en m'excusant de mener l'autre course.

Il y avait des pentes d'épaules de femme,
Des secrets d'enfants qui n'écloraient pas peut-être,
Et des yeux de vieillards à longueur de jours d'âme
Penchés sur quels courants, – et des fêtes, des fêtes !

Partout dans les vallées de chair vivante à prendre,
Et je m'en approchais sans les dire passées
En leur soufflant: «Bientôt, je pourrai redescendre
De mes longs plateaux gris crevassés de pensées.»

Je n'y lève pas même une mélancolie,
Car je dois traverser de très hautes murailles,
Bientôt je me repencherai sur votre vie
Avec une clarté recueillie dans leurs failles.

Déjà je leur criais: «Qui vous disait profanes?»
J'ai retrouvé le temps de la chair dans ma quête,
Je suis pourvu d'amour bien au-delà de l'âme,
Et doucement, il s'y fait jour, il la pénètre ...

Bientôt, bientôt ... Je ne suis pas muet encore,
Je reviendrai par la douleur à vos passées
De signes, jusqu'à vous par le signe qui dore
Même mes longs plateaux crevassés de pensée.

(*Une Somme de poésie: petit théâtre crépusculaire*)

Promise

Patrice de La Tour du Pin

And upon the evenings of those mornings of harsh search,
I went to muse on the brink of those valleys of sweet flesh,
Very far from the sad plateaux of my head,
And as if excusing myself from taking another course.

And there were hillsides like the shoulders of a woman,
And childhood secrets which perhaps would never blossom,
And the eyes of the aged, long as the soul's days,
Bent upon such streams – there were such celebrations!

Everywhere valleys of flesh for the taking,
And I approached, not thinking their day over,
Whispering to them: 'Soon I shall go down again
From my long grey plateaux, crevassed with thought.'

Melancholy is not what I gather here,
For I must pass through very high walls,
Soon I shall turn back to look upon your life
With a clarity found within their fissures.

Already I said to them: 'Who called you profane?'
The age of flesh refound in the course of my quest,
I now have a love which much exceeds the soul,
And softly it illuminates and penetrates it. . .

Soon, very soon . . . I am not yet silent,
I'll return through sorrow to your past of signs,
I'll come indeed to you by the sign which gilds
Even my long plateaux crevassed with thought.

Taupe crevée sur la route

Patrice de La Tour du Pin

Le rien qui a battu sous cette poche noire
Si plate, pas encor fondue dans le chemin,
Ce petit peu de temps qui n'est pas de l'histoire,
— Pourtant une naissance, un cours, et cette fin ...

Ce petit peu de vie à ferme d'une bête ...
Et la mienne, plus haut, cherchant à l'épouser,
Consomme son absence, et forcément sécrète
Un souffle triste et qui sait où se poser.

Venant d'un peu plus bas que le champ de nature,
Il tâtonne en mon ciel, s'accroche tout à coup
A la lueur que tout soit d'une créature,
S'entrouvre alors, et doucement revient vers nous

Porteur du rien d'une autre vie, dans ma conscience
Qui n'avait nul désir de souffler sur ce corps,
Du petit peu d'un jour où fixer l'espérance
Que les ressuscités ranimeront des morts ...

(Une Somme de poèsie: petit théâtre crépusculaire)

Mole run over on the road

Patrice de La Tour du Pin

The nothing which beat within this black bag,
Flattened, but not yet sunk into the roadway,
This fragment of time which is not history –
Yet there was a birth, a life span, and this death . . .

This tiny bit of life in a beast's shape . . .
And my own life, higher, seeking to be one with it,
Consummates its absence, and harbours, as it must,
A melancholy breath, that has nowhere to rest.

Come from a little lower than the field of nature,
It fumbles in my sky, and suddenly clings
To the glimmer that may be all that's left of a creature,
And so gapes open, and gently returns to us,

Bearer of another life's nothingness into my consciousness
Which had no wish to give breath to this corpse,
From the mere fragment of day in which to raise the hope
That those brought to life again may give life to the dead. . . .

Chansons pour des fiançailles

Jean Lescure

D'une enfance oubliée
un grenier de chiffons
une cave de bave
un silence d'effroi

ta main ne rejoint pas
la nappe de midi

pour quel repas ce cœur coupé
cette ombre hachée

pour quelle aube
ces nuits confiantes
ces nuits d'étoiles
ces nuits quittées

Pour y dormir ensemble
je dessine un jardin

je n'oublie pas l'étang
je n'oublie pas les pierres

j'y prends une douceur égale à ton épaule
une patience acquise
silence à ton silence

plus tard couchée sur moi
elle me chauffera
du feu léger des sources

Ballads for a betrothal

Jean Lescure

From an out-of-mind childhood
a rag-laden attic
with tears and fear
filling cellar and silence

your fingers don't reach
the lunch tablecloth

which meal will devour this cut-out heart
this minced-up shade

and which dawn will break
these nights deep with trust
these nights packed with stars
these nights long ago left

Just to sleep there together
I shall draw us a garden

not forgetting the pond
not forgetting the stones

finding softness in them as I do on your shoulder
taking patience from them
silence echoing yours

lying over me later
with pale fire of springs
she will bring me her warmth

pour aujourd'hui j'attelle
à ses chemins mon sang

A l'orée du bois
les filles sont claires

à l'orée du bois
un roi s'est caché

profondes allées
fausses ténébreuses
pour revoir le jour
qui ne vous suivrait

Sous un miroir d'eau
les feuilles patientent

mêlés à des pierres
tous les ciels y volent

beau regard tu veilles
sur la peau de l'eau
sur la peau du vent

pour y étaler
la nappe songeuse
des maisons heureuses

but today I shall tame
all my blood to her paths

The edge of the forest
is brilliant with girls

the edge of the forest
is hiding a king

dark forest paths
cheating mystery's depths
still seeking the light
that lingered outside

A mirror of water
lies upon patient leaves

intermingled with pebbles
every sky hovers there

vivid glances keep watch
on the skin of the water
the skin of the wind

for the moment to lay
the dreamiest cloth
of contented homes

De blanc et de gris
les journées sont faites
de bleu et de vert
la fête s'entoure

comme les morceaux
lavés d'une lettre
qui s'en vont au vent
savant des amants

comme sous l'orage
le plaisir des mouettes
mêle un peu de rire
à beaucoup de peur

Pour demain toute rose
est rose ce matin
pour sa fin tout sourire
passe dans ton sourire

ainsi que vous passez
chansons que nous aimions
dans l'or que nous formons
des cendres des journées

ainsi que vient dormir
dans l'enfant que j'aurai
l'enfant que je serai
de ce que j'ai été

Every day is made up
of grey and of white
while blue and while green
frame the holiday's span

like the washed-away scraps
of a letter are blown
ever higher on that
wise wind lovers know

as the blitheness of gulls
once caught in a storm
adds fragment of laughter
to oceans of fear

For the rosy morrow
today dawns rose
as it fades each smile
will filter through yours

as the songs that we love
are filtered across
the days we have turned
from ashes to gold

as the child I'll become
after all I have been
comes tumbling to sleep
in the child I shall have

H

225

quand je l'aurai lié
aux rondes des étés
où nous avons crié

Si la fenêtre s'ouvre
le ciel bleu se partage

les feuilles de la vigne allient un soleil d'ombre
au sommeil blanc des pierres

fleurir ne suffit pas aux roses
au fond de son miroir
il faut que l'amoureuse
les regarde la voir

(*Drailles*)

when I've helped it join in
the midsummer rites
that once rang with our cries

If the window opens
the blue sky divides

the leaves of the vine blend a shadow sun
with white stones in their slumber

no rose is happy to blossom alone
from the depths of her mirror the girl deep in love
must see the roses
watching her

Transfert nocturne

Armen Lubin

L'hôpital riche en lumières de surface
Donnait sa pâture à la bête vorace,
A la bête ventrue nommée civière,
Cornue devant et cornue derrière.

La pâture, c'était l'homme sans défense,
Rivé, cloué d'impuissance
Auquel on prêtait ce nouveau corps,
Le brancard qui va toutes défenses dehors.

Et il allait dans le silence complice,
Ayant retiré l'homme d'un bâtiment
Comme on retire pour rendre justice
Le couteau resté planté dedans.

On attaquait de nuit, d'un mauvais coin,
Et l'allée centrale crissait et comme témoin
La Voie Lactée de tout son éclat
Coulait dans le sens du brancard d'en bas.

Coulées parallèles qui visaient la mort,
Toujours impuissantes et toujours d'accord;
Celle d'en haut valait bien celle d'en bas,
Les deux porteurs accordaient leurs pas.

Ils s'accordaient dans le balancement,
La nuit restait haute, tout frissonnement,
Afin d'aspirer l'homme de l'hôpital,
Les temps étaient proches, perlaient les étoiles.

Night transfer

Armen Lubin

The hospital suffused with surface lights
Gives fodder to the voracious beast,
The potbellied beast that's called a stretcher,
Horns to the front and horns to the rear.

The fodder is a man without redress,
Riven, nailed by impotence,
To whom this new body has been lent,
This stretcher bristling at either end.

It travels through the conniving silence,
Having taken the man out of a building,
Just as the knife planted in a body
Is pulled out when justice must be done.

Deed done by night, from a dark corner;
The central pathway grated; the witness
Was the Milky Way in all its brilliance,
Flowing the same way as the strecher below.

Parallel streams, with death for their goal,
Always impotent, always in harmony;
That above worth more than that below,
The two bearers keeping in step.

They moved in harmony with the swaying,
The night stood high, all trembling,
So as to snuff up the man from the hospital,
The hour was near, the stars were sweat-drops.

Par le balancement, par l'accouplement,
L'amour le plus vaste giclait au moment
Où l'on ne sentait plus les deux porteurs,
Ils confondaient les nuits comme on meurt.

Il fut bref et il fut long mon transfert.
L'inconscient s'appelait porteur arrière.
«De quoi? disait le vent, substitution?
«Double impuissance, une seule direction!»

Même au fond de l'abîme augmentait le froid,
De l'abîme qui me creusait plus profond que moi,
Et dans la nuit haute, dans la nuit qui glace,
Tout était lumière mais lumière de surface.

(*Feux centre feux*)

Through that swaying, through that coupling,
The vastest love came spurting forth
Just when the bearers were felt no more,
They mingled with the night like an act of dying.

My transfer was both brief and long.
The second bearer was called 'the unconscious'.
"Of what?" said the wind, "of substitution?
Double impotence, one sole direction!"

It grew colder even in the depths of the abyss,
The abyss hollowing me deeper than my own depth,
And in the high night, the freezing night,
All was light, but surface light.

Sans rien autour

Armen Lubin

N'ayant plus de maison ni logis,
Plus de chambre où me mettre,
Je me suis fabriqué une fenêtre
Sans rien autour.

Fenêtre encadrant la matière
Par le tracé tendre de son contour,
Elle s'ouvre comme la paupière,
Se ferme sans rien autour.

Se sont dépouillées les vieilles amours,
Mais la fenêtre dépourvue de glace
Gagne les hauteurs, elle se déplace,
Avec son cadre étonnant,

Qui n'est ni chair ni bois blanc,
Mais qui conserve la forme exacte
D'un œil parcourant sans ciller
L'espace soumis, le temps rayé.

Et je reste suspendu au cadre qui file,
J'en suis la larme la plus inutile
Dans la nuit fermée, dans le petit jour,
Ils s'ouvrent à moi sans rien autour.

(*Feux contre feux*)

With nothing around

Armen Lubin

No house any more nor a lodging,
No room to call mine,
I've made me a window
With nothing around.

A window framing the real world
With the tender line of its contour,
It opens itself like an eyelid,
Shuts with nothing around.

The old loves are cast off,
But this window, glassless,
Moves away and soars up
With its astonishing frame,

That is neither whitewood nor flesh,
Yet keeps the exact form
Of an unblinking eye
Roving space which is conquered, time cancelled.

From that gliding frame I still dangle,
I'm its vainest teardrop
In the black night, the false dawn,
They open to me, with nothing around.

Feux contre feux

Armen Lubin

Deux surfaces, mêmes dimensions:
Mon front et le ciel étoilé.
Deux surfaces, feux contre feux.

Gâchis contre gâchis mais exaltés
Par la fusion des nuits à hautes cimes,
Mais chute aussi qui me corrige,
L'écart rétabli, fini le prestige.

Comme on est malhabile, convalescent,
Rejeté ainsi, hors de l'élément!

Froidement vidé je me sentis
Quand retomba ma dépouille,
Poches retournées je me sentis.

Par la fusée et la fusion lointaines,
Dans les hauteurs où tout est urgent,
J'ai vu le ciel, il livrait le domaine.

J'ai vu le point nul du sacre:
Absorption, déchirement, simulacre
De tout ce qu'ici-bas
Nous ne pouvons pas posséder,
Ici-bis et en ces lieux
Où fuse l'amour: feux contre feux.

Gâchis contre gâchis mais exaltés
Jusqu'à la plus haute source des larmes,
Mais chute aussi qui me corrige,
L'écart rétabli, fini le prestige.

234

Fire against fire

Armen Lubin

Two surfaces, dimensions the same:
My forehead and the starry heaven.
Two surfaces, fire against fire.

Mire against mire, but exalted
By the mingling of high-crested nights,
But also the fall to chastise me,
The gap restored, end of illusion.

How clumsy one is, convalescent,
Thrown down thus, out of one's element!

I felt myself empty and cold
When my body fell back,
Void as a pocket turned out.

Through the faraway fuse and fusion,
High up, where everything's urgent,
I saw the sky, it surrendered its realm.

I have seen ceremony's null point,
Absorption and rending, simulacrum
Of all which down here
Eludes us,
Down here, in these places
Where love fuses: fire against fire.

Mire against mire but exalted
To tears' loftiest source,
But also the fall to chastise me,
The gap restored, end of illusion.

Comme on est vain, presque mort,
Poches retournées, dedans dehors.

(*Feux contre feux*)

How vain one is, nearly dead,
empty pockets, turned inside out.

Pourquoi serpent

Armen Lubin

Pourquoi serpent et serpent qui mord?
Pourquoi cette plaie pire que la mort?

Tous les jours je guette un homme important
Avec des yeux perçants qui sont dans ma tête.

Parfois je lui donne un nom, une silhouette,
Seul le mal n'arrive pas, il est déjà présent.

Ainsi le vent soumet, la main sur le collet,
L'arbre qui se débat tout au fond de l'allée.

L'arbre qui a un cœur gravé dans son écorce,
Rien de ceci n'existe la nuit et pour cause!

Inexistant l'arbre, inexistant le vent,
Mais le cœur saigne dessus l'inexistant.

Et la pendule qui égrène jamais ne s'endort,
Toujours serpent et serpent qui mord.

(*Feux contre feux*)

Wherefore a snake

Armen Lubin

Wherefore a snake, and one that bites?
Wherefore this wound that's worse than death?

I watch each day an important man
With piercing eyes inside my head.

Sometimes I give him a name, a shape,
But evil does not come, being here.

Thus the wind arrests, hand upon collar,
The struggling tree at the lane's end.

The tree with a heart carved in its bark
Cannot exist at night – with reason!

Nonexistent the tree, so too the wind,
But the heart bleeds on the nonexistent.

Tick of a clock which never sleeps,
Always a snake and one that bites.

The thin man

Henri Michaux

PETIT
petit sous le vent
petit et lacunaire
pressé et sachant que vite il faut qu'il sache
dans sa petite galaxie
faisant le quart
dans son cockpit perpétuellement
dans son peu de paix
dans son pas de paix du tout
bruissant sous la douche de milliers d'avertisseurs
sonné
sassé
sifflé
frappé
percé
se croyant de la chair
se voulant dans un palais
mais vivant dans des palans
dans les rafales
innombrable,
frêle,
horloger aussi et foetus aussi
visé
entamé
agrippé
agriffé

frappé à coups redoublés
gravé comme une plaque
cliquetant comme un téléscripteur
déplacé
dévié

240

The thin man

Henri Michaux

LITTLE
little beneath the wind
little and lacunary
driven forward and knowing that he soon must know
in his little galaxy
keeping watch
perpetually in his cockpit
in his little bit of peace
in his total lack of peace
rustling under the downpour of thousands of alarms
summoned
sifted
hissed
struck
pierced
believing himself to be flesh
longing to live in a palace
but living in the rigging
in innumerable
squalls,
frail,
both watchmaker and foetus
endorsed
tamed
snatched
clutched

struck with redoubled blows
inscribed like a plaque
clicking like a teleprinter
displaced
disorientated

son miroir mille fois brisé
affolé
à l'écoute
ne voulant pas être perdu
traçant des plans
des plans contradictoires
des plans étrangers
des plans rebondissants
des plans à l'infini
luttant avec des plans
jamais tout à fait submergé
luttant
et même il va bientôt sourire
et puis croire que la vie est bonheur et soupirs
et doux corps rapprochés
autour de l'être éperdu

puis à nouveau renversé
redressé
puis de nouveau alerté et près d'être submergé
sur place paralysé mortellement

refaisant des plans
des contre-plans
des plans d'opposition
dans l'obscur
dans le futur
dans l'indéterminé
pilote tant qu'il pourra, jusqu'à la fin
pilote ou plus rien

his mirror smashed a thousand times
frightened
keeping an ear cocked
not wishing to be lost
making plans
contradictory plans
strange plans
plans that boomerang
plans ad infinitum
struggling with plans
never quite going under
struggling
and yet he'll soon smile
and then believe that life is sunshine and showers
and gentle bodies brought near together
around the distracted being

then once more knocked over
picked up again
then once more on the alert and near to going under
there and then paralysed fatally

remaking plans
counter-plans
plans of opposition
in the darkness
in the future
in the undetermined
pilot as best he may be, right to the end
pilot or else nothing

cible en plein vol, qui scrute
qui trace des plans,
toujours des plans
des PLANS

Celui qui est né dans la nuit
souvent refera son Mandala.

(from *Botteghe oscure*, XX, Autumn 1957)

target in full flight, who scrutinizes
who makes plans
always plans
PLANS

He who is born in the night
will often refashion his Mandala

Parmi des langues étrangères

Jean Pérol

Première; seconde. Où allons-nous ce soir? Il aime ce parfum
à ses côtés dans l'ombre. Troisième. Sa main libre retrouve sa
place, au bas du ventre et sur la jupe. Dès la sortie de la ville on
voit des rizières tourner au bout des phares. D'un bout du monde
à l'autre comme on erre la nuit! Bouche ce trou avec des yeux,
avec des mèches de cheveux! Ce n'est pas la peur qui le troue,
mais le fer rouge d'être bien. Une revanche de bernés, cent
millions de mensonges écrasés du talon. Et maintenant croire aux
autres, à la seule vérité des bras, des épaules. Ce soir encore au
bout d'un paysage, quand le moteur s'est tu, il est là, dans la
pénombre d'un bar vide, en face d'une femme, avide, curieux de
l'autre, avant la marche sur la plage, avant la chambre, tenant deux
mains entre les siennes, curieux d'un autre, s'en approchant parmi
des langues étrangères.

(*Le Coeur véhément*)

Among foreign languages

Jean Pérol

First; second. Where are we going this evening? The perfume beside him in the darkness pleases him. Third. His free hand finds its resting place again, in the hollow of the dress at the groin. As soon as the town is left behind, they can see ricefields spinning away from the tips of the headlights. How we roam the night from one end of the world to the other! Plus this hole with eyes, with locks of hair! It is not fear that burns a hole in him, but the red-hot iron of well-being. A revenge of the hoaxed, a hundred million lies crushed underfoot. And now believe in others, in the sole truth of arms, of shoulders. This evening, once again, at the end of a landscape, when the engine has fallen silent, he is there, in the semidarkness of an empty bar, sitting opposite a woman, greedy, curious about her, before the walk along the beach, before the room, holding two hands between his own, curious about another, coming closer to that other among foreign languages.

Ginza

Jéan Petrol

Sa lèvre inférieure la révèle assez, des générations et des générations se terminent ici, épuisées. La chair rongée sur l'incendie. L'armure les siècles l'ont enlevée. Petit oiseau lyrique, tu vas encore pleurer ce soir au bord de la mer. Il reste si peu sur ce feu qui s'affole. Que la mince peau fine qui n'isole plus rien. Et son parfum, dit de Paris.

Lui, passant les portes électroniques, il avance au-devant des perles et des fourrures. Des rubis des émeraudes et aussi des camées, vers le shop scintillant du building, vers ses cavernes climatisées. Dans une allée de mannequins en kimono ou en tailleur Chanel, il avance, il avance vers elle. Là c'est la Seine, le pont des Arts, ici la rue de la Roquette, qui se reposent, noir et gris, dans du vison. Elle hoche la tête, elle sourit, elle est légère sur ses talons. Sans être reine elle est mignonne, elle pourrait trotter au milieu de Paris. Les deux longs crochets noirs de ses cheveux se renferment sur son cou. De sa robe verte sans manches surgissent des bras maigres. Les mains longues et nerveuses. Il sait son torse, aussi, les seins durs et petits qui s'accrochent aux côtes, leurs bouts comme des figues brunes. Maintenant elle a faim. Il la regarde grignoter du bout des dents un sandwich minuscule en forme de triangle.

Petit oiseau lyrique, un: tu manges, deux: tu pleures, trois: tu meurs.

(*Le Coeur véhément*)

Ginza

Jean Pérol

Her lower lip betrays her, countless generations have come to a full stop here, exhausted. Her flesh eaten away by the flame. The centuries have stripped her of her armour. Little song-bird, you will weep once more this evening by the sea's edge. So little remains to fuel this raging fire. Just this thin fine skin which no longer insulates anything. And her perfume, Parisian so-called.

Passing through the electronic doors, he plunges among the pearls and furs. Rubies, emeralds and cameos too, and through towards the building's sparkling arcades, towards its air-conditioned caverns. He strides along an avenue of dummies dressed in kimonos or Chanel costumes, on towards her. Over there is the Seine, the Pont des Arts, over here is the rue de la Roquette, all taking a rest, swathed black and grey in mink. She nods her head, she smiles, she rests lightly on her high heels. No queen, certainly, but sweet, she could mince charmingly through the centre of Paris. The two long black hooks of her hair curve back to meet at the nape of her neck. Thin arms emerge from her sleeveless green dress. Long, nervous hands. He knows her torso, too, the small hard breasts clinging to her ribs, their tips like brown figs. Now she is hungry. He watches her nibble with the tips of her teeth at a tiny triangular sandwich.

Little songbird, one: you eat, two: you weep, three: you die.

Des ennuis qu'il peut y avoir …

Georges Perros

Des ennuis qu'il peut y avoir
à ne pas vouloir ou savoir
interrompre parole d'homme
ou par trop délicatesse
choquer l'amour-propre d'autrui.

I

Je rentrais dans ce café-là
assez chic ce n'est pas mon genre
mais j'avais envie de pisser
et tout autre projet cessant
Dès l'entrée je trouvais assis
un grand Russe de mes amis
ou plutôt de mes connaissances
Très racé courtois cultivé
Il me proposa le fauteuil
qui faisait face au sien Je n'eus
pas le courage de lui dire
je reviens de suite merci
et je m'assis Lui très heureux
reprit le cours d'une parlote
Tolstoï en petite culotte
Dostoïevski Gogol Pouchkine
ses grands et moins grands bisaïeuls
Mon envie allait grandissant
goutte à goutte dans ma sueur
je retenais tant que possible
ce qui me rendait écarlate
Lui pensait Il m'écoute bien

The things that happen to one when . . .

Georges Perros

The things that happen to one when
one does not want does not know how
to interrupt when someone's talking
cannot from excess of tact
hurt the self-esteem of others

I

I went into a café which
was rather smart so not my style
I was longing for a pee
stopping everything for that
A big Russian who's a friend
or rather someone whom I know
distinguished courteous well-read
offered me the chair across
from where he sat My courage failed
to say o thanks I'll be right back
So I sat down and he much pleased
chatted about Tolstoy's childhood
Gogol Pushkin Dostoevsky
his ancestors both great and not
And more and more and drop by drop
I sweated and I longed to pee
I held it just as long as I
could manage going very red
My friend thought he listens well
he's deeply moved But in the end
when we went out after our drink
I left a damp patch where I'd sat

Il est ému Mais à la fin
quand nous sortîmes après boire
ma place était humide et rien
ne me ferait retourner là
où mon urine a fait cela.

I I

Voici des moules proposées
trop gentiment pour refuser
et qu'il faut manger devant celle
qui eut ce beau geste Pourtant
l'une d'entre elles sous les dents
c'est comme un poison que l'on croque
Mais on l'avale cependant
pour faire plaisir Après quoi
on rentre vivement chez soi
pour y faire son testament
trouvant absurde de mourir
pour une moule pire encore
pour l'avoir manger afin de
ne pas froisser qui c'est peu dire
se moque de votre destin.

Il arrive que les héros
soient d'un ordre ainsi clandestin.

(*Une Vie ordinaire*)

And nothing now could take me back
to the place where I did that

II

Mussels offered much too nicely
to refuse One has to eat them
there with her who planned the treat
But one you pop into your mouth
tastes like poison when you bite
all the same you gulp it down
hurry home to make your will
finding it a little silly
to die for a mussel and worse still
for having eaten it in order
not to injure someone's feelings
who though this is not saying much
cares not a fig about your fate

Heroes so it sometimes happens
are of this clandestine sort

Je ne saurais vous dire tout …

Georges Perros

Je ne saurais vous dire tout
Et ne pourrais car le mystère
c'est bien cela vouloir tout dire
et s'apercevoir à la fin
que la marge est tout aussi grande
qui nous sépare du prochain
Pendant qu'on écrit l'existence
que l'on dit avoir bouge et change
et quand on parle à un poète
de son dernier recueil il est
depuis longtemps miné par l'autre
aussi brûlant définitif
qu'il nous fera lire demain
Si nous vivions siècles durant
on n'en finirait pas d'aller
au seuil de notre vérité
qui recule quand on la presse
et nous envahit quand on dort.

(*Une Vie ordinaire*)

Don't expect me to tell all . . .

Georges Perros

Don't expect me to tell all
I can't do it The mystery
lies in wishing to tell all
and discovering in the end
that the gap is still as wide
which divides us from our fellows
Even as one writes the existence
one claims to lead is shifting and changes
When one's talking to a poet
about his latest book he has
long been hung up on the next
just as urgent and as final
which he'll make us read tomorrow
Though we lived whole eons through
we should never quite arrive
at the threshold of our truth
which recedes as we pursue it
and invades us as we sleep.

L'usage de la nudité

André Pieyre de Mandiargues

Toute nue feuille sans tige
Elle gît au creux de la dune
Entre les herbes et les joncs
Inclinant cent chasse-mouches
Pour saluer la beauté lisse,

Auprès de sa joue le sable
Que les orages ravinèrent
Fait un petit Colorado
Où galope le pollen
Descendu des graminées sèches
Comme un étalon de blondeur,

La frappe du soleil
A rompu toutes attaches
Avec le meilleur ou le pire
Le frais le pur ou le pourri
Les haillons les perles roses
La blanchaille des caresses
Les pièges enneigés,

Oublieuse de ses limites
Floue devenue ni plus ni moins
Que la vague ou que les bouillons
Démarrée dans le temps
Décrochée dans l'espace
Elle est sargasse et flotte
Sous la face du ciel,

Le bonheur de brûler
S'unit à la déraison bleue,

The use of nakedness

André Pieyre de Mandiargues

Stark naked leaf with no stem
She lay in the hollow of the dune
Among the tufts and rushes
That dipped a hundred fly-whisks
To greet the sleek beauty,

Near her cheek the sand
Which the storms had furrowed
Makes a little Colorado
In which the pollen swept down
From the dry grasses
Gallops like a stallion of blondness,

The force of the sun
Has broken all links
With the better or worse
The fresh the pure or the corrupt
The rags the pink pearls
The whitebait of caresses
The snares snowed-up,

Forgetful of her frontiers
Indistinct now neither more nor less
Than the wave or the bubbles
Unmoored in time
Unfixed in space
She is gulf-weed and floats
Under the face of heaven,

The bliss of burning
Is one with the blue unreason,

I

Estoc à la vacuité
Voici le pas d'un homme affreux
Qui effondre le menu monde
Voici la pioche d'un regard
Qui enracine la gisante
Noue les beaux membres dénoués,

Voici les mots terreux de l'homme
Qui vont lui remettre en mémoire
L'usage de la nudité,

La bauge qu'elle fut
Dans la brousse des nuits
Les tentures fiévreuses
L'eau dégouttant
Le sapin roux
Qui boise les chambres triviales,

Et plus de cent faux-fuyants
Qu'elle offrit à l'élan sauvage.

(*Le Point où j'en suis*)

Sword thrust in the emptiness
Here's the footstep of a hideous man
Who overthrows the tiny world
Here's the mattock of a glance
Giving roots to the prostrate figure
Stiffening the beautiful supple limbs,

Here are the man's earthy words
Which will make her remember
The use of nakedness,

The lair which was herself
In the thicket of nights
The feverish tapestries
The trickling water
The red pine
That panels the trivial rooms,

And more than a hundred ruses
Which she proffered to the savage impulse.

Verdammnis ist im Wesen

Marcelin Pleynet

I

Et l'homme qui faisait ce personnage avait à chaque main
Un flambeau allumé
Par où la Reine passait
Dans les couvertures
Tendues depuis le haut des tours
Aujourd'hui encombrées d'échafauds

Le plus élevé était censé le paradis

Au-dessous du faux corps
Ce limbe contenait Adam et Ève
Et avait deux grands yeux d'acier
Sur le bord du théâtre
Où l'on place maintenant une trappe
Dite chronique bleue

Il suffisait de s'asseoir pour être censé absent

2

Christ dit: Voici la Neige

3

        Mais il est décidé de chercher
Dans une paisible indolence
    Et tous deux se promettent de vivre

Verdammnis ist im Wesen

Marcelin Pleynet

1

And the man who played this character held in each hand
A lighted torch
Whereby the Queen went
Under the awnings
Hung from the tops of the towers
Cluttered today with scaffolding

The highest part was thought of as paradise

Beneath the hollow structure
This limbo contained Adam and Eve
And possessed two great steel eyes
At the edge of the theatre
Where they are now installing a trapdoor
Called blue chronicle

It was enough to sit down to be thought of as off-stage

2

Christ says: Here's the Snow

3

       But it is decided to investigate
A peaceful indolence
   And both make up their minds to live

4

Parlons disent-ils
                    Ou taisons-nous
            De froid
Fait illisible encore   mais vous
Le nappe d'acier
                Ils apprenaient à vivre
— ce ne sont plus ici —

5

Elle dans une grotte
C'est-à-dire par l'effet d'une noire mélancolie
Comme ils pouvaient la vaincre également
Muni du secret de faire paraître les absents

6

Il parle de l'haleine

7

Par exemple l'homme qui s'agite en marchant
Remue lorsqu'il boit
                    Autant de lingots d'or qu'il y a
de grains de sable dans la mer

(*Paysages en deux*)

4

Let's talk they say
                    Or let's keep quiet
        From cold
Still unreadable deed   but you
The steel sheet
            They learned to live
– these are no longer here –

5

She in a grotto
That's to say as the result of a black melancholy
Since they too had the means to conquer it
Furnished with the secret of making the absent appear

6

He talks about breath

7

For example the man who becomes agitated while walking
Stirs when he drinks
                    As many gold ingots as there are
grains of sand in the sea

Comme, *extrait*

Marcelin Pleynet

Derrière cet arbre guettant celle qui ne parle plus il cherche une
rumeur sur la page   autre chose
un peu de lui-même
une forme interrogative (ou le livre ouvert-fermé)

Le même en quelque sorte celui-ci (ou un autre) mais un autre
qui ne serait plus pour lui (je vous l'avais bien dit) vous l'écrivez

Pourtant ce qui est ouvert est fermé
Ce qui est debout est droit
au centre avec ce qui passe (insiste)
le langage ne dit rien qu'ici maintenant ce qu'il dit
et ce qui ouvert et fermé brûlerait le livre
ou encore cette poussière (ce désir) sur les choses

Elle parle
Elle porte un livre
Elle ne se souvient plus de nous
(L'impuissant ferme le livre qui s'ouvre)
sur cette herbe humide
dans ce pays dont la voici maintenant traversée

à cet âge il doit savoir ce qui semble plaisir
et tourner autour du fouet un regard gris

Comme, *extract*

Marcelin Pleynet

Behind this tree lying in wait for her who speaks no more he seeks
an echo on the page   something else
a little of himself
an interrogative form (or the open-closed book)

The same in some ways this person (or someone else) but someone
else who would no longer be for him (I told you so didn't I) you
write him

Yet what is open is closed
What is upright is at right angles
to the centre with what passes (insists)
language says nothing except here now what he says
and what is open and closed would burn the book
or perhaps this dust (this desire) on things

She speaks
She carries a book
She no longer remembers us
(The impotent closes the books that opens up)
on this damp grass
in this country by which she is now in fact crossed

at this age he should know what seems pleasure
and cast a gloomy glance around the whip

Ce qui est spontané quand elle parle c'est la disparition et ce qui disparaît et ce qui apparaît est dit sur la ligne Le sujet lui-même si vous imaginez pouvoir l'écrire s'abîme dans ce qu'il pense à chaque bout un livre en prend la charge et l'étend et ce n'est plus le passé qui parle (ce n'est plus nous qui parlons d'une femme d'un livre) c'est dans son épaisseur toute l'écriture qui vient à nous se dit Les mythes les enfants les dieux la fin et l'origine surgissent de ce qui est écrit Tout fuit rien ne reste mais d'un mot la mémoire surgit comme surgit d'un monde le mot Rien ne se fait mais dans l'épaisseur tout est dit que le soleil se lève et qu'il disparaît et que j'écris dans l'étendue / ici / qu'un livre tient un livre qui tient un livre qui ... et que les signes communiquent en surgissement (ou en abîme) Hier aujourd'hui demain ce qui nous détermine et ce qui nous emporte se fait ici et se fera non plus chronologie mais puissance impuissance rêve et désirs et déjà ils fixent la terre ou le soleil (qui tourne) et déjà disparaissent ... (ils ne finissent pas) ... les spectacles se donnent mais c'est à la fois une plage un étang la mémoire la prophétie c'est aussi bien un couple qu'une leçon un spectacle qu'un drame ligne après ligne page après page tout se refuse et se donne ceux qui sont lus et ceux qui sont parlés les caractères les livres les statues les mots sur les statues l'histoire les idées et les mots et la fragmentation de ce qui dans son projet unit la plus vaste perception ... ainsi tourné au nord les temples singent la réalité qui n'est qu'un double ... Et n'importe le froid le sublime est à peine sec que la lumière s'enfuit. Sous ce ciel couvert (l'horizon nous le savons n'existe pas) les ruines abritent encore un monument un crime surgit encore du tombeau qui parle

et tout cela est vrai

(*Comme*)

What is spontaneous when she speaks is the disappearance and what disappears and what appears is said on the line The subject himself if you imagine you can write him is engulfed by what he thinks at each end a book takes it over and stretches it out and it is no longer the past that speaks (it is no longer we who speak of a woman of a book) it is in its thickness all the writing that comes to us tells itself Myths children gods the end and the origin arises from what is written Everything flees nothing remains but memory arises from a word just as the word arises from a world Nothing develops but in the thickness all is said that the sun rises and that it vanishes and that I write in the stretch / here / that a book holds a book which holds a book which . . . and that signs communicate as uprisings (or in a gulf) Yesterday today tomorrow what determines us and what carries us away develops here and will become not chronology any longer but power impotence dream and desires and already they stare at the earth or the sun (which turns) and already they disappear . . . (they never finish) . . . performances are given but it is simultaneously a beach a pond memory prophecy it is a couple as much as a lesson a performance as much as a drama line after line page after page everything holds back and surrenders those who are read and those who are spoken the characters the books the statues the words on the statues the story the ideas and the words and the fragmentation of what in its project unites the most immense perception . . . thus facing north the temples ape reality which is only a double. . . And despite the cold the sublime is scarcely dry when the light flees. Under the overcast sky (we know the horizon does not exist) the ruins still shelter a monument a crime still arises from the tomb that speaks

and that is all true

267

La nouvelle araignée

Francis Ponge

Au lieu de tuer tous les Caraïbes, il fallait peut-être les séduire par des spectacles, des funambules, des tours de gibecière et de la musique.

(VOLTAIRE)

Dès le lever du jour il est sensible en France — bien que cela se trame dans les coins — et merveilleusement confus dans le langage, que l'araignée avec sa toile ne fasse qu'un.

Si bien — lorsque pâlit l'étoile du silence dans nos petits préaux comme sur nos buissons —

Que la moindre rosée, en paroles distinctes,

Peut nous le rendre étincelant.

Cet animal qui, dans le vide, comme une ancre de navire se largue d'abord,

Pour s'y — voire à l'envers — maintenir tout de suite

— Suspendu sans contexte à ses propres décisions —

Dans l'expectative à son propre endroit,

— Comme il ne dispose pourtant d'aucun employé à son bord, lorsqu'il veut remonter doit ravaler son filin :

Pianotant sans succès au-dessus de l'abîme,

C'est dès qu'il a compris devoir agir autrement.

Pour légère que soit la bête, elle ne vole en effet,

Et ne se connaît pas brigande plus terrestre, déterminée pourtant à ne courir qu'aux cieux.

Il lui faut donc grimper dans les charpentes, pour — aussi aériennement qu'elle le peut — y tendre ses enchevêtrements, dresser ses barrages, comme un bandit par chemins.

The new spider

Francis Ponge

Instead of slaughtering all the Caribs, it might be better, perhaps, to win them over with entertainments: tightrope walkers, jugglers, musicians.

(VOLTAIRE)

From the first grey light of dawn, it becomes apparent in France – although the plot is being woven in obscure corners – and in a marvellously confused language, that the spider and its web form a single unity.

This is so true that – when the star of silence grows pale in our little backyards as upon hedgerows –

The lightest dew, spelling its words out carefully,

Can make this oneness sparkle for us.

This animal which first launches itself into space like a ship's anchor,

Then immediately – though still upside down – holds on there

– Hanging, without context, from its own decisions –

In high hopes and right side up,

Is obliged – since there is no one on board to lend a hand – to swallow its thread again if it wants to haul itself up:

Strumming in frustration above the abyss,

It realizes at last that it ought to try a fresh tack.

Light as the beast may be, it does not fly, is not light-fingered,

And has no ambitions to be a footpad, determined on the contrary to track its prey in the skies.

Thus it must climb up into the roof-timbers to – as aerially as possible – display its entanglements there, set up its barriers, like a highwayman.

Rayonnant, elle file et tisse, mais nullement ne brode,
Se précipitant au plus court;
Et sans doute doit-elle proportionner son ouvrage à la vitesse de sa course comme au poids de son corps,
Pour pouvoir s'y rendre en un point quelconque dans un délai toujours inférieur à celui qu'emploie le gibier le plus vibrant, doué de l'agitation la plus sensationnelle, pour se dépêtrer de ces rets:
C'est ce qu'on nomme le rayon d'action,
Que chacune connaît d'instinct.

Selon les cas et les espèces — et la puissance d'ailleurs du vent —,
Il en résulte:
Soit de fines voilures verticales, sorte de brisebise fort tendus,
Soit des voilettes d'automobilistes comme aux temps héroïques du sport,
Soit des toilettes de brocanteurs,
Soit encore des hamacs ou linceuls assez pareils à ceux des mises au tombeau classiques.

Là-dessus elle agit en funambule funeste:
Seule d'ailleurs, il faut le dire, à nouer en une ces deux notions,
Dont la première sort de corde tandis que l'autre, évoquant les funérailles, signifie souillé par la mort.

Dans la mémoire sensible tout se confond.
Et cela est bien,
Car enfin, qu'est-ce que l'araignée? Sinon l'entéléchie, l'âme immédiate, commune à la bobine, au fil, à la toile,
A la chasseresse et à son linceul.

Radiant, it spins and weaves, but never embroiders,
As it hastens along its short cuts;
And it has doubtless to adapt its work output to the speed of
its trajectory as well as the weight of its body,
In order to make its way to another point, always in less time
than that taken by the most furiously struggling prey, capable of
the most sensational agitation, to free itself from these toils:
This is what is called the radius of action,
Which everyone knows instinctively.

Depending on the circumstances and the species – and, indeed,
the wind velocity –
The result will be:
Either fine vertical sails, like tightly-stretched window-
curtains,
Or female motorists' hat-veils from the sport's heroic early
days,
Or the get-ups of junk dealers,
Or, again, hammocks or shrouds rather like those depicted in
classic entombments.

The creature performs thereon like a funereal funambulist:
The only creature, incidentally, able to link these two notions,
The first of which evokes the gloom of death, while the second
derives initially from the word for rope.

In a receptive memory all is inextricably blended.
Which is as it should be,
For after all, what is a spider but the entelechy, the core or
soul, common to the spool, the thread, the web,
To the huntress and her shroud.

Pourtant, la mémoire sensible est aussi cause de la raison,
Et c'est ainsi que, de *funus* à *funis*,
Il faut remonter,
A partir de cet amalgame,
Jusqu'à la cause première.

Mais une raison qui ne lâcherait pas en route le sensible,
Ne serait-ce pas cela, la poésie:

Une sorte de *syl-lab-logisme*?
Résumons-nous.

L'araignée, constamment à sa toilette
Assassine et funèbre,
La fait dans les coins;
Ne la quittant que la nuit,
Pour des promenades,
A fin de se dégourdir les jambes.

Morte, en effet, c'est quand elle a les jambes ployées et ne
ressemble plus qu'à un filet à provisions,
Un sac à malices jeté au rebut.

Hélas! Que ferions-nous de l'ombre d'une étoile,
Quand l'étoile elle-même a plié les genoux?

La réponse est muette,
La décision muette:

(L'araignée alors se balaye ...)

At the same time, receptive memory is also the cause of
ratiocination,
And thus, from *funus* to *funis*,
It is necessary to reascend
From this amalgam
Back to the prime cause.

But there is surely one kind of ratiocination that would not let
go of sentient receptivity in mid-journey,
And that is poetry:

A sort of *syl-lab-logism*?
Let us recapitulate.

The spider, constantly at its toilet,
Its murderous and baleful toilet,
Goes at it in corners;
Stopping only at night
To stretch its legs
By strolling around.

But when dead its limbs are curled inwards and all it looks like
is a string bag,
A bag of malice thrown on the rubbish heap.

Alas! What should we do with the shadow of a star,
When the star itself has its knees bent?

The reply is silent,
The decision silent:

(The spider simply sweeps off . . .)

Tandis qu'au ciel obscur monte la même étoile — qui nous conduit au jour.

(*Le Grand Recueil, pièces*)

While in the dark sky the same star rises – and guides us towards day.

L'ardoise

Francis Ponge

L'ardoise — à y bien réfléchir c'est-à-dire peu, car elle a une gamme de reflets très réduite et un peu comme l'aile du bouvreuil passant vite, excepté sous l'effet des précipitations critiques, du ciel gris bleuâtre au ciel noir — s'il y a un livre en elle, il n'est que de prose: une pile sèche; une batterie déchargée; une pile de quotidiens au cours des siècles, quoique illustrés par endroits des plus anciens fossiles connus, soumis à des pressions monstrueuses et soudés entre eux; mais enfin le produit d'un métamorphisme incomplet.

Il lui manque d'avoir été touchée à l'épaule par le doigt du feu. Contrairement aux filles de Carrare, elle ne s'enveloppera donc ni ne développera jamais de lumière.

Ces demoiselles sont de la fin du secondaire tandis qu'elle appartient aux établissements du primaire, notre institutrice de vieille roche, montrant un visage triste, abattu: un teint évoquant moins la nuit que l'ennuyeuse pénombre des temps.

Délitée, puis sciée en quernons, sa tranche atteinte au vif, compacte, mate, n'est que préparée au poli, poncée: jamais rien de plus, rien de moins, si la pluie quelquefois, sur le versant nord, y fait luire comme les bourguignottes d'une compagnie de gardes, immobile.

Pourtant, il y a une idée de crédit dans l'ardoise.

Humble support pour une humble science, elle est moins faite pour ce qui doit demeurer en mémoire que pour des formulations précaires, crayeuses, pour ce qui doit passer d'une mémoire à l'autre, rapidement, à plusieurs reprises, et pouvoir être facilement effaceé.

De même, aux offenses du ciel elle s'oppose en formation oblique, une aile refusée.

Quel plaisir d'y passer l'éponge.

Il y a moins de plaisir à écrire sur l'ardoise qu'à tout y effacer

276

Slate

Francis Ponge

If one reflects well on slate – in other words, not very much, since its range of reflections is very limited and not unlike the wing of a bullfinch in full flight, except under the effect of critical precipitations, of skies changing from blue-grey to black – one may come to the conclusion that any book it may contain will consist entirely of prose: a dry cell; a drained battery; a pile of newspapers reaching back through the centuries, illustrated in places by some of the oldest known fossils which, though submitted to monstrous pressures, and now welded into the pile, are still the product of an incomplete metamorphosis.

It suffers from having never been touched on the shoulder by the finger of fire. Unlike the daughters of Carrara, therefore, it will never swathe itself in light nor radiate light.

These damsels come from the end of the secondary, whereas slate belongs to the establishments of the primary, and is our old-time governess, stony-hearted, showing a sad, dejected face: a complexion less evocative of night than of the dull penumbra of the ages.

Cut along the line of stratification, then sawn into square blocks, slate's compact, dull-hued cross-section, once the quick has been reached, is simply prepared for polishing, pumiced: never anything more or anything less, except perhaps when the rain sometimes makes it shine, on the northern slope, like the vizorless helmets of a company of royal guards at attention.

Nevertheless, a great deal of credit attaches to slate, is put on the slate.

A humble prop for a humble science, it is designed less for what must be retained by the memory than for precarious, chalky formulations, for what must be transmitted from one memory to another, rapidly, repeatedly, for what can easily be obliterated.

d'un seul geste, comme le météore négateur qui s'y appuie à peine et qui la rend au noir.

Mais un nouveau virage s'accomplit vite; d'humide à humble elle perd ses voyelles, sèche bientôt:

«Laissez-moi sans souci détendre ma glabelle et l'offrir au moindre écolier, qui du moindre chiffon l'essuie.»

L'ardoise n'est enfin qu'une sorte de pierre d'attente, terne et dure.

Songeons-y.

(*Le Nouveau Recueil*)

In the same way, it resists the sky's transgressions deviously, at an angle, keeping one wing hidden.

Let's say no more about it. Clean slate!

There is less pleasure to be gained in writing on a slate, on the subject of slate, than in obliterating one's words, one's thoughts, with a single gesture, like that corrective weather phenomenon the sudden squall which has only to brush up against it for a moment to turn it black, painting a gloomy picture of it in an instant.

But it quickly changes colour again, loses its vowels between moistness and modesty, soon dries:

'Let me unknit my brow and offer its smooth surface to the humblest schoolboy, who may wipe it with the humblest rag.'

A slate is really nothing but a kind of temporary stone, lustreless and hard.

Worth contemplating.

Les ombres

Jacques Prévert

Tu es là
en face de moi
dans la lumière de l'amour
Et moi
je suis là
en face de toi
avec la musique du bonheur
Mais ton ombre
sur le mur
guette tous les instants
des mes jours
et mon ombre à moi
fait de même
épiant ta liberté
Et pourtant je t'aime
et tu m'aimes
comme on aime le jour et la vie ou l'été
Mais comme les heures qui se suivent
et ne sonnent jamais ensemble
nos deux ombres se poursuivent
comme deux chiens de la même portée
détachés de la même chaine
mais hostiles tous deux à l'amour
uniquement fidèles à leur maître
à leur maîtresse
et qui attendent patiemment
mais tremblants de détresse
la séparation des amants
qui attendent
que notre vie s'achève
et notre amour

Shadows

Jacques Prévert

There you are
looking at me
in the light of love
And here
am I
looking at you
with the music of happiness
Yet on the wall
your silhouette
shadows every moment
of my days
while mine does the same
to yours
spying on your freedom
And yet I love you
and you love me
as we love the days of life and the summer
But just as the hours that follow each other
never strike at the same time
so our two silhouettes shadow each other
like a pair of twin puppies
unleashed from the same chain
both hating love
and obedient only to their master
to their mistress
and who wait in patience
though trembling with distress
for the lovers' parting
who wait
for our life to come to an end
with our love

et que nos os leur soient jetés
pour s'en saisir
et les cacher et les enfouir
et s'en fouir en même temps
sous les cendres du désir
dans les débris du temps

(*Histoires*)

and for our bones to be thrown to them
so that they can snap them up
hide them and bury them
and at the same time bury themselves
under the ashes of passion
in the ruins of time

Comme par miracle

Jacques Prévert

Comme par miracle
Des oranges aux branches d'un oranger
Comme par miracle
Un homme s'avance
Mettant comme par miracle
Un pied devant l'autre pour marcher
Comme par miracle
Une maison de pierre blanche
Derrière lui sur la terre est posée
Comme par miracle
L'homme s'arrête au pied de l'oranger
Cueille une orange l'épluche et la mange
Jette la peau au loin et crache les pépins
Apaisant comme par miracle
Sa grande soif du matin
Comme par miracle
L'homme sourit
Regardant le soleil qui se lève
Et qui luit
Comme par miracle
Et l'homme ébloui rentre chez lui
Et retrouve comme par miracle
Sa femme endormie
Émerveillé
De la voir si jeune si belle
Et comme par miracle
Nue dans le soleil
Il la regarde
Et comme par miracle elle se réveille
Et lui sourit
Comme par miracle il la caresse

Just like a miracle

Jacques Prévert

Just like a miracle
Oranges on the branches of an orange tree
Just like a miracle
A man comes along
Walking just like a miracle
By putting one foot in front of the other
Just like a miracle a house built of white stone
Is standing on the ground behind him
Just like a miracle
The man stops walking underneath the orange tree
Plucks an orange peels it and eats it
Scatters the peel far and wide and spits out the pips
Quenching just like a miracle
His tremendous early morning thirst
Just like a miracle
The man smiles
Looking at the sun
Rising and shining
Just like a miracle
And full of delight the man goes back indoors
And just like a miracle finds his wife still there
Still asleep
Full of wonder
At seeing how young and beautiful she is
He looks at her
Naked in the sunlight
And just like a miracle she wakes up
And smiles at him
Just like a miracle he puts his hand out to her

Et comme par miracle elle se laisse caresser
Alors comme par miracle
Des oiseaux de passage passent
Qui passent comme cela
Comme par miracle
Des oiseaux de passage qui s'en vont vers la mer
Volant très haut
Au-dessus de la maison de pierre
Où l'homme et la femme
Comme par miracle
Font l'amour
Des oiseaux de passage au-dessus du jardin
Où comme par miracle l'oranger berce ses oranges
Dans le vent du matin
Jetant comme par miracle son ombre sur la route
Sur la route où un prêtre s'avance
Le nez dans son bréviaire le bréviaire dans les mains
Et le prêtre marchant sur la pelure d'orange jetée par l'homme
    au loin
Glisse et tombe
Comme un prêtre qui glisse sur une pelure d'orange et qui
    tombe sur une route
Une beau matin.

(*Histoires*)

And just like a miracle she lets him take her in his arms
Then just like a miracle
Birds of passage fly by overhead
As birds of passage do fly by overhead
Just like a miracle
Birds of passage flying by overhead on their way to the sea
Flying very high
Over the house built of stone
Where the man and the woman
Just like a miracle
Are making love
Birds of passage flying by over the garden
Where just like a miracle the orange tree is rocking its oranges
In the morning breeze
Throwing just like a miracle its shadow across the road
Across the road where a priest is coming along
His nose in his missal his missal in his hands
And the priest puts his foot on the orange peel scattered far
    and wide by the man
Slips and falls over
Like a priest skidding on a piece of orange peel and falling
    over on a road
On a fine and beautiful morning.

Ce n'est pas moi qui chante . . .

Jacques Prévert

Ce n'est pas moi qui chante
c'est les fleurs que j'ai vues
ce n'est pas moi qui ris
c'est le vin que j'ai bu
ce n'est pas moi qui pleure
c'est mon amour perdu.

(*Fatras*)

It's not me who goes singing . . .

Jacques Prévert

It's not me who goes singing
But the flowers I walk past
It's not me who goes laughing
But the wine I still taste
It's not me who goes weeping
But the love I have lost

Le porc

Raymond Queneau

Le porc est un ami de l'homme
il lui ressemble énormément
pour des dents on le dit tout comme
aussi point de vue aliments

le porc est un ami de l'homme
on l'égorge communément
on saigne sans nulle vergogne
on se régale de son sang

goret animal adorable
et gracieux lorsque tu deviens
quelque chose de consommable
on oublie ton charme enfantin

on te suspend par les deux pieds
on te laisse le cou coupé
hurler hurler hurler hurler
toute une longue matinée

et lorsqu'enfin tu es bien mort
on se réjouit du bon boudin
que l'on extraira de ton corps
et voilà, porc, quelle est ta fin

pour toi point d'autres funérailles
tu dormiras pas allongé
en gardant pour toi tes entrailles
et tes jambons bien enterrés

(*Battre la campagne*)

The pig

Raymond Queneau

With man the pig's most popular
they hardly differ – if at all
their teeth are very similar
their tastes in food identical

the pig's a friend to all of us
we slaughter him communally
he bleeds but we don't make much fuss
and on his spoils feast regally

sweet piglet you're adorable
and full of grace but once you've grown
into a shape that's edible
you'll find your youthful charms have flown

you're hung up by your toe and heel
with throat cut like a crescent moon
to squeal and squeal and squeal and squeal
from crack of dawn till blaze of noon

then when you're dead as dead can be
the best black pudding we shall blend
from your select anatomy
and that dear pig is how you'll end

no ceremony else in fact
your corpse will not be laid to sleep
with brains and liver left intact
and hambones buried six feet deep

Buccin

Raymond Queneau

Dans sa coquille vivant
le mollusque ne parlait pas
facilement à l'homme
mort il raconte maintenant
toute la mer à l'oreille de l'enfant
qui s'en étonne
qui s'en étonne

(Fendre les flots)

Whelk

Raymond Queneau

The mollusc living in its shell
never found very much to say
to man
but dead it tells the ocean's tale
to ears of children listening
in hushed surprise
in hushed surprise

Le livre de bord

Raymond Queneau

La reine Victoria donna
des jumelles à mon grand-père
pour avoir sauvé un marin
que voulait noyer la tempête
un marin anglais bien sûr sinon
que viendrait faire là
la reine Victoria

Le vaisseau s'appelait l'Arabie
il allait à la Chine
il restait trois ans (au moins) parti
souvenirs de porcelaine

Hommes et femmes au Japon
se baignaient nus ensemble
est-ce un récit de voyageur?
Les grands livres noirs de bord
ont disparu je ne sais quand
mais les jumelles toujours présentes
permettent de voir quoi?
de voir quoi?

(*Fendre les flots*)

The log

Raymond Queneau

Queen Victoria presented
my grandpa with a pair
of binoculars for saving
a drowning sailor from the storm
an English sailor otherwise
what would Queen Victoria
be doing in this story

The ship called the Arabia
sailed across the Chinese main
and stayed away three years (or more)
memories frail as porcelain

In Japan the men and women
took their bath together naked
is this just a traveller's tale?
The big black ship's books disappeared
some time ago I don't know when
the glasses though are still around
revealing what to us today?
revealing what?

Une traversée en 1922

Raymond Queneau

Pourquoi donc tant de gens ont-ils le mal de mer
telle était la question qu'à moi-même posait
la vue âcre de ceux qui en chœur vomissaient
faisant route à vapeur vers la grande Angleterre
on se trouvait alors loin du cap d'Antifer
mais me trompé-je ici? n'était-ce pas à Dieppe
que j'embarquai ce jour pour aller monoglotte
apprendre autre langage en dansant l'one-step?
Oui c'était bien à Dieppe et les gens vomissaient
quel spectacle attristant quand on est sur la flotte
La beauté de la nuit respire ces odeurs
machines ou cambouis et surtout les senteurs
qu'étend l'individu avec l'in-digestion
je tirais vanité de ce mal être indemme
j'avais le pied marin et l'estomac de même
Vanité vanité: malades, bien portants
arrivèrent ensemble au port des anglicans
et je ne sus alors que dire yes ou bien no
bien au hasard d'ailleurs ne comprenant que pouic
à ce que racontaient les douaniers britanniques
qui lisaient de travers mon nom Raymond Queneau
et lorsque je revins un mois ou deux plus tard
en sachant prononcer deux ou trois autres mots
les douaniers me semblaient toujours dans le brouillard
le même qui cernait les contours du bateau
de nouveau quelques gens en chœur redégueulèrent
vanité vanité je reviens d'Angleterre
ayant le pied marin mais ne sachant pas mieux
que lorsque je partis la langue de Chexpire

(Fendre les flots)

296

Crossing the channel in 1922

Raymond Queneau

How can so many people be seasick at once
was the question I found myself forced to enquire
by the sight of an acridly vomiting choir
steaming over to England and leaving fair France
far from Cap d'Antifer though there's quite a good chance
that I've got it all wrong and the quays at Dieppe
saw my monoglot self climb on board to perfect
its English along with the good old one-step
Yes just outside Dieppe the big breakers rose higher
and the seasick grew sicker till seascapes were wrecked
Through the beauty of night wafts the stench from below
bringing engine-oil galley-grease ill winds that blow
from those souls with dyspepsia much overwrought
their distress made me smug their ills I'd never catch
having natural sea-legs and stomach to match
Boastful vanity: whether with seasickness fraught
or immune one way led to the anglican port
all I knew how to say then was yes sometimes no
indiscriminately and there wasn't an ounce
of good sense I could make from attempts to pronounce
by the King's customs-men my name Raymond Queneau
and when I went home one month later or two
hardly adding a word to my minuscule score
those customs-men still lacked the foggiest clue
and were quite in the dark like our ship with its crew
and its chorus on deck being seasick once more
Boastful vanity: leaving old England's grey shore
with my marvellous sea-legs there wasn't a doubt
I knew Shakespeare's tongue no more than when I'd set out

Matin d'octobre

Jacques Réda

Lev Davidovitch Bronstein agite sa barbiche, agite
Ses mains, sa chevelure hirsute; encore un peu, il va
Bondir de son gilet et perdre ses besicles d'érudit,
Lui qui parle aux marins de Cronstadt taillés dans le bois mal
Équarri de Finlande, et guère moins sensibles que
Les crosses des fusils qui font gicler la neige sale.
Il prêche, Lev Davidovitch, il s'époumone, alors
Que sur le plomb de la Néva lentement les tourelles
Du croiseur *Aurora* vers la façade obscure du
Palais d'Hiver se tournent.
                    Quel bagou; quel ciel jaune;
Quel poids d'histoire sur les ponts déserts où parfois ronfle
Une voiture aux ailes hérissées de baïonnettes.
A Smolny, cette nuit, les barbes ont poussé; les yeux,
Brûlés par le tabac et le filament des ampoules,
Chavirent, Petrograd, devant ton crépuscule, ton silence
Où là-bas, au milieu des Lettons appliqués et farouches,
Lev Davidovitch prophétise, exhorte, menace, tremble
Aussi de sentir la masse immobile des siècles
Basculer sans retour, comme les canons sur leur axe,
Au bord de ce matin d'octobre.
                        (Et déjà Vladimir
Ilitch en secret a rejoint la capitale; il dormira
Plus tard, également grimé, dans un cercueil de verre,
Immobile toujours sous les bouquets et les fanfares.
Cependant Lev Davidovitch agite sa tignasse,
Rattrape son lorgnon,
                  — un peu de sang, un peu de ciel
Mexicain s'y mélangeront le dernier jour, si loin
De toi boueux octobre délirant au vent des drapeaux rouges.)

(*Amén*)

October morning

Jacques Réda

Lev Davidovitch Bronstein's goatee beard quivers,
His hands quiver, so does his shaggy hair; in a moment he's
    going to
Pop out of his waistcoat and lose his professorial eyeglasses,
He who talks to the sailors of Kronstadt carved from roughly
Squared Finnish timber and almost as tough as
The rifle butts which make the dirty snow spurt up.
He preaches, Lev Davidovitch, shouts himself hoarse, while
Slowly the turrets of the *Aurora* turn upon the leaden Neva
Towards the Winter Palace's dark frontage.
                    What a smooth tongue, and what a yellow sky;
What weight of history on the empty bridges where sometimes
A car rumbles, wings bristling with bayonets.
At Smolny, tonight, the beards have grown; eyes
Smarting with tobacco and the light bulbs' glare
Show their whites, Petrograd, facing your silence
Where amid the fierce, attentive Letts,
Lev Davidovitch prophesises, exhorts, threatens, trembles
Too as he feels the centuries' immobile mass
Swing once and for all around, like guns upon their axes,
At the very edge of this October morning.
                                (And already Vladimir
Ilyitch has secretly reached the capital; he will sleep,
Later, made up for the same part, in a glass coffin,
For ever motionless beneath the bouquets and ovations.
Meanwhile, Lev Davidovitch jerks back his tousled hair,
Clutches his spectacles,
                    – a little blood, a little
Mexican sky will mingle there on his last day, so far
From you, muddy October, rapturous in the wind of the red
    flags.)

Le bracelet perdu

Jacques Réda

Maintenant je reviens en arrière avec vous,
Cherchant des yeux ce bracelet dans la poussière,
Par un midi si dur que la lumière semble
Elle-même se dévorer, bientôt absente
En son vaste brasier qui se volatilise.
                                        Et vous,
Qui vous agenouillez dans l'herbe blanche et les cailloux,
Votre profil, perdu sous l'horizon de vent qui nous entoure,
Fait de ce chemin creux une barque en dérive
Où nous serons ensemble à jamais maintenant,
Oubliés par le temps que la grandeur du jour immobilise,
Tandis que le sang bat à votre poignet nu.

(*Amén*)

The lost bracelet

Jacques Réda

Now I go back with you,
Eyes seeking the bracelet in the dust,
Upon a noon so harsh that the light seems
To devour itself, and soon is gone
In the hot vapour of its own great brazier.
                                    And you
Kneeling amid the white grass and the pebbles,
Your profile, lost beneath the horizon of wind that rings us,
Makes of this sunken path a ship adrift
Where we shall be together always,
Forgotten by time which the day's huge brightness stops,
While the blood beats at your naked wrist.

La distance du feu

Jean-Claude Renard

Le feu qui peint ce soir la chambre ensevelie
Circule autour de moi comme un bouclier noir vivant
   où je ne marche
Mais vivant où je suis si je deviens vivant.
Son obscure chaleur qui s'en vient et s'en va comme
   un cerf dans la neige
Ma présence peut-être me la rendra présente.
Ou faut-il que la flamme à peine prise au froid
S'éteigne intimement
Pour inviter ma mort à inventer sans cesse une lumière d'être,
Un sens et un mystère plus puissants que la nuit?
Ou la faut-il ici foncière mais future
Comme de cet écart où le sol sec éclate
Et forme une fontaine
Et la montagne pure avoisine la mer
Pour inviter en moi ce que je crée de libre en m'inventant
   moi-même avec chaque présence
A inventer sans cesse la vérité du feu?

(*La Terre du sacre*)

Fire's distance

Jean-Claude Renard

The fire which this evening paints the buried room
Flows round me like a black shield alive where my steps halt
But alive where I am if I come alive.
Perhaps my presence will render present to me
Its dark warmth that comes and goes like a deer in the snow.
Or must the flame thinly burning in the cold
Flicker out intimately
Inviting my death to create continuously a brightness of being,
A meaning and mystery mightier than the night?
Or must the flame deep-rooted but future be here
As in that lonely spot where the parched ground splits
And makes a fountain
And the pure mountain borders the sea
Inviting into me whatever is free that I create by moulding
    myself anew with each presence
To create continuously the truth of fire?

Récit 4

Jean-Claude Renard

Si d'étranges colombes ne s'étaient posées là,
Dans cette lande rousse lainée d'un champ de pierres
   où je cherchais un signe,
Il n'y aurait pas eu (pourquoi?) sur les ruisseaux
Tant de fougères mortes.

Une chambre peinte de pommes, de cruches, de soleils
Connaissait les mots noirs qui consument la mer
Et forent sous les os, à l'envers de l'amour,
De grands pays déments.

Quelqu'un qui ne parlait que de choses secrètes
Y enterra le feu,
— Tournant vers le silence les arbres d'un ravin
Où se perdirent les sources.

Le soir, dans les genêts,
Toute piste de cerf s'écartait de son corps qui profanait le sacre,
Pourrissait l'herbe pure
Et transmuait le sang en quel sang possédé.

Quand les branches furent sèches
Et la peur d'exister assez prête au néant
Les ténèbres y prirent — puis brûlèrent les agneaux
Descendus des collines.

Plus tard, près des falaises,
A travers la mémoire des puits antérieurs et l'écriture des astres,
Une main humiliante approcha de l'angoisse
Un livre ouvert au vide, au sommeil et au froid.

Récit 4

Jean-Claude Renard

If strange doves had not alighted there,
On this russet heath napped by a field of stones where I was
    looking for a sign,
The brooks would not have carried (why?)
So many dead ferns.

A room painted with apples, pitchers, suns
Knew the black words which eat up the sea
Then tunnel under the bones, on love's other side,
Of great demented lands.

Someone who spoke only of secret things
Buried fire there,
– Turning towards silence the trees of a ravine
Where the springs vanished.

That evening, in the thickets of broom,
The deer tracks all kept clear of his body which was
    profaning the consecration,
Rotting the pure grass
And changing blood into what blood of the possessed.

When the branches were dry
And the fear of life ready enough for the void
The shadows caught at them – then burned the lambs
Just down from the hills.

Later, near the cliffs,
Traversing the memory of earlier well-springs and the stars'
    handwriting,
A humiliating hand confronted anguish with
A book open to the void, to sleep and cold.

D'épaisses lâchetés
Durent avec le pain manger la cendre acide
Des dieux momifiés
D'où s'éloignaient les pluies.

Il fallut aux racines
La patience de l'eau filtrant dans les cavernes
Pour retrouver au fond du métal et du sable
La lumière arrachée.

Mais de ces tiroirs rouges — ce lit d'initiation
Là-bas, dans une armoire dont les puissances veillent et vivent
  de tuer,
Remonte encore parfois, comme une odeur d'alcool,
La fascinante absence d'un langage détruit.

(*La Braise et la rivière*)

Jostling ignominies were forced
To eat a bread mingled with the sour ash
Of the mummified gods
From places where the rains held back.

The roots required
The patience of the water seeping through the caverns
To find once more, deep in metal and sand,
The torn-out light.

But from these red cupboard-drawers – this bed of initiation
    Down there, in a cupboard whose prowling powers live by
    killing,
There still re-arises sometimes, like an odour of alcohol,
The fascinating absence of a ruined language.

Avec de grands gestes ...

Armand Robin

Avec de grands gestes,
J'ai jeté pendant quatre ans mon âme dans toutes les langues,
J'ai cherché, libre et fou, tous les endroits de vérité,
Surtout j'ai cherché les dialectes où l'homme n'était pas dompté.
Je me suis mis en quête de la vérité dans toutes les langues.

Le martyre de mon peuple on m'interdisait
        En français.
J'ai pris le croate, l'irlandais, le hongrois, l'arabe, le chinois
        Pour me sentir un homme délivré.

J'aimais d'autant plus les langues étrangères
        Pour moi pures, tellement à l'écart:
Dans ma langue française (ma seconde langue) il y avait eu
        toutes les trahisons
        On savait y dire oui à l'infamie!

J'ai senti le martyre de mon peuple dans les mots de tous les
        pays:
J'ai souffert en breton, français, norvégien; têhèque, slovêne,
        croate;
        Et surtout en russe:

Je me suis étendu sur la grande terre russe,
J'entendais les chants d'un peuple immense qui voulait bien
        mourir

Et là, crucifié, je ne sentais pas de mal,

With sweeping gestures . . .

Armand Robin

With sweeping gestures
For four years I threw my soul into the midst of all languages,
Free and mad, I sought for truth wherever it was to be found,
Most of all sought for those dialects where man was not tamed,
I went in quest of truth in the midst of all languages.

The martyrdom of my people I was forbidden to speak of
       In French.
I took Croatian, Irish, Hungarian, Arabic, Chinese
   To feel myself a free man.

I loved foreign languages so much the more
   Because to me pure, so much set apart:
In my own French (my second tongue) there have been so many
  treasons
   Men could say yes in it to infamous things!

I felt the martyrdom of my people in the words of every
   land:
I suffered in Breton, French, Norwegian, Czech, Slovene,
  Croatian;
   But most of all in Russian:

I stretched myself out on the great Russian earth,
I heard the songs of a huge people that was resigned to
  death

And there, crucified, I felt no pain,

Là, fatigué, je ne sentais que de la rosée,
Là, fatigué de moi, je me sentais reposé,

Là fatigué, j'ai tout senti en rosée.

(*Le Monde d'une voix*)

There, weary, felt only the dew,
Weary of myself, felt reposed,

Weary, sensed all things in dew.

Tou Fou

Armand Robin

Il y a plus de mille ans, dans le non-temps du chant,
Errant sans moi, sans ma vie, j'ai rencontré Tou Fou criant.

Loin de tout pays, de tout temps, nous fûmes amis à l'instant.

Il aida ma jonque d'instants oscillants
Il fut, plus dur pour moi que moi, mes instants déchirants
(Il fut plus bas que l'eau mes instants déchirants).

Dans les ruines de Tchang-Ngang j'eus ma patrie,
De village en village avec lui j'ai fui.

Il avait sur lui les massacres, les ruines, la guerre,
Il ne savait pas plaire.

(*Le Monde d'une voix*)

Tu Fu

Armand Robin

It is more than a thousand years, in the no-time of song,
Since, wandering without myself, without my life, I met Tu Fu
   crying.

Far from all lands, all ages, we were friends in a moment.

He succoured my junk of oscillating moments
He was, harsher for me than myself, my terrible moments
(He was, in the depths, my terrible moments).

In the ruins of Chang-an I found my own country,
From village to village with him I fled away.

He had to bear massacres, ruin and war.
Upon pleasing he set no store.

Théâtre des agissements d'Eros, *extrait*

Denis Roche

Théâtral acte d'Amour: 1re *chance*

hors du bouillonnement de l'instrument, sem-
blable à cette phrase mal tournée de notre suicide
Ensemble, à l'Épée-de-rose — enseigne verte, on
Voit un peu de verdure de Sologne au travers —,
... n'osant donner de l'héroïne aux vers afin que
Nul ne meure d'une telle agronomique erreur:

Une jupe fleurie qui crée un Amour à chaque pas,
Dérobe à nos yeux de ravissants appas; et cette
Cuisse comme à Vénus potelée ... A mille beautés,
A mille appas vivants, atours, vous ne substituez que
Des empêchements! ... Et ce soulier mignon, qui
Couvre un pied d'Hébé, de Vénus, tout provocant qu'il
Est, vaut-il ses charmes nus? ...
Tu en as menti, ô fleur de mes lèvres, les
Haricots et les bulles des folles, ton cul bien
Droit fait vers moi quelques périphrases (inuti-
les aujourd'hui) en forme de tire-bouchons.

*

Théâtral acte d'Amour: 2e *chance*

                                  que
Des bords d'une nappe de coton j'essuyai
L'arme encore coupante de ta puanteur:

Eros possessed: theatricals, *extract*

Denis Roche

Demonstrative act of Love: 1st chance

outside the seething of the tool, which re-
sembles this clumsy phrase of our suicide
Together, at The Rose Sword – green sign, you
see a little Sologne greenery through it —,
. . . not daring to give heroin to the worms lest
Any die of such an error of husbandry:

A flower'd gown that creates a Cupid at each step
Hides from our eyes delectable charms; and this
Thigh as round as Venus'. . . . A thousand beauties,
A thousand living charms, and ornaments, you replace but with
Hindrances! . . . And this darling slipper, that
Encloses a foot like Hebe's or Venus', alluring as it
Is, can it match her naked grace? . . .
You lied about it, o flower of my lips, the
Beans and the crazy women's bubbles, your arse perfectly
Upright performs towards me a number of circumlocutions (use-
less today) having the shape of corkscrews.

*

Demonstrative act of Love: 2nd chance

that
With the edges of a cotton cloth I wiped
The still-sharp weapon of your stink:

(ici la citation de Mathurin Régnier)
Le blé plus facile des peintres était tout-
à-fait saccagé quand nous nous sommes relevés.
Quelle poésie enfin enfoncée dans un trou de
Glaise n'aime pas les jupes dont on fait les
Bouchons? — «Voudriez-vous me faire un
Plaisir, Mademoiselle? — Oui, oui, oui. —
De donner ces deux-là ... — Je sais, je sais ...»
J'ai beau y mettre des ronds-de-jambe, des
Sphères, des Pulcinelles, au besoin la balan-
çoire même en signe de puritaine sentine,
La poésie, d'une crémière, ou du bond qu'un
Augustin ferait sur icelle, n'en revêtira jamais
Pour autant l'habit que je te passe quand il ne
Tient qu'à moi de remettre l'assaut (sic).

Théâtral acte d'Amour: immédiatement après la 2e chance

Quand on vient d'écrire des phrases comme celles
De la page précédente je suis avec des brindilles
Ma compagne la plus avancée pensant amasser mon

(here the quotation from Mathurin Régnier)*
The more accessible wheat of the painters was thor-
oughly pillaged when we stood up again.
What poetry, finally shoved into a hole of
Clay, dislikes the skirts from which cork-
screws are made? — 'Would you grant me one
Delight, milady? — Oh yes, oh yes. —
To yield that pair . . . — I know, I know . . .'
It doesn't matter if I add court manners,
Spheres, Pulcinellas, or if needed the
Swing itself as a token of puritan bilge,
Poetry, concerning a dairymaid, or the leap that
A friar would make upon her, would never for all that
Be adorned with the raiment I lend you when it's
Entirely up to me to resume the attack (*sic*).

Demonstrative act of Love: immediately after the 2nd chance

When one has just written sentences like those
On the preceding page I am with the twigs
My most up-to-date mistress thinking she will hoard my

* already quoted by the author in a section here omitted:
L'Amour est une affection
Qui, par les yeux, dans le cœur entre,
Et, par forme de fluxion
S'escoule par bas de ventre.

For Love is an affection
That finds the heart through th'eyes,
Then, by way of fluxion,
Runs out between the thighs.

Doute comme le prétexte d'un moulin dans une
Dans une campagne ancienne (si tu peux te faire à l'idêe
Du papier et de l'encre de l'empire chinois
Dans un siècle encore plus ancien que ne l'aurait
Été le moulin) J'emplis l'appareil de ce phénomè-
ne d'un grand nombre de ressorts communs à mon
Imagination. Comme le pied posé précautionneuse-
ment sur le rebord de la baignoire la main gauche
Rabattant le gant de toilette vers les plis qui sont
Au niveau de son estomac. Etc. Bien sûr, sinon
Quelle importance, de la verdure ou de la fontaine?
Rien n'emporterait plus ce que j'avais à te dire
En t'entourant les jambes. Conseil enfin: continuer
Par le titre suivant

Interlude dans les chances: des voyelles et de l'érosion

«J'avoue le 20 que je me trouve dans un état
mort.» *Des mets divins du poème charmant,* comme
Le bagage dont s'apprête à disposer l'aubergiste,
Prennent en plein quelque reflet. Le tonnerre
Est à peine venu. Je reconsidère l'avancée
Brutale cette fois de la terre, celle en fri-
che celle dont les gens sont morts où restent
Des abricotiers où la mort mais pas la leur tombe
Creusée dans les pois lieu des arrestations fos-
Et ainsi de suite la parole n'étant rien.
La fatigue pourrait-elle n'être qu'une sorte de
Discipline? Qui me rendrait aveugle quand j'
Écris? Les jeunes voisines de ta beauté

Doubt as the pretext for a mill in an
In an ancient countryside (if you can get used to the idea
Of paper and ink in the Chinese empire
At a time more ancient than the
Mill would have been) I fill the instrument of this won-
der with a large number of incentives familiar to my
Imagination. Such as the foot placed cautious-
ly on the rim of the bathtub, the left hand
Lowering the washcloth towards the folds that are
At the level of her stomach. Etc. Of course, otherwise
Who cares, about greenery or the fountain?
No longer would it matter at all what I had to tell you
When I embraced your legs. Advice finally: continue
With the next title

Interlude between chances: of vowels and erosion

'On the 20th I confess to finding my condition that of one
dead.' *Ambrosia of the enchanting poem*, like
Luggage that the innkeeper prepares to remove,
Receives a certain direct glint. Thunder
Hardly came. I reconsider the earth's
Progression (this time abrupt), that which was left fal-
low that by which people died where there remain
Apricot-trees where death but not theirs falls
Furrowed into the peas place of arrests grav-
And so forth, speech being nothing.
Could fatigue be only a kind of
Discipline? That might blind me when I
Write? The girls who are your beauty's neighbours

Pourraient en rire de notre colloque ne voyant
Pas ce que nos mains font des mets divins du
Poème charmant ――――――――――――

★

Après une exposition prolongée au soleil,
Rideau

Mais ma parole douce, confondante, où pire
Existence *la seconde chope lui affirme que*
C'est vrai, sur le penchant de ma ruine, mon
Absolution. Pêcheur modeste, orduriers mots,
Ordurière appellation, seule une musique enchan-
teresse se soutient près de moi. Son trépas
Résolu, la mélodie imaginant ma lente montée
Vers les prés de son existence, la rencontre
Fortuite du mélange de cette vision colorée
(couleurs des cheveux, des pots sur scène)
Et de ma maladie, tout cela rejoint mon pas
Sans audace, l'hyperbole, mon enjambement de
Balcon en balcon vert, en droite ligne je me
Prolonge comme le paysage vers une nouvelle
Fournée mortuaire, vers sa tombe de toute façon.
(Détumescence-sourire)

(*Eros energumène*)

Might laugh over our exchange not seeing
That our hands create ambrosia of the
enchanting poem ⸻⸻⸻⸻

★

After prolonged exposure to the sun,
Curtain

But my tender, confounding speech, where worse
Existence *the second tankard tells him that*
It's true, on my ruin's inclination, my
Absolution. Modest angler, words foul,
Designation foul, only a bewitching mus-
ic survives near me. Its decease
Settled, the tune that imagines my slow ascension
Towards the meadows of its being, the chance
Encounter of the medley of this florid vision
(colours of tresses, of pots on stage)
And my disease, all this overtakes my step
Without presumption, the hyperbole, my straddling
Balcony to green balcony, in a straight line I
Extend myself like the landscape towards a new
Shipment for burial, in any case towards her grave.
(Detumescence-smile)

Menteur

Robert Sabatier

Menteur, tu mets des oiseaux dans ta robe
Et jettes l'ombre à la tête des loups.
Tu dis le nom d'un ange pour un autre,
Tu te dis pierre et tu n'es que caillou,
Menteur, menteur, tu ne sais plus ton rôle.

Tu prends les mots, ta main les dissimule
Et ta voix triche en te défigurant.
Ta phrase est ivre et ton livre postule
Un monde mort où tu vas délirant,
Menteur, menteur, le temps brûle tes urnes.

Menteur, menteur, je ne peux plus te suivre.
Tu mets l'automne au-dedans de l'été,
Tous les printemps ne sont pas faits de cuivre,
L'hiver existe et le temps ne peut vivre
Que par les jours qu'on peut multiplier.

Menteur, menteur, tu dis des choses telles
Qu'on reconnaît le monde qui n'est pas.
Tu te dis vol et tu manges tes ailes,
Tu te dis marche et tu détruis tes pas.
Menteur, menteur, il faudra bien te taire.

Menteur, menteur, jusque dans ton silence,
Tu troubles l'homme en le recommençant.
Dans ton miroir, tant de ténèbres dansent!
Mais toi, menteur, tu regardes ton sang,
Tu le dis vert et repars en chantant
Toujours suivi de licornes et d'anges.

(*Les Châteaux de millions d'années*)

322

Liar

Robert Sabatier

Liar, you put birds in your robe and
Throw the shadow in the wolves' teeth.
You name one angel for another,
Call yourself stone when merely pebble,
Liar, no longer know your part.

You take words, sleight of hand conceals them,
Your voice cheating as it mars you.
Drunken your phrase, your book supposes
A dead world where you move frenzied,
Liar, time burns your funeral vases.

Liar, liar, I cannot follow you.
You put the autumn into summer,
All springtimes are not made of copper,
Winter exists and time lives only
Through those days we can multiply.

Liar, you utter things that make me
See the world that's nonexistent.
'Fly' you tell yourself, then eat your
Wings up; 'walk', destroy your footsteps.
Liar, it's time that you fell silent.

Liar, you, even in your silence,
Confuse man, starting him anew.
So many shadows dance in your mirror!
You gaze upon your blood and call it
Green and go off singing, always
Followed by unicorns and angels.

Le sablier

Robert Sabatier

Mourir est une fête
Pour les vainqueurs du temps.

Les suicidés s'en vont
Deux par deux sous la lune.
Lèvre pour lèvre, échange
De baisers, de murmures.

Oiseau, dit la complainte.
Tigre, dit le poème.
Humain, dit le silence.

La nuit, les femmes brûlent
Pour renaître au matin.
De longs serpents se glissent
Dans les rêves des morts.

Les mots mangent la bouche
De celui qui les dit.

Papillon? — Crépuscule.
Rumeurs? Non, quelques pierres
Parmi les trous d'un crâne.
Vases, bijoux, calices
Et nourritures mortes.

Et sans un cri, la mer.
Sans un regret, le ciel.
Sans un sourire, un arbre
Tremblant de son bois sec.

The hourglass

Robert Sabatier

Dying is a holiday
For the conquerors of time.

The suicides stroll
Two by two beneath the moon.
Lip for lip, exchange
Of kisses, murmurs.

Bird, says the song.
Tiger, says the poem.
Human, says the silence

Each night, the women are consumed by fire
To be reborn next morning.
Long snakes glide
Into the dreams of the dead.

Words eat the mouth
Of him who utters them.

Butterfly? – Twilight.
Far-off sounds? No, a few stones
Rattling in the hollows of a skull.
Urns, jewels, chalices
And dead sustenance.

The sea without a cry.
The sky without a regret.
A tree without a smile,
Shaking under the weight of its dry wood.

Cheveux de gazon vert,
Cheveux de neige et d'ombre,
Vibrez dans le vent noir.

(*Les Châteaux de millions d'années*)

Hair of green grass,
Hair of snow and shadow,
Flutter in the black wind.

Oiseaux, *extraits*

Saint-John Perse

> ... *Quantum non milvus oberret.*
> (... Plus que ne couvre le vol d'un milan.)
> *Aulus Persius Flaccus. Sat. IV*, 5, 26.

I

L'Oiseau, de tous nos consanguins le plus ardent à vivre, mène aux confins du jour un singulier destin. Migrateur, et hanté d'inflation solaire, il voyage de nuït, les jours étant trop courts pour son activité. Par temps de lune grise couleur du gui des Gaules, il peuple de son spectre la prophétie des nuits. Et son cri dans la nuit est cri de l'aube elle-même: cri de guerre sainte à l'arme blanche.

Au fléau de son aile l'immense libration d'une double saison; et sous la courbe du vol, la courbure même de la terre ... L'alternance est sa loi; l'ambiguïté son règne. Dans l'espace et le temps qu'il couve d'un même vol, son hérésie est celle d'une sseule estivation. C'est le scandale aussi du peintre et du poète, assembleurs de saisons aux plus hauts lieux d'intersection.

Ascétisme du vol! ... L'oiseau, de tous nos commensaux le plus avide d'être, est celui-là qui, pour nourrir sa passion, porte secrète en lui la plus haute fièvre du sang. Sa grâce est dans la combustion. Rien là de symbolique: simple fait biologique. Et si légère pour nous est la matière oiseau, qu'elle semble, à contre feu du jour, portée jusqu'à l'incandescence. Un homme en mer, flairant midi, lève la tête à cet esclandre: une mouette blanche ouverte sur le ciel, comme une main de femme contre la flamme d'une lampe, élève dans le jour la rose transparence d'une blancheur d'hostie ...

Oiseaux, *extracts*

Saint-John Perse

> . . . *Quantum non milvus oberret.*
> (. . . More than a kite can fly over.)
> *Aulus Persius Flaccus. Sat. IV*, 5, 26.

I

The Bird, of all those related in blood to us the most ardent for
life, conducts upon the confines of the day a singular destiny.
A migrant, haunted by solar inflation, he travels by night, the
days being too short for his activity. In grey moonlight, the
colour of Gaulish mistletoe, he peoples the prophecy of the
nights with his spectre. And his cry in the night is the cry of the
dawn itself; the cry of a holy war waged with naked steel.

Upon the balance of his wings the immense libration of a
double season; and beneath the arc of his flight the very curvature
of the earth. . . Alternation is his law; ambiguity his kingdom.
In the space and time that he hatches in a single flight, his heresy
is that of a single aestivation. The poet and painter, assemblers
of the seasons at their highest points of intersection, are also
moved by the scandal of it.

Asceticism of flight! . . . The bird, of all our compeers the
most avid for existence, is a being who, to feed his passion,
carries secretly within himself the blood's hottest fever. His
grace lies in combustion. No symbolism there: a simple biological
fact. And bird-substance seems so weightless to us that, when
seen against the sun, it looks as if it will burst into flames. A man
at sea, sensing the stroke of noon, lifts his head to find this out-
rage: a white gull open against the sky, like a woman's hand
against the flame of a lamp, lifts in the sunlight the rosy trans-
parency of a host's whiteness. . .

Aile falquée du songe, vous nous retrouverez ce soir sur d'autres rives !

2

Les vieux naturalistes français, dans leur langue très sûre et très révérencieuse, après avoir fait droit aux attributs de l'aile — «hampe», «barbes», «étendard» de la plume; «rémiges» et «rectrices» des grandes pennes motrices; et toutes «mailles» et «macules» de la livrée d'adulte — s'attachaient de plus près au corps même, dit «territoire» de l'oiseau, comme à une parcelle infime du territoire terrestre. Dans sa double allégeance, aérienne et terrestre, l'oiseau nous était ainsi présenté pour ce qu'il est: un satellite infime de notre orbite planétaire.

On étudiait, dans son volume et dans sa masse, toute cette architecture légère faite pour l'essor et la durée du vol: cet allongement sternal en forme de navette, cette chambre-forte d'un cœur accessible au seul flux artériel, et tout l'encagement de cette force secrète, gréée des muscles les plus fins. On admirait ce vase ailé en forme d'urne pour tout ce qui se consume là d'ardent et de subtil; et, pour hâter la combustion, tout ce système interstitiel d'une «pneumatique» de l'oiseau doublant l'arbre sanguin jusqu'aux vertèbres et phalanges.

L'oiseau, sur ses os creux et sur ses «sacs aériens», porté, plus légèrement que chaume, à l'excellence du vol, défiait toutes notions acquises en aéro-dynamique. L'étudiant, ou l'enfant trop

Falcate wing of dream, you will discover us again this evening upon other shores!

2

The old French naturalists, in their marvellously exact and reverent language, after having done justice to the wing's attributes – 'stems', 'barbs' and 'standards' of the feathers; 'remigers' and 'rectifers' of the propulsive pinions; and all the 'specklings' and 'maculations' of the adult bird's livery – applied themselves yet more closely to the body of the creature, called the 'territory' of the bird, as to an infinitely small trace of terrestial territory. In its double alleigance, aerial and terrestial, the bird was thus presented to us for what he is: a tiny satellite of our planetary orbit.

They studied, in its volume and mass, this whole lightweight architecture created so that flight might soar and endure: the eternal prolongation in the form of a shuttle, the strongroom of the heart accessible only to the arterial flux, and the whole encagement of this secret strength, rigged with the most delicate of muscles. They admired this winged, urn-shaped vase for all the ardent, subtle things which are consumed there; and to hasten the combustion, all the close-set system of hollow tubes within the bird, exact replica of the blood stream, down to the vertebrae and phalanxes.

The bird, borne more lightly than straw upon his hollow bones and his 'aerial sacs', towards excellence in flight, defied all established notions about aerodynamics. The student, or too

curieux, qui avait une fois disséqué un oiseau, gardait longtemps mémoire de sa conformation nautique: de son aisance en tout à mimer le navire, avec sa cage thoracique en forme de carène et l'assemblage des couples sur la quille, la masse osseuse du château de proue, l'étrave ou rostre du bréchet, la ceinture scapulaire où s'eugage la rame de l'aile, et la ceinture pelvienne où s'instaure la poupe …

8

Oiseaux, et qu'une longue affinité tient aux confins de l'homme … Les voici, pour l'action, armés comme filles de l'esprit. Les voici, pour la transe et l'avant-création, plus nocturnes qu'à l'homme la grande nuit du songe clair où s'exerce la logique du songe.

Dans la maturité d'un texte immense en voie toujours de formation, ils ont mûri comme des fruits, ou mieux comme des mots: à même la sève et la substance originelle. Et bien sont-ils comme des mots sous leur charge magique: noyaux de force et d'action, foyers d'éclairs et d'émissions, portant au loin l'initiative et la prémonition.

Sur la page blanche aux marges infinies, l'espace qu'ils mesurent n'est plus qu'incantation. Ils sont, comme dans le mètre, quantités syllabiques. Et procédant, comme les mots, de lointaine ascendance, ils perdent, comme les mots, leur sens à la limite de la félicité.

A l'aventure poétique ils eurent part jadis, avec l'augure et

curious child, once having dissected a bird, long remembered
its nautical conformation: the ease with which everything about
a ship was mimicked, with the thoracic cage in the form of a
hull and the assemblage of the ribs upon the keel, the bony mass
of the prow, the stem or ship's bow of the breastbone, the
scapular girdle where the wing's oar slots in, and the pelvic
girdle where the poop erects itself. . .

8

Birds, whose long affinity for man keeps them at his farthest
limits. . . Behold them, armed for action, like the daughters of
the spirit. Behold them, made for trance and pre-creation, more
nocturnal than is to mankind the great night of clear dreaming
wherein the dream's logic operates.

In the maturity of a huge text always in process of formation,
they have ripened like fruit, or, better still, like words: even to
the sap and original substance. They are indeed like words with
their magic charge: nuclei of force and action, sources of
lightning bolts and discharges of energy, bearing far away initia-
tive and premonition.

Upon the white page with infinite margins, the space they
measure is more now than incantation. They are, as in metre,
syllabic quantities. Proceeding, like words, from remote ancestry,
they lose, like words, their meaning at the limit of felicity.

Formerly they played a part in the poetic adventure, in

l'aruspice. Et les voici, vocables assujettis au même enchaînement, pour l'exercice au loin d'une divination nouvelle ... Au soir d'antiques civilisations, c'est un oiseau de bois, les bras en croix saisis par l'officiant, qui tient le rôle du scribe dans l'écriture médiumnique, comme aux mains du sorcier ou du géomancien.

Oiseaux, nés d'une inflexion première pour la plus longue intonation ... Ils sont, comme les mots, portés du rythme universel; ils s'inscrivent d'eux-mêmes, et comme d'affinité, dans la plus large strophe errante que l'on ait vue jamais se dérouler au monde.

Heureux, ah! qu'ils tendent jusqu'à nous, d'un bord à l'autre de l'océan céleste, cet arc immense d'ailes peintes qui nous assiste et qui nous cerne, ah! qu'ils en portent tout l'honneur à force d'âme, parmi nous! ...
L'homme porte le poids de sa gravitation comme une meule au cou, l'oiseau comme une plume peinte au front. Mais au bout de son fil invisible, l'oiseau de Braque n'échappe pas plus à la fatalité terrestre qu'une particule rocheuse dans la géologie de Cézanne.

13

Oiseaux, lances levées à toutes frontières de l'homme! ...

L'aile puissante et calme, et l'œil lavé de sécrétions très pures, ils vont et nous devancent aux franchises d'outre-mer, comme aux Échelles et Comptoirs d'un éternel Levant. Ils sont pélerins de longue pérégrination, Croisés d'un éternel An Mille. Et aussi

company with the augur and the haruspex. And here they are, vocables subject to the same rules of linkage, for the distant practice of a new divination. . . In the evening of antique civilizations, it is a wooden bird, the cross-shaped arms held by the officiant, which plays the role of scribe in mediumistic writing, as in the hands of the sorcerer or the geomancer.

Birds, born of a first inflection for the longest intonation. . . They, like words, are carried along by the universal rhythm; inscribing themselves of their own accord, as if from affinity, in the largest wandering strophe that the world has ever seen unfolding.

Happy are they, as they hold out to us, from one shore to the other of the celestial ocean, the huge arc of painted wings which helps us and rings us in! May they bring the full honour of it among us, by strength of soul! . . .
A man carries his own weight like a millstone round his neck, the bird like a feather painted upon a forehead. But, at the end of his invisible thread, Braque's bird will no more escape from terrestial fatality than a rocky particle in the geology of Cézanne.

13

Birds, lances lifted upon all the frontiers of mankind! . .

Wings powerful and calm, eyes bathed with the purest of secretions, they go before us to the franchises of the lands of the Crusades, as to the ports and counting houses of an eternal Levant. They are pilgrims of long peregrination, crusaders of an

bien furent ils «croisés» sur la croix de leurs ailes ... Nulle mer portant bateaux a-t-elle jamais connu pareil concert de voiles et d'ailes sur l'étendue heureuse?

Avec toutes choses errantes par le monde et qui sont choses au fil de l'heure, ils vont où vont tous les oiseaux du monde, à leur destin d'êtres crées ... Où va le mouvement même des choses, sur sa houle, où va le cours même du ciel, sur sa roue — à cette immensité de vivre et de créer dont s'est émue la plus grande nuit de mai, ils vont, et doublant plus de caps que n'en lèvent nos songes, ils passent, nous laissant à l'Océan des choses libres et non libres ...

Ignorants de leur ombre, et ne sachant de mort que ce qui s'en consume d'immortel au bruit lointain des grandes eaux, ils passent, nous laissant, et nous ne sommes plus les mêmes. Ils sont l'espace traversé d'une seule pensée. .

Laconisme de l'aile ! Ô mutisme des forts ... Muets sont-ils, et de haut vol, dans la grande nuit de l'homme. Mais à l'aube, étrangers, ils descendent vers nous: vêtus de ces couleurs de l'aube — entre bitume et givre — qui sont les couleurs même du fond de l'homme ... Et de cette aube de fraîcheur, comme d'un ondoiement très pur, ils gardent parmi nous quelque chose du songe de la création.

(from *Nouvelle Revue française*, no. 120, December 1962)

eternal Millenium. Indeed, they have taken the cross, with the cross of their wings. . . Has any sea of ships ever known a like concert of sails and wings upon its happy expanse?

Together with all things that wander through the world and are carried off by the current of time, they go where all the birds of the world are going, to their destiny as created beings. . . Where the very movement of things goes, upon its wave, or the sky's course, upon its wheel – they go to that immensity of living and creating which occupies the grandest night of May, and doubling more capes than our dreams raise up, they pass by, leaving us to the Ocean of things free and unfree. . .

Ignorant of their own shadows, knowing no death but that which the immortal consumes to the distant sound of great waters, they go, leaving us behind, and we are no longer the same. They are the space traversed by a single thought.

Brevity of wings ! Muteness of the strong ! They are silent, and fly high, in the great night of mankind. But when dawn comes, they soar down towards us like strangers, clothed in the colours of dawn – between bitumen and rime – which are the very colours of man's essence. . . And from this fresh dawn, as from a truly pure baptism, they preserve among us something of the dream of the Creation.

Silencieuse et grandissante

Jean-Philippe Salabreuil

Silencieuse et grandissante bercée m'aura veillé la végétale
parure au jour et à la nuit. Je suis venu. C'est un matin blanc de
rosée. Dans la sphère albumineuse de l'œil ouvert s'ordonne en
lys un lieu sauvage d'insomnie. Une larme y roule sa lueur
tremblante. Et parmi la hauteur merveilleuse des végétaux
flamboyants (fatigué du voyage) seul incliné j'ai vomi les filets
d'une bile d'argent. Rejailli dans la gloire de l'aube mon front les
songes le caressent. Mémoires me blanchissent l'épaule vos mains
(l'une en l'autre) qui sont les ailes d'un ange mort. Je m'éclaire et
je vais par les pans d'ombre de ce parc ainsi clair. Et me rappelle
qui vivais une enfance éclatante. Aussi je m'émerveille. Il est
troublant que l'angle le plus noir du rêve ait refleuri de pensées
belles et blanches. Mais le présent des astres à la terre maussade
est une eau radieuse. Et de florissantes clartés s'élèvent. Un reflet
m'environne parmi l'arbrée natale aux résines d'or. Élevés dans
le plein flux de ma vue pleine ô riches sapins sombres vous brillez.
Refondus soudain par le céleste éclat. Je regarde et ne vous vois.
Mais de hauts flots d'un lac étincelant qui écument très haut:
grandissez les rayons de la joie ! Le torrent passe les chevreuses
aux poudres de soleil. L'onde floconne éblouissante en-deçà les
chaux de la sifflante rive-Dieu. Ce que je vois ! Sa chevelure (elle
me fut glissée des mains) qui se déroule et qui ruisselle. O neiges
de l'oubli ! J'étais aux sources de l'amour avec le temps de ne
prendre qu'à peine encontre-moi sinistre sa blancheur. Et ce fut
un berceau de silence au-dessus de notre liée que sapins (que sapins
sombres et bercés). L'aigle s'abaisse de l'été profond. Comme elle
s'en va boire liquide sa propre ombre glacée ! Les merveilles de ces
murs chantants sont de croulants amours. Je m'avance dans
l'avenue d'alarme aux plus beaux jours de la terrestre année.
L'ombrage est consolé parfois d'une clairière. Y flambe un feu de
joie couronné de cortèges d'enfants en rond. Sans fin ! Le lisse de

Silent and growing

Jean-Philippe Salabreuil

The garland of vegetation will have watched over me by day and night rocked silent and growing to and fro. I arrived. A morning white with dew. In the albuminous sphere of the eye a savage region of insomnia arrayed itself in lily shape. There a tear rolled its trembling gleam. And amidst the marvellous height of the flaming plants (wearied by the voyage) bent solitary I vomited up the filaments of a silvery bile. Gushed out in the dawn's glory my forehead dreams caressed it. Memories whitened my shoulder your hands (clasped) that are the wings of a dead angel. I become bright and go through the shadows in this park which is thus made bright. And recall who had a brilliant childhood. I am thus astonished. It is confusing that the darkest corner of the dream should have flowered once more with white and beautiful thoughts. But the present made by the stars to the sullen earth is radiant water. And flourishing brightnesses arise. A reflection encompasses me amid the natal grove with its golden resins. Lifted into the full flux of my full view you shine o rich dark pines. Suddenly remade by the celestial brightness. I look and do not see you. Instead, the tall waves of a sparkling lake which foams on high: may the rays of joy grow greater! The torrent goes by the sun-powdered brakes. The fleecy dazzling wave on the hither side of the whistling God-coast. What I behold! Her hair (it had slipped from my hands) unrolling, flowing down. O snows of forgetfulness. I was at the wellsprings of love with scarcely the time to take counter to my sinister self her whiteness. It was as if the pine-trees (dark and rocking pine-trees) made a bower of silence above our bond. The eagle stoops from the depths of summer. How she swoops away to drink liquid her own frozen shadow! The marvels of these singing walls are made from crumbling loves. I go down the avenue of alarm in the finest days of the

l'âme s'altère. Et venu de si loin je me blesse aux éclats de figures serrées. Simulacres d'amour et nymphes vaines: soyez rompus aux glaces du prochain hiver. Je ne serai plus là mais vous n'y serez plus. Maintenant je ne prends garde qu'à peine aux pensées d'un étroit promenoir. Et la rocaille démente s'accroît. Je me retranche de ce monde vieux par les degrés d'une terrasse aux confins de brouillards.

(*L'Inésperé*)

terrestial year. The shade is sometimes consoled by a clearing. Where flames a bonfire crowned by troops of children, ring-a-rosy. Endlessly ! The plane of the soul is changed. And come from so far to wound myself on the splinters of pinched faces. Simulacra of loves and vain nymphs: be broken upon the ice of the next winter. I will no longer be there but you will not exist. Now I hardly take much notice of the thoughts of a narrow corridor. And the mad rockwork increases. I retreat from this old world by the steps of a terrace upon the very edge of fog.

Harengs et bouleaux

Jude Stéfan

Trois harengs
et quatre arbres
quatre arbres sur le pré
sous des monceaux de nuées
l'un défeuillé et l'autre ébréché
l'un ployé et l'autre tout entier
encore offert aux vents
sous des nuées bigarrées
trois harengs dans un plat
près d'un bol en porcelaine
à midi pour le déjeuner
et quatre arbres roux
dressés au soleil décoloré
le soir en automne
trois harengs morts
et quatre arbres là.

(*Cyprès*)

Herrings and birch trees

Jude Stéfan

Three herrings
and four trees
four trees in the meadow
under heaps of clouds
one leafless and one split
one bent and one whole
still offered to the winds
under the many-coloured clouds
three herrings on a plate
near a porcelain bowl
at noon for luncheon
and four russet trees
standing in the pale sun
at evening in autumn
three dead herrings
and four trees there.

Litanie

Jude Stéfan

Par désespoir de l'amour qui n'est
pas échu Par désespoir de la mort
qui déjà m'a prévu Par désespoir
du sexe qui nous fut à charge Par
désespoir de l'homme qui n'est que
misère Par désespoir du temps qui
n'est que poussière Par désespoir de
l'art qui n'a pas visité Par dés-
espoir de l'âme que l'on n'a pas
trouvée Par désespoir de soi
qui ne sut que honte Par désespoir
de la vanité du futur Par
désespoir du suicide qui n'est qu'
alibi Par désespoir du monde
illusion Par désespoir où
s'enfouir? Dans l'étude par oubli
dans le stupre par malchance mais
dans la mer pour s'y laver.

(*Cyprès*)

Litany

Jude Stéfan

Through despair of love which is not
my lot Through despair of death
which already expects me Through despair
of sex which weighed us down Through
despair of man who is misery
incarnate Through despair of time which
is merely dust Through despair of
art which did not come Through des-
pair of the soul which one has not
found Through despair of oneself
who knew only shame Through despair
of the future's vanity Through
despair of suicide which is only an
alibi Through despair of the illusion
world Through despair where
to bury oneself? In study through
forgetfulness in lechery by
mishap but in the sea
to wash oneself.

La mort du poète

Jude Stéfan

Il suffit du trépas d'un singe
savant pour apitoyer la société
ayant revêtu son habit de gala
gisant sur un lit d'auberge
n'ayant pu résister moribond
à l'extrême élan de son cœur:
se donner en spectacle
à un groupe de misère
sous un préau délabré.
Ainsi le poète du Médiocre
obscur en son temps
un jour est étendu au sol
ayant perdu son être
il entend chanter
les anges du Néant.

(*Cyprès*)

Death of the poet

Jude Stéfan

The death of a performing
monkey is enough to move society
dressed in his gala costume
laid out on the bed of an inn
when already dying having been unable
to resist the warm impulse of his heart:
which was to make an exhibition of himself
before a group of wretches
under a tattered awning.
Thus the poet of the Mediocre
obscure in his own time
is one day stretched on the ground
having lost his being
he hears singing
the angels of the void.

Une femme un oiseau

Jean Tardieu

L'oiseau très grand qui survolait la plaine
au même rythme que les creux et les collines,
longtemps nous l'avions vu planer
dans un ciel absolu
qui n'était ni le jour ni la nuit.
Une cigogne? Un aigle? Tout ensemble
le vol silencieux du chat-huant
et cette royale envergure
d'un dieu qui se ferait oiseau ...

Nos yeux un instant détournés
soudain virent descendre la merveille:
c'était la fille de l'aurore et du désir
ange dans nos sillons tombé avec un corps
plus féminin que l'amour même et longue longue
posant ses pieds à peine sur le sol car le vent de ses ailes
la soulevait encore. Enfin le lisse et blanc plumage
sur cette femme de cristal se replia. Elle semblait ne pas nous voir
ni s'étonner qu'un lac
au-devant de ses pas s'étendit ... déjà

(*Histoires obscures*)

A Woman a bird

Jean Tardieu

This huge bird flying over the plain
keeping the same rhythm as the valleys and hills,
long we watched it hovering
in an absolute heaven
that was neither day nor night.
A stork? An eagle? Both
the brown owl's silent flight
and the royal wingspan
of a god become bird. . .

Our eyes for one moment averted
suddenly saw the marvel descending:
it was the daughter of dawn and desire,
an angel fallen into our fields with a body
more feminine than love itself, and tall, tall,
scarcely putting her feet to the ground for the wind of her wings
still lifted her. At last the smooth white feathers
of this woman of crystal were folded. She seemed not to see us,
nor to be astonished that a lake
stretched before her footsteps . . . already

Mémoire morte

Jean Tardieu

Près des lambris dorés des bureaux
où les corridors filent dans les miroirs sans fin
chaque porte, chaque pilier
cache un tueur qui s'ennuie et bâille:
le temps est long et le gage est mince.

Cependant au-dehors dans l'ombre des immeubles
plus d'un portail abrite de la pluie
une femme debout brillante comme une vitrine
qui regarde avec des yeux vides.

— Allô!... — Oui c'est moi!... — Il est temps!...
— Écoutez... Où êtes-vous?... Où êtes-vous?...
— Qui parle?... qui est là?... Je n'entends pas!...
La mer a roulé par ces avenues:
demain le sable sous le pas des caravanes.
Alors l'archéologue dans les roches
confondra nos siècles et nos jours
et la conque d'un téléphone rouillé
ne lui livrera aucun secret
sur le bourdonnement de nos paroles.

(*Histoires obscures*)

Dead memory

Jean Tardieu

Near the gilded panelling of the offices,
where the corridors slip away in mirrors without end,
each door, each pillar
hides a killer, bored, yawning:
the hours are long and the wage is small.

Meanwhile outside in the shadow of the buildings
more than one portal is sheltering from the rain
a woman who stands there shining like a shopwindow,
staring with empty eyes.

– Hello! . . . – Yes, it's me! . . . – It's time! . . .
– Listen . . . Where are you? . . . Where are you? . . .
– Who's speaking? . . . who's there? . . . I can't hear! . . .
The sea has rolled through these avenues:
tomorrow the sand beneath the footsteps of caravans.
Then the archaeologist among the rocks
will mix up our centuries and days
and the conch of a rusty telephone
will yield him no secrets
about the buzzing of our words.

Les objets perdus

Toursky

Qu'il est amer, le compte
des cheveux arrachés
par le peigne, des dents
tombées, des cicatrices !

Voici que le miroir
indifférent me charge
des amenuisements
dont la somme est la vie.

(Elles entraient en robes
claires, toutes ces rides !
Lasses de rire, lasses
de boire, elles s'enlisent

définitivement.)

Un hanneton réveille
l'image des tilleuls,
des bassins et du sable
dans le jardin d'enfants.

Hanneton sur le dos,
saoul de pollen, grotesque
prisonnier qui tournoie
autour de sa colère.

Les pattes ne rencontrent
qu'un air distrait, les ailes
vont se figer. Cet or
qui plongeait dans les roses

Things lost

Toursky

Bitter, this accounting
of hairs pulled out
in the comb, of lost
teeth, of scars!

How the indifferent
mirror burdens me
with the diminutions
whose total is life!

(All these wrinkles
came in bright garments!
Tired of laughter and
drinking, they got stuck here

definitively.)

A cockchafer wakens
the image of the limes,
of the pools and sand
of the children's playground.

Cockchafer on its back,
drunk with pollen, grotesque
prisoner whirling
around its own anger.

Its feet find only
Vacant air, the wings
will stiffen. This gold
which plunged among the roses

va cesser d'être lourd.

Le briquet, le canif,
ont eu raison des poches.
Ton prénom a dû prendre
ce chemin ... Liane ou Line?

Les doublures trouées
réservent à la main
une bise venue
d'en bas, du sol hostile.

Tout le désert occupe
l'espace d'un objet
perdu. Le dénuement
est de ne plus avoir

un rien qui rassurait.

Les anciens tatouages,
même poncés, lavés,
remontent si l'on fouette
l'avant-bras qu'ils ornèrent.

Ils reviennent fantômes,
pareils aux mauvais coups
ratés. Si je ranime
ce qui de toi me reste,

will cease to be heavy

The lighter, the pocketknife,
have got the better of the pockets.
Your Christian name must have taken
this same path. . . Liane or Line?

The holed linings
reserve for the hand
a draught from below,
from the hostile ground.

The whole desert takes
the room of a lost
object. Destitution
is to possess no longer

some reassuring trifle.

Old tattooings,
scrubbed and pumiced,
still show if one strikes
the forearm they adorned.

They come back to haunt us
like deeds gone wrong.
So, if I revive
what's left to me of you,

ce sont des lettres blanches.
Qui serre les paupières
contre un assaut de phares
croit effacer ... Le fond

de l'œil est mis à vif.

Une veste qui s'use,
des montres qui s'arrêtent,
m'épaulent davantage
que la résignation.

Nous acceptons de vivre
parce qu'autour de nous
s'effilochent, s'éliment,
de pauvres serviteurs,

compagnons qui rejoignent
la matière orpheline,
anneaux sans annulaires,
alors que je conserve

mes mains pour te les tendre !

(*Un Drôle d'air*)

it's letters traced in white.
A man who screws his eyes up
against the blaze of headlights
thinks he's blotting out . . The depths

of the eye are brought to life.

A jacket that's fraying,
watches that stop,
give me more help
than resignation.

We consent to live
because around us
poor servants
unravel and wear out,

companions who return
to orphaned matter,
rings without ring-fingers,
while I still have

hands to hold out to you!

Je voudrais pas crever

Boris Vian

Je voudrais pas crever
Avant d'avoir connu
Les chiens noirs du Mexique
Qui dorment sans rêver
Les singes à cul nu
Dévoreurs de tropiques
Les araignées d'argent
Au nid truffé de bulles
Je voudrais pas crever
Sans savoir si la lune
Sous son faux air de thune
A un côté pointu
Si le soleil est froid
Si les quatre saisons
Ne sont vraiment que quatre
Sans avoir essayé
De porter une robe
Sur les grands boulevards
Sans avoir regardé
Dans un regard d'égout
Sans avoir mis mon zobe
Dans des coinstots bizarres
Je voudrais pas finir
Sans connaître la lèpre
Ou les sept maladies
Qu'on attrape là-bas
Le bon ni le mauvais
Ne me feraient de peine
Si si si je savais
Que j'en aurai l'étrenne
Et il y a z aussi

I don't want to croak

Boris Vian

I don't want to croak
Until I've got to know
The black dogs of Mexico
Who sleep without dreaming
The bare-arsed apes
Devouring the tropics
The silver spiders
In nests stuffed with bubbles
I don't want to croak
Without knowing whether the moon
Under its tricky air of being a nickel
Is concealing a pointed side
Whether the sun is cold
Whether the four seasons
Are really only four
Without having tried
Strolling along the boulevards
Wearing a dress
Without having squinted
Down the squint-hole of a sewer
Without having put my pecker
Into strange neighbourhoods
I don't want to push off
Without getting to know leprosy
Or the seven diseases
One catches down there
The good and the bad ones
Would cause me no pain
If if if I were sure
That I'd have first refusal
And then of course there's

Tout ce que je connais
Tout ce que j'apprécie
Que je sais qui me plaît
Le fond vert de la mer
Où valsent les brins d'algue
Sur le sable ondulé
l'herbe grillée de juin
La terre qui craquelle
L'odeur des conifères
Et les baisers de celle
Que ceci que cela
La belle que voilà
Mon Ourson, l'Ursula
Je voudrais pas crever
Avant d'avoir usé
Sa bouche avec ma bouche
Son corps avec mes mains
Le reste avec mes yeux
J'en dis pas plus faut bien
Rester révérencieux
Je voudrais pas mourir
Sans qu'on ait inventé
Les roses éternelles
La journée de deux heures
La mer à la montagne
La montagne à la mer
La fin de la douleur
Les journaux en couleur
Tous les enfants contents
Et tant de trucs encore
Qui dorment dans les crânes

360

Everything I've learned
Everything I've learned to like
What I know what pleases me
The sea's green depths
Where strands of seaweed waltz
Over the rippling sand
June's scorched grass
The crackling earth
The smell of pine trees
And the kisses of her
Whom I this and I that
My beautiful other
My bear's cub, my Ursula
I don't want to croak
Before having consumed
Her mouth with my mouth
Her body with my hands
The rest with my eyes
I'll say no more must
Remain reverential
I don't want to croak
Before someone has invented
Everlasting roses
The two-hour day
The seaside in the mountains
Mountains at the seaside
The end of all pain
Rainbow-coloured newspapers
All children contented
And so many other schemes
Sleeping in the brains

Des géniaux ingénieurs
Des jardiniers joviaux
Des soucieux socialistes
Des urbains urbanistes
Et des pensifs penseurs
Tant de choses à voir
A voir et à z-entendre
Tant de temps à attendre
A chercher dans le noir

Et moi je vois la fin
Qui grouille et qui s'amène
Avec sa gueule moche
Et qui m'ouvre ses bras
De grenouille bancroche

Je voudrais pas crever
Non monsieur non madame
Avant d'avoir tâté
Le goût qui me tourmente
Le goût qu'est le plus fort
Je voudrais pas crever
Avant d'avoir goûté
La saveur de la mort ...

(*Je voudrais pas crever*)

Of ingenious engineers
Of gay gardeners
Of solicitous socialists
Of urbane urbanists
And of thoughtful thinkers
So many things to see
To see and zmmm to hear
So much time to wait
To grope around in the dark

As for me I can see the end
Swarming barging in
With its ugly mug
And like a bandy-legged frog its arms
Outstretched to grab me

I don't want to croak
No sir no madam
Until I have sampled
The taste which torments me
The strongest taste of all
I don't want to croak
Until I have savoured
The taste of death. . .

Un jour

Boris Vian

Un jour
Il y aura autre chose que le jour
Une chose plus franche, que l'on appellera le Jodel
Une encore, translucide comme l'arcanson
Que l'on s'enchâssera dans l'œil d'un geste élégant
Il y aura l'auraille, plus cruel
Le volutin, plus dégagé
Le comble, moins sempiternel
Le baouf, toujours enneigé
Il y aura le chalamondre
L'ivrunini, le baroïque
Et toute un planté d'analogues
Les heures seront différentes
Pas pareilles, sans résultat
Inutile de fixer maintenant
Le détail précis de tout ça
Une certitude subsiste: un jour
Il y aura autre chose que le jour.

(*Je voudrais pas crever*)

One day

Boris Vian

One day
There'll be something other than day
Something freer, which will be called the dilly
And something else translucid as the sunbow
Which people will screw into their eye with an elegant gesture
There'll be the rawl, more ruthless
The springle, more relaxed
The haven, less sempiternal
The froon, for ever snowbound
There'll be the solamaunder
The squiffaroony the quarious
And a whole scuttering of relevations
The hours will be different
Asymmetric, inconclusive
Pointless to pin down yet
All the precise details
One thing's certain though: one day
There'll be something other than day.

Notes on the Authors with Select Bibliographies

Only works of poetry by the authors are listed, although in some cases the word 'poetry' must be taken to include not only verse but other less easily classifiable forms such as the prose-poem, *récit* and poem-play (as opposed to verse drama). Plaquettes of verse have not always been listed, especially where they have subsequently been incorporated by the author into a collective volume. There has been no attempt to list all poems published *hors commerce*, or in numbered, limited editions complementing the graphic work of contemporary artists. The place of publication of a book is Paris unless otherwise stated. The listing of existing translations into English is restricted to those that have been published in book form, and excludes those that have appeared only in journals or magazines. The recommendations for further reading about individual authors are by no means exhaustive: they include only those monographs or critical essays which deal with the author's work as a poet and have been published in book form, excluding studies that have appeared only in journals or magazines. The following works on contemporary French literature/poetry contain studies of, or discusss, most of the authors included in this anthology and may be consulted with profit:

Alyn, Marc, *La Nouvelle Poésie française* (1968).
Boisdeffre, Pierre de, *Une Histoire vivante de la littérature d'aujourd'hui (1939–1964)* (5th ed., 1964).
Boisdeffre, Pierre de, *Une Anthologie vivante de la littérature d'aujourd'hui (1945–1965)* (1965).
Boisdeffre, Pierre de, *La Poésie française de Baudelaire à nos jours* (1966).
Boisdeffre, Pierre de (ed.), *Dictionnaire de littérature contemporaine* (1963).
Bosquet, Alain, *Verbe et vertige* (1961).
Gros, Léon-Gabriel, *Présentation de poètes contemporains* (2 vols., 1951).
Majault, J., Nivat, J. M., and Geronimi, C. (eds.), *Littérature de notre temps* (3rd rev. ed., 1966); *Ecrivains français* I, II and III (three dossiers of separate folios on authors to complement *Littérature de notre temps*).
Onimus, Jean, *La Connaissance poétique* (1966).

Picon, Gaëtan, *Panorama de la nouvelle litterature française* (1960).
Richard, J.-P., *Poésie et profondeur* (1955).
Richard, J.-P., *Onze études sur la poésie moderne* (2nd ed., 1964).
Rousselot, Jean, *Poètes français d'aujourd'hui* (1959).
Rousselot, Jean (ed.), *Dictionnaire de la poésie française contemporaine* (1968).

Also three anthologies of contemporary French poetry:
Bédouin, Jean-Louis (ed.), *La Poésie surrealiste* (1964).
Nadeau, Maurice (ed.), *Anthologie de la poésie française*: Vol. II, *Le XXe siècle, tome I;* Vol. 12, *Le XXe siècle, tome II* (1967).
Seghers, Pierre (ed.), *Le Livre d'or de la poésie française*. Seconde partie: de 1940 a 1960 (2 vols., verviers, 1969).

Also three English-language anthologies which contain translations of the work of a number of the poets included in the present volume:
Aspel, Alexander and Justice, Donald, *Contemporary French Poetry* (Ann Arbor, 1965) which includes poems by Francis Ponge, Henri Michaux, Jean Follain, René Char, André Frénaud, Guillevic, André Pieyre de Mandiargues, Yves Bonnefoy, André du Bouchet, Philippe Jaccottet and Jacques Dupin.
Gavronsky, Serge (ed.), *Poems and Texts* (New York, 1969), which includes poems by Yves Bonnefoy, André du Bouchet, Jean Follain, André Frénaud, Guillevic, Marcelin Pleynet, Francis Ponge and Denis Roche.
Watson Taylor, Simon (ed.), *French Writing Today* (Harmondsworth, 1968 and New York, 1969) which includes poems by Raymond Queneau, Francis Ponge, Henri Michaux, René Char, Jacques Prévert, André Pieyre de Mandiargues, André Frenaud, Jean Lescure, Guillevic, Alain Bosquet, Yves Bonnefoy, André du Bouchet, Boris Vian, Philippe Jaccottet, Jacques Dupin, Olivier Larronde, Denis Roche, Michel Butor, Michel Deguy, Jean Pierre Faye and Marc Alyn.

MARC ALYN

Born 1937 in Rheims. At the age of seventeen founded a short-lived review *Terre de feu*, followed by several plaquettes of poems which were collected into one volume, *Le Temps des autres*, in 1957 (Prix Max Jacob). Military service and the Algerian war 1957–9. Is the editorial director, at Editions Flammarion, of a poetry series, and has for several years been the poetry critic of *Le Figaro littéraire*. Has written numerous essays on poets and poetry, and a critical survey of modern French poetry from its origins, *La Nouvelle Poésie française* (1968). Apart from his poetry, he has written a novel, *Le Déplacement* (1964), compiled an anthology of sixteenth-century French poetry (*Poètes du XVIe siècle*, 1962), and critical studies of the work of Gérard de Nerval (1963), François Mauriac (1960), Dylan Thomas (1962) and André de Richaud (1966).

Alyn's earlier work was inspired by the radicalism and lyricism of Paul Eluard's form of surrealism, but he has recently swung towards an almost Hugoesque romanticism with mystical religious overtones. As against the widespread praise accorded his first collections of verse, his later work has encountered resistance for what has appeared to some critics as an increasing traditionalism and an air of detachment from the problems of the present.

Main works of poetry:
Le Temps des autres (1957), *Cruels divertissements* (1958), *Brûler le feu* (1959), *Délébiles* (1962), *Nuit majeure* (1968).

ARAGON (Louis Aragon, known as)

Born 1897 in Paris. Mobilized in 1917, met André Breton while studying military medicine at the Val-de-Grâce. In 1919 he joined Breton and another young poet, Philippe Soupault, in founding the review *Littérature*. Active in the dada movement and then in surrealism. Broke with Breton and the surrealists in 1931 over political issues, and proclaimed his total and unswerving adherence to the Communist Party, with which he has remained closely associated ever since. Numerous voyages to the Soviet Union 1930–6. Editor of *L'Humanité* 1933–4. Secretary (with Malraux, Chamson and Bloch) of the 'Association Internationale des écrivains pour la defence de la Culture' in 1935. Codirector of *Ce soir* (1937–40 and 1944–9). Mobilized in 1939: Dunkerque, Croix de Guerre, Medaille Militaire, prisoner of war, escaped to 'Free Zone'. During the Occupation was a leading figure in the Resistance, helping to found the clandestine reviews *Étoiles* and *Les Lettres françaises*. Member of the Central Committee of the French Com munist Party 1954, awarded Lenin Peace Prize that same year, President of the Confédération Nationale des Ecrivains in 1957. At present director of *Les Lettres françaises*. His late wife, Elsa Triolet, whom he met in 1928, provided the direct inspiration for all his poetry. He is also a prolific novelist, essayist and journalist.

Though Aragon remains one of the great figures of the contemporary French literary scene, his very considerable verse output has, in recent years, contained much which seems barren of real poetic inspiration. Essentially, in the years since the war, Aragon has continued to use the direct, popular style he first developed at the time of the French defeat in order to express what all men were then feeling. He has, however, found it difficult to discover post-war issues which would unite the whole public with a sense of their importance. It has been remarked, appositely, by a French critic, that Aragon 'rarely agrees to forget his own virtuosity'.

The three poems printed here show some of the more attractive aspects of Aragon's recent work. The poem about Picasso's Blue Period painting *The Embrace* is a beautiful tribute to Guillaume Apollinaire, who certainly had a great influence on Aragon's work, while the section taken from the *Ode à Pablo Neruda* also demonstrates Aragon's power of empathy where other poets and artists are concerned.

Main works of poetry:
Feu de joie (1920), *Le Mouvement perpétuel* (1925), *La Grande Gaîté* (1929), *Persécuté Persécuteur* (1931), *Hourra l'oural* (1934), *Le Crève-Coeur* (1941), *Cantique à Elsa* (1942), *Les Yeux d'Elsa* (1942), *Le Musée Grévin* (1943), *La Diane française* (1945), *Le Nouveau Crève-Coeur* (1948), *Les Yeux et la mémoire* (1954), *Le Roman inachevé* (1956), *Elsa* (1959), *Les Poètes* (1960), *Poésie: Anthologie 1917–1960* (1960), *Le Fou d'Elsa* (1963), *Le Voyage en Hollande* (1964), *Elégie à Pablo Neruda* (1966).

To consult:
Roger Garaudy, *L'Itinéraire d'Aragon* (1961); Hubert Juin, *Aragon* (1960); Pierre de Lescure, *Aragon romancier* (1960); Georges Raillard, *Aragon* (1963); Claude Roy, *Aragon* (1945); Jean Sur, *Aragon* (1966).

JULIEN BLAINE

Born 1942 in Rognac (Bouches du Rhône). Desultory studies at the

University of Aix-en-Provence, followed by voyages abroad. In 1962 founded in Aix the review *Les Carnets de l'Octéor* as an organ for 'semeiotic poetry' (emphasizing the importance of calligraphy, typography and texture in the creation of a poem). Settled in Paris in 1963 after a long voyage through Europe and the Middle East. In 1966 founded, with J. F. Bory, the review *Approches* (four issues to date) to conduct research into the elemental and material structure of poetry. In 1967 founded, with Jean Clay, *Robho* (four issues to date) a journal of information about international movements (theatre, happenings, plastic arts, architecture, poetry) using their powers of invention to affect social reality in the direction of revolution. Organized, in June 1967, an exhibition in Paris of the 'First International Inventory of Elementary Poetry', bringing together authors who have made use of poetic elements in calligraphy, typography, photography, collage, graphic art, etc. Has contributed concrete and spatialist poems to a large number of anthologies and reviews in France, England, Belgium, Italy, Germany, Holland, Argentine, United States, Japan, etc. Has also participated in numerous collective exhibitions of experimental poetry. Has published one gramophone record, *Text und Aktionsabend II* (Switzerland, 1968), and produced two films, *Destruction des forces cycliques* (1967) and *Rouge Improvise* (1969). Believes now that poetry must be transformed into action in the street, rather than committed to the printed page.

Main works of poetry (pictural as well as graphic) include:
W M Quinzième (1966), *Essai sur la sculpture* (1967), *Cette carte et autres faits* (1968), and *Petit Précis d'érotomanie* (1969).

To consult:
Pierre Garnier, *Poésie concrète* (1968).

EDITH BOISSONNAS

Born in Switzerland. Her father was a doctor. Started writing at the age of eight. Educated in France, her family having moved to the Var region when she was still a child. Visits to Spain and England before marriage followed by two years in the United States. Has lived in Paris since her return. A regular contributor to the *NRF* (prose, poetry, critical texts), and to a number of other reviews.

Mme Boissonnas' poetry strikes a particularly individual note in France today. She has strong affinities with the metaphysical poets of the seventeenth century, but her work is characterized by a slight air of dishevelment, with turns of phrase and images which seem to jar with one another. It is these, in fact, which set the tone. Through these discords the poet expresses the sensibility of her own century.

Main works:
Paysage cruel (1946), *Demeures* (1950), *Le Grand Jour* (1955), *Passioné*, with a lithograph by Georges Braque (1958), *Limbe*, with lithographs by André Masson (1959), *L'Embéllie* (1966).

YVES BONNEFOY

Born 1923 in Tours. Took a degree in philosophy at the University of Paris. Associated with the surrealists 1945–7. Has travelled widely: Italy, England, Greece, Spain, United States. A visiting professor at Brandeis University (USA) 1962–4. Apart from his poetry, he has written art history and literary essays, and translated a number of Shakespeare's plays. In 1967 he founded (with André du Bouchet, Gaëtan Picon and Louis-René des Forêts) the poetry review *L' Ephémère*.

Bonnefoy has been one of the most widely praised of contemporary French poets in France, and may be considered one of the few to have made a genuine impact in other countries. Part of the reason for the sustained interest in his work, both in France and abroad, is doubtless its almost obsessional unity of theme and structure. Another reason for his wide popularity is his extremely fine ear. Bonnefoy is a romantic who echoes all the most approved models in the poetry of the immediate past, among them Baudelaire, Mallarmé, Valèry and Jouve. His characteristic obscurity and his obsesession with the idea of death (he once declared that the 'material of poetry after attempting so many paths is meditation upon death'), are qualities that have impressed some readers as much as they have infuriated others. A certain polarization of opinion about Bonnefoy's work already gives indications that his reputation is due for hostile reappraisal; he nevertheless remains an important figure in modern French poetry.

Main works:

POETRY: *Du mouvement et de l'immobilité de Douve* (1953), *Hier régnant désert* (1958), *Pierre écrite* (1965).

ESSAYS: *Les Tombeaux de Ravenne* (1953), *Peintures murales de la France gothique* (1954), *L'Improbable* (1959), *Arthur Rimbaud par lui-même* (1961), *La Seconde Simplicité* (1961), *Anti-Platon* (1963), *L'Affirmation et l'écume* (1967), *Un Rêve fait à Mantoue* (1967).

To consult:
Philippe Jaccottet, *L'Entretien des Muses* (1968); Jean-Pierre Richard, *Onze études sur la poésie moderne* (1964).

Translations:
Selected Poems by Yves Bonnefoy, translated by Anthony Rudolf (London, 1968).

ALAIN BOSQUET

Born 1919 in Odessa. Was five years old when his parents left Russia for Belgium, where he spent his youth. University studies at Brussels. Mobilized in 1940, served in the Belgian campaign, then the French campaign. Went to the United States in 1941; edited the Free French journal *La Voix de France* in New York, 1941–2. Attached to the Allied HQ, England, 1943–5, then a member of the Control Commission in Berlin 1945–51. Has lived in Paris from 1951 onwards. Apart from his poetry, he is a novelist (seven novels, including *La Confession méxicaine*, Prix Interallié 1966), essayist (several studies of poets), anthologist, translator, broadcaster and literary critic (*Combat*, *Le Monde*). In 1968 he was awarded the Grand Prix de Poésie of the Académie Française.

Bosquet began in the surrealist camp, and though he has long since abandoned any kind of ties with orthodox surrealism, his work still shows the evidence of these beginnings. His great strengths as a poet are his power over imagery and his sense of elegance, qualities which are rarely found together in the verse of the present day. This witty and fluent writer tends to be regarded with considerable reserve in certain quarters in France, precisely because of these admirable but suspect characteristics, no doubt.

Main works:

POETRY: *Syncopes* (New York, 1943), *La Vie est clandestine* (1945), *A la mémoire de ma planète* (1948), *Langue morte* (1951: Prix Apollinaire), *Quel royaume oublié* (1955), *Premier Testament* (1957: Prix Saint-Beuve), *Deuxième Testament* (1959: Prix Max Jacob), *Maître Objet* (1962), *Quatre Testaments et autres poèmes* (1967). *100 Notes pour une solitude* (1970).

ESSAYS: *Saint-John Perse* (1953), *Emily Dickinson* (1957), *Walt Whitman* (1959), *Pierre Emmanuel* (1959), *Verbe et vertige* (1961: Prix Fémina-Vacaresco), *Robert Goffin* (1966).

ANTHOLOGIES: *Anthologie de la poésie américaine* (1956), *35 jeunes poètes americains* (1960), *Poésie du Quebec* (1968).

Translations (poetry): *Selected Poems*: a selection of poems by Alain Bosquet, translated by Samuel Beckett, Charles Guenther, Edouard Roditi and Ruth Whitman (New York, 1962).

To consult:
Charles Le Quintrec, *Alain Bosquet* (1964).

ANDRE DU BOUCHET

Born 1924 in Paris. Studied in Paris until his departure for the United States in 1941. Graduated from Harvard in 1943. Returned to Paris in 1948. One of the co-founders of the review *Ephémères* in 1967, and a member of the present editorial board (with Yves Bonnefoy, Paul Celan, Louis-René des Forêts, Jacques Dupin and Michel Leiris). Apart from his poetry, he has written literary and art criticism, translated Hölderlin, Shakespeare (*The Tempest*) and James Joyce (a fragment of *Finnegans Wake*), and written a study of the drawings of Alberto Giacometti (1968).

Du Bouchet is deeply concerned with the problem of human identity. Examining the sometimes tenuous relationship that can be established between man and the objects that surround him, and between man and a universe of light and space, he is a 'spatialist' poet in the true sense of the word: wide typographical spacing of the poem on the page is an essential element in the way he records his intensely visual and non-metaphorical perception of a cosmic reality in which man is

373

only one frail element. His techniques link him to the more hermetic wing of contemporary French poetry.

Main works:
Dans la chaleur vacante (which includes three previously published plaquettes: *Le Moteur blanc, Face de la chaleur, Sur le pas*) (1961: Prix des Critiques), *Où le soleil* (which includes two previously published plaquettes: *Ajournement, L'Inhabité*) (1968).

To consult:
Philippe Jaccottet, *L'Entretien des Muses* (1968).

MICHEL BUTOR

Born 1926 in Mons-en-Baroeul. Educated in Paris, studied philosophy at the Sorbonne under Gaston Bachelard and Jean Wahl, obtained degree. Professor at Minieh (Egypt) 1950–1, at Manchester University 1951–3, at Salonika 1954–5, at Geneva 1956–7. Three visits to the United States in 1960, 1962 and 1965. Spent 1964 in Berlin. He is, of course, better known as one of the most distinguished practitioners of the *nouveau roman* (his 1957 novel *La Modification* won the Prix Renaudot). He has also published several volumes of essays (*Le Génie de lieu, Repertoire I, Histoire extraordinaire, Repertoire II, Essais sur les modernes, Portrait de l'artiste en jeune singe, Repertoire III, Essais sur les essais, Essais sur le roman*) and an opera (*Votre Faust*, 1964).

Perhaps it was inevitable that his reputation as a novelist should have obscured the fame of his poetry. But, although it is true that the poems must be read as part of an *oeuvre* of which the novels, essays and *stéréoscopies* form the most substantial segments, it must be borne in mind, nevertheless, that Butor himself has always given a place of primary importance to his poetry. And although the techniques which are already familiar to readers of the novels may readily be recognized in the poems, it is equally appropriate to note that in those novels, and in the essays also, Butor's explanation of his stereoscopic universe has tended increasingly to be couched in poetic terms; he has himself emphasized his 'quest for new forms of imaginative writing (*formes romanesques*) containing a greater power of integration [of man with his universe].'

374

Main works of poetry:
La Banlieu de l'aube à l'aurore (written 1948, published 1968), *Illustrations* (1964), *Paysage de répons*, suivi de *Dialogues des règnes* (1968), *Illustrations II* (1969).

To consult:
R. M. Albérès, *Butor* (1964); Claude Mauriac, *L'Alittérature contemporaine* (1969); Georges Raillard, *Michel Butor* (1968); Jean Roudaut, *Michel Butor ou le livre futur* (1969).

RENE CHAR

Born 1907 at L'Isle-sur-Sorgue (Vaucluse). He has spent his whole life, apart from the war years, at his birthplace. Active in the surrealist movement 1929–34, signing the various manifestos and tracts, and writing, with Breton and Eluard, a collective work, *Ralentir travaux* (1930). The poems he published during this surrealist period were collected together in 1934 under the title *Le Marteau sans maître*. Mobilized in 1939, he fought in Alsace. After the armistice he returned home, then joined the *maquis* where he became a Resistance leader in the field. 1944–5, attached to Allied HQ, Algiers, in charge of parachute missions into France. As well as poems and essays, he has written on the art of Miró and Braque.

Char is one of the great names in French verse. The reputation first made with *Le Marteau sans Maître* was confirmed and greatly extended by the poetry he wrote during the war. His work stands in contrast to that of Aragon through its compression and its hermeticism, and it is Char rather than Aragon who has up till now had the greatest influence on younger French writers; this influence has extended far outside the borders of metropolitan France, and has for instance been strongly felt among French-Canadian poets. In recent years, Char has often seemed to be a victim of the temptation towards self-imitation, a hazard which must always confront the inventor of an extremely idosyncratic literary style, and his most recent work, expressing a fastidiously restricted range of ideas, has not done much for an already great reputation.

Main works since 1945:
POETRY: *Seuls demeurent* (1945), *Premières Alluvions* (1946), *Feuillets d'Hypnos* (1946), *Fureur et mystère* (1948), *Les Matinaux* (1950), *La*

Parole en archipel (1962), *Commune Présence* (1964), *Retour amont* (1966), *Dans la pluie giboyeuse* (1968). *Poèmes et proses choisis* (1957) presents a selection of texts published originally between 1935 and 1957.

ESSAYS: *A une sérénité crispée* (1951), *Lettera amorosa* (1953), *Recherche de la base du sommet* (1955), *Sur la poésie* (1958).

Translations:
Hypnos Waking: a selection of poems by René Char, ed. by J. Mathews (New York, 1956).

To consult:
Pierre Guerre, *René Char* (1961), Philippe Jaccottet, *L'Entretien des Muses* (1968); Georges Mounin, *Avez-vous lu Char?* (1946); Greta Rau, *René Char ou la poésie accrue* (1957).

MICHEL DEGUY

Born 1930 in Paris. 1948–50, studied at the Lycée Louis-le-Grand, Paris, and voyaged throughout Europe. 1953, degree in philosophy from the Sorbonne, where he is at present teaching. He is also a *lecteur* at Editions Gallimard. A member of the editorial board of the review *Critique*, founder and editorial director of the *Revue de poésie*, regular contributor to the *Nouvelle Revue française*. Apart from his poetry, he has written an essay on Thomas Mann (*Le Monde de Thomas Mann*, 1962) and translated (in collaboration) Heidegger's *Approches d'Hölderlin* (1962).

Deguy reveals a great deal about his poetic method by his phrase about poetry being something in which 'a thought was like a planetary system'. Like the linguistic philosophers who have influenced him, he is fascinated by the notion of language as a thing constantly in a state of becoming, and like them he is interested in what lies almost at the borders of specific meaning. As a result, his poetry can bewilder by the variety of the means which it employs. His primary concerns are two-fold: the poetic and its language, and poetry as a legitimate expression of life's realities. These have led him to a number of different prosodic approaches, experimental constructions and philosophical reflections.

Main works:
Les Meurtrières (1959), *Fragments du cadastre* (1960), *Poèmes de la presqu'île*

376

(1961), *Biefs* (1963), *Ouï dire* (1966). Two essays on poetry, combined with illustrative poems: *Actes* (1966), *Figurations* (1969).

To consult:
Philippe Jaccottet, *L'Entretien des muses* (1968).

JACQUES DUPIN

Born 1927 in Privas (Ardèche). Settled in Paris 1945. After studying law and political science, began to write poetry and art criticism. Author of studies on Miró and Giacometti (which have been translated into English), Tapiés and other contemporary artists. Is editorial director of the Galerie Maeght publications in Paris.

Like several poets of his generation, Dupin is in direct line of descent from René Char, but his metaphysically oriented vision is both tougher and more anguished than Char's. Dupin has described the poetic process as 'a limitless and unattainable experience [or, experimentation] which feeds itself on our own contradictions'; the cry '*Ignorez-moi passionément!*' ('Ignore me . . .' but also 'remain unaware of me passionately') which concludes the poem 'L'Ordre du jour' in his first published collection has become as well-known as any single line in modern French verse. His investigation of the possibilities of poetic language produces a texture as rock-like and crystalline as the human landscapes he describes, and an atmosphere tense with hidden violence.

Main works:
Cendrier du voyage (1950), *Art poétique* (1956), *Les Brisants* (1958), *L'Epervier* (1960), *Saccades* (1962), *Textes pour une approche* (1963), *Gravir* (which includes *Cendrier du voyage, Les Brisants, L'Epervier* and *Saccades*) (1963), *Le Corps clairvoyant* (1965), *La Nuit grandissante* (1967), *L'Embrasure* (1969).

To consult:
Philippe Jaccottet, *L'Entretien des muses* (1968).

JEAN-PIERRE DUPREY

Born 1930 in Rouen, died 1959 in Paris. Arrived in Paris 1948. During 1949 wrote the series of texts which were to compose *Derrière son double* and *Spectreuses*, and a dramatic poem *La Forêt sacrilège* (of which a fragment appeared the following year in the second edition of André Breton's *Anthologie de l'humoir noir*). In 1951, he abandoned poetry to take up painting and sculpture, and spent 1951–2 as an apprentice iron-worker in various workshops in Paris and Pantin. From 1953 to 1958 participated in a number of exhibitions of painting and sculpture and held several one-man shows of his iron sculptures. In 1959 he returned to poetry, and put together his last collection of poems, *La Fin et la manière*. He committed suicide that same day after addressing the manuscript to Breton. It was published posthumously, with a preface by Alain Jouffroy.

Duprey was one of the very last poets in the main surrealist stream to possess an original and viable message. Alone among the younger followers of André Breton, Duprey seemed successful in making use of the traditional surrealist tool of automatism to provoke genuine poetic imagery and reveal a powerfully disturbed imagination. One feels, as with none of the other surrealist poets who were first heard from in the immediate post-war era, that this mode of poetic expression provided a vital and ineluctable release-mechanism for his obsessed and anguished sense of personal fatality. The fact that he was deeply torn between poetry and the plastic arts, returning to poetry only to make a final confession of despair, makes him something very different from a 'professional' poet, in the sense that that word can be applied to many of the other writers here represented. This very fact may have something to do with the continuing vitality of his work.

Main works:
Derrière son double, suivi de *Spectreuses* (1950, revised edition 1964), *La Fin et la manière* (1965).

To consult:
André Breton, *Anthologie de l'humour noir* (1950); Alain Jouffroy, *Une Révolution du regard* (1964).

PIERRE EMMANUEL (Noël Mathieu, known as)

Born 1916 in Gan (Basses-Pyrénées). Went to Paris in 1935 and studied at the Sorbonne's Faculté des Lettres, where he was a pupil of Jean

Wahl. His first meeting with Pierre Jean Jouve in 1938 encouraged him to continue writing poetry, and his first poem, 'Christ au tombeau', was published that year. From 1940 to 1944 he was a professor at Dieulefit (Drôme) and collaborating in the clandestine publishing activities of the poets engaged in the Resistance. In 1945 he entered Radiodiffusion Française and became director of the English services of the radio. In 1959 he started working actively for the Congress for Cultural Freedom, making frequent visits abroad on behalf of the organization. Elected to the Académie Française in 1968. Apart from his poetry, he has written several volumes of essays, an autobiography (*Qui est cet homme?* 1948), a study of Baudelaire, and a novel.

Emmanuel is one of the few living French poets to enjoy a well-established reputation abroad. He is also one of that important group of French writers which is deeply indebted to the Christian experience – he has close links, for example, with both Jouve and La Tour du Pin. Writing on the theme of 'Poetry as a Spiritual Exercise', Emmanuel has said: 'The image is inseparable from the breath which gives it life: its beauty resides in great part in the adaptation of the language to its function, which is to create myths. The broadly human poetry which we are waiting for will be the work of a few great men of intuition, who will have understood that a writer's work, like in myth, develops following an internal law, biologically.'

Emmanuel has tried to follow this prescription in his own work, and has recently turned away from the epic and apocalyptic peoetry which made his name, in favour of something which, to use his own phrase, tries to get closer to 'the essence of the word'.

Main works of poetry:
Elégies (Brussels, 1940), *Tombeau d'Orphée* (1941), *XX Cantos* (Algiers, 1942), *Jour de colère* (Algiers, 1942), *Le Poète et son Christ* (Neuchâtel, 1942), *Combats avec tes défenseurs* (1942), *Orphiques* (1942), *Sodome* (1944), *La Liberté guide nos pas* (1945), *Tristesse ô ma patrie* (Algiers, 1946), *Chansons du dé à coudre* (1947), *Babel* (1952), *Visage nuage* (1956), *Versant de l'âge* (1958), *Evangéliaire* (1960), *La Nouvelle naissance* (1963), *Ligne de faîte* (1966).

To consult:
Alain Bosquet, *Pierre Emmanuel* (1959).

JEAN PIERRE FAYE

Born 1925 in Paris. His first poems were published in 1945 in the *Cahiers de la Table Ronde*. In 1950 entered the Sorbonne, where his fellow students included Michel Butor and Michel Foucault. Degree in philosophy, a subject which he has subsequently taught. Apart from his poetry, he has written four novels (*L'Ecluse* won the Prix Renaudot in 1964), four plays (*Ames et Pierres* was performed at the Odéon in 1965) and two collections of 'auto-critical' essays about writing (*Analogues*, 1964, and *Le Récit hunique*, 1967). A member of the editorial committee of the review *Tel Quel* until 1967, when he resigned from the group. Participated in the Cultural Congress at Havana in 1967 and visited Soviet Russia in 1968. In November 1968 founded the review *Change* (with Maurice Roche, Jacques Roubaud and others).

Although, as a novelist, Faye has sometimes been lumped in with the practitioners of the *nouveau roman*, his purpose, which he has called 'the invention of our time', has nothing in common with Robbe-Grillet's kind of systematized theorization. In a sense, Faye's novels, plays, *récits* and poems form different but complementary strands of a single preoccupation, namely the identity and meaning of the signs that constitute the intermediary between idea and man. Literature, then, is 'the ability to say by which signs our reality approaches us'. Hence the great importance for Faye of myth and fable, which might be called history in terms of signs (symbols): in French, *histoire* signifies equally 'history' and 'story'. 'To capture in flight this *pattern* which passes between words and things' – 'to discover and invent, ceaselessly, this sort of *physicality* of meaning' is the ambition that lies behind all his work, envisaged as *récit* (narration) in one form or another. For Faye, the *récit* is 'a machine to *stock* meaning', latent meaning in the form of signs that will cut through at any moment to the surface of the narrative, which is conceived as a network of such intersections.

Faye's poetry may be considered an attempt to situate reality at a point of intersection between things and images, between the present and 'memory' of the past: a point where the written word retains an intrinsic value independent of the ideas and actions it may be expressing, a substance that the reader is free to manipulate as he wishes.

Main works of poetry:
Fleuve renversé (1959), *Couleurs pliées* (1965), 'Le Change' in *Change* no. 1 (November 1968).

JEAN FOLLAIN

Born 1903 in Canisy (Manche). Studied law at the Faculté de Droit of Caen 1921–3. Settled in Paris in 1921, continuing law studies. Called to the bar in 1928, and began to publish poems that year. Became a member of the P.E.N. Club in 1949. In 1951 appointed to the magistrature, and became a district judge. Since his retirement, he has travelled widely: voyages to Japan in 1958, to South America (Brazil, Bolivia, Peru) in 1960, and to the United States in 1966. Apart from his poetry he has written various books including a study of Peru (1963) and a *Petit Glossaire de l'argot*.

Follain's poetry combines the concrete and the metaphysical in a particularly individual way. It is rooted, despite his wide travels, in the countryside of his childhood; each poem (they are always very brief) is a compression of experience and reflection which hints at far more than it states directly. A possible criticism of Follain's poetic resources would be that, though extremely special, they are also somewhat limited. Paradoxically, the passionate attachment to the past which is one of the principal emotions to be discovered in Follain's work links him to the practitioners of the *nouveau roman*, who have in fact been influenced by him. Follain's sensual attachment to what he remembers leads him to a concern with the identity of the object in relation to the everyday world. He ritualizes reality as a way of celebrating it.

Main works of poetry:
Cinq poèmes (1933), *La Main chaude* (1933), *Huit poèmes* (1935), *Le Gant rouge* (1936), *La Visite du domaine* (1936), *Chants terrestres* (1937), *L'Epicerie d'enfance* (1938), *Ici-bas* (Brussels, 1941), *Canisy* (1942), *Inventaire* (1942), *Usage de temps* (which includes *La Main chaude, Chants terrestres, Ici-bas*, together with an unpublished suite *Transparence du monde*) (1943), *Exister* (1947), *Chef-lieu* (1950), *Les Choses données* (1952), *Territoires* (1953), *Objets* (Limoges, 1955), *Tout instant* (1957), *Des heures* (1960), *Poèmes et Proses choisis* (1961), *Appareil de la terre* (1964), *D'après tout* (1967). *Exister*, suivi de *Territoires* (1969). *Les Poésies*, suivi de *Portrait de Jules* et de *Recit de l'an zéro* (1969).

To consult:
André Dhôtel, *Jean Follain* (1956); Philippe Jaccottet, *L'Entretien des muses* (1968).

381

ANDRE FRENAUD

Born 1907 in Montceau-les-Mines (Saône-et-Loire). Studied philosophy and law, taught French at the University of Lwów in 1930, travelled extensively throughout Europe. Became a civil servant in 1937. Mobilized in 1940, captured that same year, escaped from a German POW camp in 1942 and joined the Resistance. The poems contained in his first book, *Les Rois Mages* (1942), were all written in captivity. Since his retirement from the civil service has made voyages to Canada and the United States. Apart from his poetry, he has written a number of prefaces to the work of contemporary artists.

Frénaud's poetry spans a wide variety of styles, and is often strong in gesture and highly coloured. He has said of himself: 'I do not hope, I strive', and it is indeed an ironic humanism and generosity which characterizes his work at its best and most typical. Eluard remarked: 'Sociability is one of the dominant characteristics of the poetry of André Frénaud . . . it is not a stranger speaking, but my friend André Frénaud. I hear him imagine, put to the test, and confirm the strong words that are the life of others and the militant truth of the poet.' Frénaud was probably the most important poet to emerge from the war. His early work was widely acclaimed for the vigorous reaction it represented against surrealist obscurantism. On the other hand, his more recent work has not found favour with those younger poets influenced by linguistic philosophy.

Main works:

Most of André Frénaud's poetry has now been reassembled in three volumes: *Les Rois Mages* (new revised edition, 1966), *Il n'y a pas de Paradis* (1967) and *La Sainte Face* (1968). Other works include: *Vache bleue dans une ville* (1944), *Malamour* (1945), *Soleil irreductible* (Neuchâtel, 1946), *Poèmes de Brandebourg* (1948), *Poèmes de dessous le plancher* suivie de *La Noce noire* (1949), *Source entière* (1952), *Passage de la visitation* (1956), *Tombeau de mon père* (1961), *L'Etape dans la clairière* (1966).

To consult:

Georges-Emmanuel Clancier, *André Frénaud* (1963).

JEAN GROSJEAN

Born 1912 in Paris. Followed various occupations after leaving school, both in France and in the Middle East – Egypt, Palestine, the Lebanon –

where he spent the two years 1936–7: learned Arabic, Aramaic, Hebrew. After theological studies at a seminary, he was ordained a priest in 1939. Mobilized in 1940 and taken prisoner that same year; two years in a German POW camp. On his return to France, he was named vicar in various parishes in the neighbourhood of Paris, and participated in the Worker-Priest experiment. He left the Catholic Church in 1950. In 1967 he was invited to join Jean Paulhan and Marcel Arland in the editorial direction of the *Nouvelle Revue française*. In addition to his poetry, he has published two collections of essays, and translated Hebrew and Islamic sacred texts and the tragedies of Aeschylus and Sophocles.

Grosjean is one of the principal heirs of Paul Claudel, and despite his amicable parting from the Catholic Church, is one of the most important of contemporary French religious poets. He also bears the impress of Rimbaud, who was a major influence on Claudel himself. In fact, Grosjean's profoundly unorthodox temperament recalls Rimbaud, and the comparison helps to explain not only Grosjean's writing, but his chequered spiritual career. Another aspect of his poetry can be deduced from the texts which he has chosen to translate: from the Hebrew, the Old Testament Prophets; from the Arabic, the Koran; from Ancient Greek, the loftiest of the tragedians. In a preface to one of his books, he speaks of language 'completing that which it speaks of, terminating in that silent text whose words the reader will perhaps hear returning towards their source within himself.'

Main works:
Terre du temps (1946), *Hypostases* (1950), *Le Livre du juste* (1952), *Fils de l'homme* (1954), *Majestés et passants* (1956), *Apocalypse* (1962), *Hiver* (1964), *Elégies* (1967), *La Gloire*, précédé de *Apocalypse, Hiver* et *Elégies* (1969).

To consult:
Philippe Jaccottet, *L'Entretien des Muses* (1968).

GUILLEVIC (Eugène Guillevic, known as)

Born 1907 in Carnac (Morbihan). His father was a sailor and, later, a gendarme. Secondary school education, baccalauréat, passed examination into civil service: from 1935 onwards held post in the Ministry of

Finance until his retirement. Joined the clandestine Communist Party during the war. His 1954 collection of poems, *Trente et un sonnets*, was prefaced by Aragon. He has travelled very widely since 1947: Algeria, Tunisia, Czechoslovakia, Hungary, the Soviet Union, Roumania, etc. Apart from his poetry, he has translated or adapted many poems from the German, Russian, Hungarian, etc.

Guillevic is a Breton, and his poetry has the qualities of compactness, density and precision that are evoked by his native landscape, with its rows of menhirs ranged along a craggy shoreline. Guillevic demands, simply, forcefully and untiringly, that poetry should clarify the relationship between man and the world. The remarkable unity of his entire *oeuvre* (one may except a brief 'socialist-realist' divagation at the time of the *Trente et un sonnets*) comes from his constant, single-minded attempt to use words to bridge what seems to him a tragic gulf between man and an ill-disposed natural environment. At its best, the resulting verse is among the most direct, compelling and tender being written in France today.

Main works:
Requiem (1938), *Terraqué* (1942), *Elégies* (1946), *Amulettes* (1946), *Fractures* (1947), *Exécutoire* (1947), *Coördonnées* (Basle, 1948), *Gagner* (1949), *Les Chansons d'Antonin Blond* (1949), *Les Murs* (1950), *Envie de vivre* (1951), *Terre à bonheur* (1952), *Trente et un sonnets* (1954), *L'Age mûr* (1955), *Carnac* (1961) *Sphère* (1963), *Avec* (1966), *Euclidiennes* (1967), *La Ville* (1969).

Translations:
Guillevic, a selection edited and translated by Teo Savory (Santa Barbara, 1968); *Selected Poems*, with parallel translations by Denise Leverstov (New York, 1969).

To consult:
Philippe Jaccottet, *L'Entretien des Muses* (1968); Jean-Pierre Richard, *Onze études sur la poésie moderne* (1946); Jean Tortel, *Guillevic* (1953).

PHILIPPE JACCOTTET

Born 1925 in Moudon, Switzerland. Studied liberal arts at the university of Lausanne. Went to Paris in 1946, travelled in Spain and Italy.

Has lived in France since 1953. Apart from his poetry, he has translated Homer and many contemporary German and Italian authors, and has written extensively as a literary critic for magazines and newspapers.

Jaccottet's poetry has, in general, been characterized by an artful simplicity, with an underlying religious note which has prompted one critic to compare him to Jammes. The simplicity is a matter of art because, as the translator soon discovers, the poet's effects are very much bound up with the nature, and indeed the structure of the French language. The diaphanous quality of Jaccottet's more recent poetry suggests the possibility that it be read aloud rather than analysed; only thus, perhaps, can the individual decide whether this fine-spun verse has anything to say to his own ear.

Main works:
POETRY: *L'Effraie et autres poèmes* (1953), *L'Ignorant, poèmes 1952–6* (1957), *Airs* (1967), *Leçons* (1969).

ESSAYS: *Eléments d'un songe* (1961), *L'Obscurité* (1961), *La Semaison, carnets 1954–62* (1963), *L'Entretien des muses* (a collection of essays on contemporary French poets) (1968).

ALAIN JOUFFROY

Born 1928 in Paris. Participated in the activities of the surrealist movement 1947–8; his first poems appeared in the surrealist review *Néon* in 1947. Between 1954 and 1959, he divided his time between Paris and Venice. Apart from his poetry, he has written two novels, a volume of essays on the dada and surrealist painters and the avant-garde in modern art (*Une Révolution du regard*, 1964), studies of Henri Michaux, Victor Brauner and other artists, introduced and edited an anthology of the work of Saint-Pol Roux, translated the poetry of Salvatore Quasimodo, and compiled a special poetry issue of the Belgian review *Apparatus* (no. 63–67, Brussels, 1966).

In an essay on André Breton, who has always remained for him an essential poetic inspiration, Jouffroy describes poems as 'meetings, events, history living and still to be lived . . . , a revolution settled minute by minute, wherever it is freely manifested *without limits* . . . Poetry arises from the direction and trajectory of words, that is, it is *the dictation of words in action*.' This description explains very clearly the twin elements of radically-oriented *reportage* and surrealist technique in Jouffroy's verse, especially from *Trajéctoire* onwards. It also explains why Jouffroy has been the advocate in France of Ginsberg and the Beat poets. But though it is not difficult to find various influences at work in his poetry (Saint-John Perse may once have been one of them), the basic emotional and psychological thread which unites Jouffroy's work is surrealism, and specifically the surrealism of Breton. Jouffroy himself has said that his faithfulness to the concept of surreality (and to a future surreality which will not even bear that name) is in exact proportion to the distance he has kept between himself and the manifestations of the official surrealist group.

Main works of poetry:
A Toi (1958), *Déclaration d'Indépendance* (San Francisco, 1961), *Tire à l'arc*, illustrated by Victor Brauner (Milan, 1962), *L'Epée dans l'eau*, illustrated by Fontana (Milan, 1962), *Aube à l'antipode*, illustrated by René Margritte (1966, poems written 1947–8), *Trajéctoire* (1968), *Libertés de la liberté*, illustrated by Joan Miró (1970).

An anthology:
La Poésie de la Beat Generation (with Jean-Jacques Lebel) (1965).

PIERRE JEAN JOUVE

Born 1887 in Arras. First influenced as a poet by the symbolists, published a symbolist review, *Les Bandeau d'or*, 1906–8. In touch during those years with the humanist 'Groupe de l'Abbaye'. His reading in 1915 of Romain Rolland's *Jean-Christophe* influenced him deeply: he became a friend of Rolland and a follower of his 'unanism'. Published between 1912 and 1923 a number of collections of poems which he disavowed *in toto* in 1924 when he published *Les Mysterieuses Noces*. Thenceforward, his work was to be marked by its mixture of extreme Christian sensibility and an awareness of eroticism in terms of Freudian psychoanalytic theory. Apart from his poetry, he has written a number of novels, several volumes of essays on poets, painters and musicians, and has translated Shakespeare (*Othello*, the *Sonnets*) and Hölderlin. He received the Grand Prix des Lettres in 1964, and the Grand Prix de Poésie of the Académie Française in 1966.

Jouve is unquestionably one of the leading poets in France, and has long been so, though his reputation has only now begun to travel abroad. In a manifesto, published in 1934, he said: 'The revolution, like the religious act, has need of love. Poetry is an interior vehicle of love. We poets must therefore produce that bloody sweat which is the raising up into such profound and elevated substances, proceeding from destitution, of the beautiful power of human eroticism.'

Main works of poetry:
Noces (1928), *Les Noces* (1931), *Sueur de sang* (1933), *Hélène* (1936), *Matière céleste* (1937), *Kyrie* (1938), *Porche à la nuit des saints* (Neuchâtel, 1942), *Gloire* (Algiers, 1942), *La Vierge de Paris* (Fribourg, 1946), *Hymne* (Fribourg, 1947), *Diadème* (1949), *Ode* (1951), *Lyrique* (1956), *Mélodrame* (1957), *Inventions* (1958), *Moires* (1962).
Most of these volumes have been reassembled, in revised versions, in four volumes of *Oeuvre Poétique* (1967), as follows: *Poésie I–IV* (1925–38): *Les Noces, Sueur de sang, Matière celeste, Kyrie; Poésie V–VI* (1939–47) *La Vierge de Paris, Hymne; Poésie VII–IX* (1949–54) *Diadème, Ode, Langue; Poésie X–XI* (1956–66) *Mélodrame, Moires.*

Translations:
An Idiom of Night, selected poems of Pierre Jean Jouve translated by Keith Bosley (London, 1968).

To consult:
Léon-Gabriel Gros, *Poètes contemporains* (*Marseille,* 1944); René Micha, *Pierre Jean Jouve* (1956); Jean Rousselot, *Pierre Jean Jouve ou le rôle sanctificatieur de l'oeuvre d'art* (1956); Jean Starobinsky, Paul Alexandre, Marc Eigeldinger, *Pierre Jean Jouve, poète et romancier* (Neuchâtel, 1946); Philippe Jaccottet, *L'Entretien des muses* (1968).

OLIVIER LARRONDE

Born 1927 in La Ciotat (Bouches du Rhône), died 1965 in Paris. His father, Carlos Larronde, was a poet, journalist and one of the founders of French radio. He arrived in Paris in 1944, and was immediately taken up by Cocteau, Bérard and Genet. His first collection of poems, *Les Barricades mystérieuses,* was published when he was twenty-one. Began to smoke opium as therapy for epileptic fits from which he now suffered: increasingly involved with the law over his drug-taking, arrested several time for possession of opium. After being forcibly dis-intoxicated he turned to alcohol, as a result of which his condition deteriorated. From 1956 onwards, although a victim of schizophrenia and persecution mania, he never ceased writing poems during periods of lucidity. His third collection of poems, *L'Arbre à lettres* (its title is a pun on L'Arbalète, his publisher's house-name) was published post-humously; it includes his translation of Shakespeare's 'The Pheonix and the Turtle'.

Larronde could be said to represent the continuation of the tradition of Mallarmé in the French poetry of the mid-twentieth century. If he may sometimes seem, dismayingly, more Mallarmean than his model, his poetry nevertheless frequently offers delicious or poignant rewards for the reader with a sufficient fund of patience and erudition to unravel his complex and often highly intellectual meanings.

Main works:
Les Barricades mystérieuses (1948), *Rien voilà l'ordre*, illustrated by Alberto Giacometti (1959), *Les Armes miraculeuses* (1961), *L'Arbre à lettres* (1966).

PATRICE DE LA TOUR DU PIN

Born 1911 in Paris. Of Irish descent on his mother's side, and of noble Auvergnat descent on his father's side. He spent his childhood at the family estates at Bignon-Mirabeau in Sologne. Studied the liberal arts and then political science 1929–32. Since 1935 has lived permanently at the Château de Bignon-Mirabeau, where he leads the life of a 'poetic recluse'. His first poem was published in the *Nouvelle Revue française* in 1933. Mobilized in 1940 and captured that same year, he spent 1940–3 in a German POW camp, during which time he wrote a great deal of poetry. His published poems up to 1946 have been reassembled in a single volume, *Une Somme de poésie*, the first of a continuing series of volumes intended to constitute a celebration of God and the divine nature of man; he has himself created the neologism '*théopoésie*' to describe his poetic endeavour. La Tour du Pin is one of the few French poets of his generation not to feel the influence of surrealism. Instead, he is a symbolist in the strictest sense of the word. He has pursued a quest; for him 'the lands without legends are condemned to die of cold.' Quoting this line, a contemporary French critic adds that the word 'legend' means for the poet 'precisely this passage from a chaos of incomprehensible signs to the symbolic coherence of a meaningful adventure.'

Main works:
La Quête de joie (1933), *Psaumes* (1938), *Le Jeu du seul* (1946), *Une Somme de poésie* (1946), *Les Concerts sur terre* (1946), *La Contemplation errante* (1948), *Une Somme de poésie: le second jeu* (1959), *Une Somme de poésie: petit théâtre crépusculaire* (1963).

To consult:
Eva Kushner, *Patrice de La Tour du Pin* (1961).

JEAN LESCURE

Born 1912 in Asnières. Published his first plaquette of poems, *Le Voyage immobile*, in 1938, the same year that he founded the review *Messages*. Resumed editing *Messages* in 1942, under the Occupation: several successive issues banned by the authorities. In 1943 he wrote, with Eluard, the celebrated manifesto 'L'Honneur des poètes', and became co-director of the clandestine *Lettres françaises*. Appointed the director of Radiodiffusion Française after the Liberation. Later became director of the Théâtre des Nations. Founder-director of Cinéma d'Art et Essai. Apart from his poetry, his writings include translations of Shakespeare (*Measure for Measure*) and Ungaretti, and prefaces to the work of a number of contemporary artists.

An old friend and colleague of Raymond Queneau (who was fellow-director of Radiodiffusion Française in the post-war years), Lescure shares some of Queneau's preoccupation with language as a basis for experimental transformations. In addition to manipulating the semantic resources of the French language in witty and sophisticated fashion, Lescure is equally at home in a lyrical idiom which is characterized by delicate, ironic sensibility. In poems in this latter mode, we may detect the lingering influence of surrealism, but it is surrealism in the manner of Lescure's friend Paul Eluard.

Main works of poetry:
Treize poèmes, suivie de *La Marseillaise bretonne* (1964), *Drailles* (1968).

ARMEN LUBIN

Born 1903 in Istanbul. Of Armenian parentage, he came to Paris as a refugee while still an adolescent. He has described, in imaginative terms, this period of his life in Paris in his first collection of poems, *Le Passager clandestin*. Although he has remained reticent about the details of his health, it is clear that at some unspecified period he became very seriously ill: ever since then his life has been one of enforced isolation, a continual transplantation from one hospital or sanatorium to another. He now lives on the Côte d'Azur. His later poetry inevitably reflects the poignant—and sometimes burlesque—aspects of the transient world of sickness and hospital life, but at a far from anecdotal level. Indeed, the virtue of his poetry is the manner in which he has transformed into lyrical and emotionally integrated perceptions the sad, sordid world of sickness and helplessness. The tone is often ironic, never plaintive. Before the Second World War, Lubin contributed to various literary reviews: the *Nouvelle Revue française*, *Les Cahiers de la Pléiade*, *Measures*, and since the Liberation he has contributed to *Les Cahiers des saisons*.

Main works:
Le Passager clandestin (1946), *Sainte Patience* (1951), *Transfert nocturne* (1955), *Les Haute terrasses* (1957), *Feux contre feux*, which includes revised versions of the above four collections plus a number of unpublished poems (1968).

To consult:
Philippe Jaccottet, *L'Entretien des Muses* (1968).

HENRI MICHAUX

Born 1899 in Namur, Belgium. Educated in that country. His varied occupations as a young man included those of sailor, merchant, tutor, private secretary (to Jules Supervielle), etc. His discovery of Lautréamont in 1922 proved decisive. 1928–37, travelled widely in North and South America, India, China, Japan, Egypt, Africa; he has also stayed frequently in Portugal. His 'home base' is Paris where he prefers to live in complete seclusion. He has always refused the name 'poet' for himself, remarking that: 'Poetry is always an imponderable which may be found in any means of expression, as a sudden enlargement of the world. Its density may be far stronger in painting, a photograph, a mean hut.' His work is, in fact, difficult to divide into genres, and includes travel 'notebooks', essays on art and on drug-taking as a means of provoking 'alienation of sensation'. He may be considered a surrealist in the fullest sense of the term. He is also a distinguished painter, graphic artist and book illustrator: an exhibition of his graphic work was held at the Musée National d'Art Moderne in 1965. He refused the award of the Grand Prix National des Lettres in 1965 as a matter of principle, to express his opposition to the institution of literary prizes.

Main works:
Qui je fus (1927), *Ecuador* (1929), *Mes propriétés* (1929), *Un Certain Plume* (1930), *Un Barbare en Asie* (1933), *La Nuit remue* (1935), *Voyage en Grande Garabagne* (1936), *Plume* précédé de *Lointain intérieur* (1937), *Au pays de la magie* (1942), *Epreuves, exorcismes* (1945), *Ici, Poddéma* (1946), *Apparitions*, with drawings by the author (1946), *Meidosems*, with thirteen lithographs by the author (1948), *La Vie dans les plis* (1948), *Poésie pour pouvoir* (1949), *Passages* (1950), *Mouvements*, album of drawings accompanied by texts (1951), *Face aux verrous* (1954), *Misérable miracle* (1956), *L'Infini turbulent* (1957), *Paix dans les brisements* (1959), *Connaissance par les gouffres* (1961), *Vents et poussières* (1962), *Passages*, revised edition (1963), *L'Infini turbulent*, revised edition (1964), *L'Espace du dedans*, a selection of writings 1927–59 (1966).

Translations:
Poems, a choice of poems by Henri Michaux, translated by Sylvia Beach (New York, 1949); *A Barbarian in Asia*, translated by Sylvia Beach (New York, 1949); *The Space Within*, translated by Richard Elmann (New York, 1951); *Light through Darkness*, translated by Haakon Chevalier (New York, 1963, London, 1964); *Miserable Miracle*, translated by Louise Varèse (San Francisco, 1963).

To consult:
Raymond Bellour, *Henri Michaux ou une mesure de l'être* (1965); René Bertelé, *Henri Michaux* (1965); Robert Bréchon, *Michaux* (1959); Philippe de Coulon, *Henri Michaux, poète de notre société* (1949); André Gide, *Découvrons Henri Michaux* (1941); Philippe Jaccottet, *L'Entretien des Muses* (1968); Alain Jouffroy, *Henri Michaux* (1962); Alain Jouffroy, *Une Révolution du regard* (1964); Claude Mauriac, *L'Alittérature contemporaine* (1958, revised edition 1969); N. Murat, *Michaux* (1967); Cahiers de *L'Herne*, no. 8, *Henri Michaux* (1966).

JEAN PEROL

Born 1932 at Vienne (Isère). Childhood spent in the south-east of France (between Nîmes and Lyon) in what he describes as miserable surroundings. Education: self-taught, obtained *baccalauréat* and arts degree 'outside the university system'. Was close to Roger Vailland, and considers this friendship to have been an important influence on his development as a writer. At present, teaches French in a Paris *lycée*. Spent six years in Japan (1964-9) and has returned to France profoundly affected by this experience. Apart from his poetry, he writes literary criticism for the *Nouvelle Revue française*, *Lettres françaises* and the *Magazine littéraire*. His poems have been translated into Japanese, Turkish, Polish, Roumanian, Serbo-Croatian.

Pérol lists among his poetic preoccupations: "How to make the *blood* course again in poetry!—How to keep (intelligently) one's distance from the 'intellect' in poetry, which is to say without ignoring it, but without making it the master of the whole system?—How to recover the 'modernity' of our time in poetry, in an efficacious way, with the liveliness of the cinema, for instance ('to be resolutely modern, to keep what has been gained', as Rimbaud wrote)?—How to reconcile a certain *swiftness*, *acceleration*, *brutality*, *violence*, with poetry, and the old ideas which readers have of it." Among the contemporary poets he admires, he cites Henri Michaux, Michel Deguy, Jacques Réda and Alain Jouffroy.

Main works:
Sang et raisons (1953), *Le Coeur de l'olivier* (1957), *Le Feu du gel* (1959), *L'Atelier* (1961), *Le Point vélique* (1965), *D'un pays lointain* (Tokyo, 1965), *Le Coeur véhément* (1968), *Ruptures* (1970).

GEORGES PERROS

Born 1923 in Paris. His parents moved to the country when he was six, and he attended school at Rheims, Belfort and Rennes successively. After war service, and a number of short-lived enthusiasms which included football, the piano and literature, he returned to Paris. He completed his education at the Lycée Condorcet there, then decided to become an actor. Studied at the Conservatoire, won second prize of proficiency, became a member of the Comédie Française company as an actor. After two years left to join the Théâtre Nationale Populaire as a reader for Jean Vilar. Left Paris in 1959 for Brittany, where he has since lived. In 1966 joined Editions Gallimard as a reader of poetry. Has written scripts for the radio on the work of Lichtenberg, Valéry and Stendhal.

He has written, about his own poetic intentions: 'I try to liberate, to the maximum extent possible, the new state of what serves me for language.' This laconic statement scarcely hints at the marvellous out-pouring of wit and humour that complements the resourcefulness of a disenchanted memory blessed with total recall. Perros' little suite of anti-epics constitutes the tragi-comic 'diary' of a solitary man confronted (and confounded) by an unpredictable social environment, a chronicle rich with wry but serene reflections on mortality.

Main works:
Papiers collés (1960), *Poèmes bleus* (1962), *Une Vie ordinaire* (1967).

ANDRE PIEYRE DE MANDIARGUES

Born 1909 in Paris. Lived in Monaco during the Occupation, publishing his first collection of poems, *Dans les années sordides,* in 1943. He first attracted attention, in 1946, with a collection of fantastic short stories, *Le Musée noir.* Shortly afterwards he became closely attached to André Breton, and remained on cordial terms with the surrealist group during their more active post-war years, signing some of their manifestos. Apart from his poetry, he has written several novels, some of which have been translated into English, as well as short stories, studies on art and architecture, and prefaces to the work of many contemporary artists.

Despite his close connection with the surrealist movement, the surrealist element in his own work is tenuous: as a critic has remarked, he has been 'too much of an artist to trifle for long with the failed poets who looked for genius in automatism.' On the other hand, he is a writer who likes to astonish, even to shock a little, and his work always has a keen sense of the perverse and the erotic. He himself confirms these attitudes, saying: 'The writer and the artist want to astonish. There is no work worthy of attention which does not have a little thunder and lightning.'

Main works of poetry:
Dans les années sordides (1943, revised edition 1949), *L'Age de craie*, suivi de *Hédéra* (1961), *Astynanax*, précédé de *Les Incongruités monumentales*, et suivi de *Cartolines et Dédicaces* (1964), *Le Point où j'en suis*, suivis de *Dalila exaltée* et de *La Nuit l'amour* (1964), *Ruisseau des solitudes*, suivi de *Jacinthes* et de *Chapeaugaga* (1968).

MARCELIN PLEYNET

Born 1933 in Lyons. His first collection of poems, *Provisoires amants des nègres*, published in 1962 in the Collection Tel Quel, showed a certain neo-surrealist influence. One of the founders of the review *Tel Quel*, of which he is the *secrétaire de la rédaction*. Apart from his poetry, he has written a long essay, *Lautréamont par lui-même*, for the series 'Ecrivains de toujours' (1967), as well as a number of theoretical essays on the nature of writing from the point of view of structural linguistics (Jacques Derrida, Julia Kristova, etc.). His essay 'La poésie doit avoir pour but . . .' in *Tel Quel: Théorie d'ensemble* (1968) describes poetry as 'speculative philosophy', and continues: 'Language is inevitably difficult and initiatory in its process; but the recorded evidence of this process is political. Language is inevitably difficult and initiatory in its relationship with the theory of production of language. So long as poetry fails to recognize the inscription of its text and its practice in history, so long will it remain profoundly unconvincing, like blinded (?) fortune led by its eyes wherever they think fit'.

Main works:
Provisoires Amants des nègres (1962), *Paysages en deux*, suivis de *Les Lignes de la prose* (1964), *Comme* (1965).

FRANCIS PONGE

Born 1899 in Montpellier. Educated first at Caen, then at Paris, where he completed law studies at the Sorbonne. Literary studies at Strasbourg 1919–21. In contact, intermittently, with the surrealists between 1925 and 1930. Between the wars, worked first for the *Nouvelle Revue française*, then for Librairie Hachette, then on the editorial staff of the

Lyons daily *Progrés*. Joined the Communist Party in 1937, and was active in the Resistance during the war. Director of the weekly *Action* 1945-6. Left the Communists in 1947, spent the two following years in Algeria. From 1952 to 1965 a professor at the Alliance Française in Paris; he has also made many lecture tours abroad. Now lives in retirement in Provence.

A profoundly anti-lyrical writer, Ponge has always declined to describe his imaginative prose-texts as 'poetry'. Yet, despite himself, he is unquestionably a poet, and one who has perfected the form of the poem in prose. His aim, in these self-contained prose-structures, is nothing less than the poetic re-education of language, the submission of its structures to the structures of the objects it describes. His ambition is to bestow upon the object (any object he may encounter, or that comes to hand) 'the good fortune to be born into words', to become what it is, 'to bubble and explode in terms of a language'. Ponge's slogan is: 'Recognize the object's basic rights, its inalienable rights in opposition to poetic objectives.' Hence Ponge's 'rhetoric', designed to illustrate the object's absolute resistance to the possibilities of poetic analogy. The results of this new 'rhetoric of the object' are seldom less than fascinating, if disorienting, even on such an extended level as the majestic *Soap* sequence which was composed over a period of twenty-five years. His work has had an acknowledged effect on Robbe-Grillet in the formation of the *nouveau roman*, and on Philippe Sollers and the *Tel Quel* group.

Main works:
Douze petits écrits (1926), *Le Parti pris des choses* (1942), *Le Carnet du bois des pins* (1947), *Proêmes* (1948), *La Rage de l'expression* (1952), *Pour un Malherbe* (1965), *Le Savon* (1967: started 1942, completed 1965).

The main body of his work has been assembled in:
Le Grand Recueil (3 vols., 1961) and *Le Nouveau Recueil* (1967).

Translations:
Soap, translated by Lane Dunlop (London, 1969).

To consult:
Philippe Jaccottet, *L'Entretien des Muses* (1968); Jean-Pierre Richard, *Poésie et profondeur* (1965); Jean-Paul Sartre, *Situations I* (1947); Philippe Sollers, *Francis Ponge* (1963); Jean Thibaudeau, *Ponge* (1967).

JACQUES PREVERT

Born 1900 in Neilly-sur-Seine. Participated in the activities of the surrealist group 1926–30; then devoted himself to the cinema, writing the scenarios of a number of films (some of them directed by his brother Pierre Prévert) which have remained justly famous: *Drôle de drame*, *Les Visiteurs du soir*, *Les Enfants du paradis*, etc. He has also written several short plays, including *La Famille tuyau de poêle*, and radio scripts. As an artist, he has held exhibitions of his photo-collages and published them in book form. Many of his poems may be considered songs, and have been set to music by Joseph Kosma and others.

Prévert has enjoyed the most widespread popularity with the public of any living French poet and, essentially, he represents a kind of reconciliation between the avant-garde spirit of surrealism and the favourite themes of popular culture. From his surrealist days he retains a liking for the 'surprise-image' and a facility in producing it, but Prévert has equally remained faithful to a revolutionary attitude expressed in populist terms of anti-clericalism, anti-militarism and the sanctity of love between man and woman, a love freely given and received. He has been criticized, indeed, for 'vulgarizing, to the point of making them inoffensive, the subversive properties of surrealism'. But it would be less churlish, and more sensible, to be grateful to him for all the qualities that make his poetry so endearing: frankness, forcefulness, a humour that is brutal or tender according to the context, a mastery of satire as a weapon (his *Diner de Têtes* ... is one of the modern masterpieces of satire), his innate sense of how the spoken language works.

Main works:
Des Bêtes, with photographs by Ylla (1930), *Paroles* (1946), *Histoires* in collaboration with André Verdet (1946), *Spectacle* (1951), *Le Grand Bal de printemps*, with photographs by Izis (1932), *La Pluie et le beau temps* (1955), *Fatras*, illustrated with photo-collages by the author (1965).

Translations:
Selections from *Paroles*, translated by Lawrence Ferlinghetti (San Francisco, 1965).

To consult:
Jean Queval, *Jacques Prévert* (1955).

RAYMOND QUENEAU

Born 1903 in Le Havre. Degree in philosophy from the Sorbonne in 1925. His fellow-student at the Sorbonne, Pierre Naville, introduced him to the surrealist group and he began writing for *La Révolution surréaliste*. Military service with the Zouaves 1925–7, taking part in the Riff war which gave him the background for his novel *Odile*. He broke, amicably, with the surrealists in 1929; published his first novel, *Le Chiendent*, in 1933. Between 1931 and 1933 wrote for Boris Souvarine's journal *La Critique sociale*, and, between 1936 and 1938 for the daily *L'Intransigeant*. Joined Editions Gallimard as a *lecteur* in 1938, and was appointed *secrétaire général* in 1941: he edited the first volume of the Encyclopédie de la Pléiade, *Histoire de la science*. A member of the Société Mathématique de France, and elected a member of the Académie Goncourt in 1951. Apart from his poetry, he has published seventeen novels, three collections of short stories, an imaginative investigation of the diversities of language—*Exercises de style*, studies on contemporary artists (Miró, Vlaminck), etc.

Queneau's work is all of a piece—novels and poems alike. He himself says: 'I have set myself (in the novel) rules as strict as those of a sonnet. . . . One can rhyme characters and situations as one rhymes words, one can even be satisfied with alliterations. In fact, I have never seen essential differences between the novel, of the kind I want to write, and poetry.' The two constant characteristics which one finds in Queneau's work are ironic humour, and an obsession with language in all its forms, from the most correct and classical to the most popular. A contemporary critic has said of him: 'That which characterizes Queneau's art, is the knowledge of how to hide the fear of death, fundamental pessimism, beneath the sleight-of-hand of anachronism and of the language, and of how to use all the resources of culture in order to rediscover the milk of human kindness and one of the distinguishing marks of humanity: laughter, without for one moment ceasing to be a poet.'

Main works of poetry:
Chêne et chien (novel in verse) (1937), *Les Ziaux* (1943). *Bucoliques* (1947), *Exercises de style* (1947), *L'Instant fatal* (1948), *Monuments* (1948), *Petite Cosmogonie portative* (1950), *Si tu t'imagines* (1952), *Le Chien à la mandoline* (1958, reprinted 1965), *Sonnets* (1958), *Cent mille milliards de poèmes* (1961), *Courir les rues* (1967), *Battre la campagne* (1968), *Fendre les flots* (1969).

Translations (poetry):
Exercises in Style, translated by Barbara Wright (London, 1958).

To consult:
Jacques Bens, *Raymond Queneau* (1962); Jean Queval, *Raymond Queneau* (1960); Claude Simmonet, *Queneau déchiffré* (*notes sur 'Le Chiendent'*) (1960); Raymond Queneau with Georges Charbonnier, *Entretiens* (1962).

JACQUES REDA

Born 1929 in Lunéville. Studied law at the Faculté des Droits, Paris. Between 1952 and 1955 he published several plaquettes of poems which he now characterizes as 'lightweight', then retired entirely from the Paris literary scene. For the next ten years or so he worked at a variety of jobs, including that of factory hand, remaining in touch only with the review *Cahiers du Sud,* to which he contributed a number of essays of literary criticism, and occasional poems. *Amén,* which won the 1968 Prix Max Jacob by unanimous vote, was his first volume of poems to appear for fifteen years. He has since contributed fiction and literary criticism to the *Nouvelle Revue française* and the quarterly *Cahiers du chemin.* A lifelong jazz lover, he has been writing regularly for the Paris *Jazz Magazine* since 1963.

Amén and the poems written subsequently represent a total spiritual break with his previous work, the outcome of a prolonged period of meditation and reflection. Réda's present pessimistic vision is softened by a compassionate apprehension of *la condition humaine* that is power-fully reinforced by the controlled language in which it is expressed. His solidly constructed, thematically integrated verse is probably more immediately accessible to a reader habituated to English and American prosodic norms than that of most of his French contemporaries.

Main works:
Les Inconvenients du métier (1952), *All Stars* (1953), *Amén* (1968).

JEAN-CLAUDE RENARD

Born 1922 in Toulon. When he was eight his family moved to Paris, where he has lived ever since. Arts degree from the Sorbonne 1944;

published his first collection of poems, *Juan*, the following year. During 1948–9, he experienced what he has called 'a grave spiritual crisis, involving an initiation into esoteric philosophy'. Since 1947 he has worked in publishing; he is now director of literary services for Editions Casterman. Received the Grand Prix Catholique de Littérature in 1957. Voyages to Morocco (1962) and Spain (1963 and 1966). Awarded the Prix Sainte-Beuve in 1966 for his *La Terre du sacre*.

Michel Carrouges has defined Renard's work thus: 'A great poetry of cosmic and spiritual inspiration, wherein is affirmed a strange accord between the sense of the harmony of correspondences and that of lyric violence. . . . The theme of metamorphosis predominates in it. It engenders a kind of great symphonic orchestration where man and woman . . . earth and the Heavenly City design in shining lines the fascinating ghost of their future unity.' Jean Rousselot speaks of Renard's 'instinctive pantheism with theogenic, cosmogenic and theosophical conceptions that recall simultaneously those of Jakob Boehme, Swedenborg, Saint-Martin and Teilhard de Chardin'.

Main works:
Juan (1945), *Cantiques des pays perdus* (1947, new edition 1957), *Haute-Mer* (1950), *Métamorphose du monde* (1951, new edition 1963), *Fable* (1952), *Père, voici que l'homme . . .* (1955), *En une seule vigne* (1959), *Incantation des eaux* (1961), *Incantation du temps* (1962), *La Terre du sacre* (1966), *La Braise et la rivière* (1969).

To consult:
André Alter, *Jean-Claude Renard* (1966); Léon Guichard, *Renard* (1961).

ARMAND ROBIN

Born 1912 in Brittany (nr. Plougeurnevel, Côtes-du-Nord), died 1962 in Paris. Youngest of eight children of a Breton peasant family, educated first at small village schools, then for three years at Saint-Brieuc *lycée* before winning a scholarship to Lyon university, where he studied Russian. After failing the *agrégation* (State examination for a university teaching degree), he began the wandering existence which he was to maintain for most of his life; during the years between about 1930 and the outbreak of war he visited most of the countries of Europe, including the Soviet Union, Germany, Estonia, Lithuania, the Scandinavian countries, Switzerland, Spain. Around 1940 he enrolled at the Ecole des Langues Orientales in Paris, where he learned Chinese. He was a remarkable linguist; together with Chinese, and the Greek, Latin, English, Russian and German he had learned at school and college, he studied and became fluent in Flemish, Swedish, Italian, Spanish, Arabic, Uzbek, Cheremiss (one of the two 'Volga' languages), Finnish, Hungarian, etc. As well as being a poet, he was a uniquely gifted and versatile translator of poetry into French. He also wrote a novel, *Le Temps qu'il fait* (1942), and a collection of his essays was published in 1953 under the title *La Fausse Parole*. His political sympathies remained revolutionary and anarchist, and his critical writings, poems and translations appeared frequently in the anarchist press: his best-known collection of poems, *Les Poèmes indésirables*, was published by the Anarchist Federation. He led an impoverished and often solitary existence: after the war, he gained a precarious living in Paris from the publication of a regular news bulletin based on his monitoring of world-wide short-wave radio programmes, roneo-typed by himself and sold by subscription from his attic lodgings (to a few distinguished customers who included the Vatican and the Elysée Palace). He died in mysterious circumstances, in the central police hospital in Paris, three days after being arrested for questioning on unknown charges. Neither friends nor family learned of his death until a month afterwards; his personal papers and manuscripts (including the poems which make up the posthumous collection *Le Monde d'une voix*) were rescued by friends just in time to save them being destroyed as rubbish by municipal workmen clearing out the empty lodgings.

Robin's poetry, despite his powerful equipment as a polyglot, is neither cosmopolitan nor sophisticated. Rather, it is the outcry of a solitary who found himself at odds with the world and its injustices.

Main works (poetry, translations of poetry):
Ma Vie sans moi (1940; poems by the author, and translations of poems by Essenin, Mayakovsky, Rilke, Poe, Chekhov and others), *Poèmes indésirables* (1945), *Quatre poètes russes: Blok, Essénine, Maiakovski, Pasternak* (1948), *Poèmes d'André Ady* (1951: from the Hungarian), *Poésie non traduite I* (1953: containing translations from the Chinese, Swedish, Finnish, German, Dutch, Russian, Spanish, Italian, Hungarian, sixth-century Arabic, Cheremiss, and some translations from French into Breton), *Poésie non traduite II* (1958: containing translations from the Chinese, Russian, Polish, Old Bulgarian, Hungarian,

Mongolian, sixth-century Gaulish, Spanish, German, English, Italian, Slovene, Uigur), *Le Monde d'une voix* (1968).

DENIS ROCHE

Born 1937 in Paris. Spent his early childhood in the Caribbean and South America. Returned to France in 1946. Works as an editor in the fine arts publishing department of Editions Tschou. Associated with the *Tel Quel* group since its inception, and a regular contributor to the review. Apart from his poetry, he has written a theoretical text on poetry, 'La poesie est inadmissible d'ailleurs elle n'existe pas', which appears in the *Tel Quel* anthology *Théorie d'Ensemble* (1968).

Roche is one of the most intelligent (and least loved) members of the poetic avant-garde, despite the ringing title of his 1968 essay-manifesto, 'Poetry is inadmissible, besides it does not exist'. The dense texture of his verse and its characteristic dislocations (he often begins a new line in the middle of a word) shows the preoccupation with the nature of language which he shares with other members of the *Tel Quel* group; but this structural camouflage should not be allowed to blind the reader to the underlying humour, erotic provocation and sly mythological/historical and literary allusion. Roche has written of the baleful influence of symbolism in French poetry, claiming that 'it is, generally speaking, from symbolism onwards that poetry has become the written concretization of bourgeois idealism', and that the revolution to be mounted at the heart of this 'poetics' must of necessity be grammatical or syntactical: 'any writing which does not denounce this "poetics" is worthless . . . the logic of modern writing demands that one should take a vigorous hand in promoting the death agonies of this symbolistic, outmoded ideology. Writing can only symbolize what it is in its functioning, in its "society", within the frame of its utilization. It must stick to that.'

Main works:
Forestière amazonide (1962), *Récits complets* (1963), *Les Idées centésimales de Miss Elanize* (1964), *Eros énergumène* (1968).

ROBERT SABATIER

Born 1923 in Paris. Spent part of his childhood at Saugues (Haute-Loire), came to Paris in 1936 to pursue his studies. Published his first

poems, a plaquette entitled *Les Premières voix*, in 1939. In 1943 went
into hiding to join the Saugues *maquis*: clandestine publication of his
collection of Resistance poems *Flammes*. 1945, provincial existence and
various occupations (decorator, lecturer, etc.). Founded a literary
review, *La Cassette*, in 1947 which included Eluard among its contribu-
tors. Returned to Paris in 1950, and entered the publishing profession:
his collection of poems published that year, *Fêtes solaires*, won the Prix
Antonin Artaud (the revised edition won the Prix Apollinaire five
years later). In 1964 he began writing literary criticism for *Le Figaro
littéraire*, in 1965 he was appointed literary director of Editions Albin
Michel. Apart from his poetry, he is a prolific novelist (nine novels
since 1953), has written an autobiographical essay *L'Etat princier* (1961),
a biography of Saint Vincent de Paul, and a *Dictionnaire de la mort*
(1967). He was awarded the Grand Prix de Poésie of the Académie
Française in 1969, for his entire *oeuvre*.

It has been remarked of his poetry that 'he sometimes makes one
think of a Valéry who has made his peace with surrealism'. In fact, his
poetry is essentially Orphic: the poet tries to link himself and his
utterance to the whole cosmos, to establish the profound identity of
creative purpose between man and all the elements of the universe.
The delicately romantic style in which these feelings are expressed
links Sabatier to tradition.

Main works of poetry:
Les Fêtes solaires (1950, revised edition 1955), *Dédicace d'un navire* (1959),
Les Poisons délectables (1965), *Les Châteaux de millions d'années* (1969).

SAINT-JOHN PERSE (Alexis Saint-Léger Léger, known as)

Born 1887 in Guadaloupe. Spent his childhood on the small island of
Saint-Léger-les-Feuilles owned by his parents. Came to France in
1899, studied law at Bordeaux. After voyages to Spain, Germany and
England in 1914, he entered the Foreign Service. 1916–20, Secretary of
the French Embassy at Pekin: voyages inside China, and to Korea,
Japan, Mongolia. 1921 onwards, a number of diplomatic posts at
Washington and Paris; in 1933 appointed Secretary General of Foreign
Affairs at the Quai d'Orsay. In 1940 his functions were terminated by
Paul Reynaud: he left for the United States, and in November of that

year found himself stripped of his French nationality and all his honours. In 1941, appointed Literary Adviser to the Library of Congress. Awarded France's Grand Prix National des Lettres in 1959, and the Nobel Prize for literature in 1960. He divides his time between France and the United States. A great deal of his writing is dispersed in French and foreign reviews; the main body of his work has been assembled in two volumes of *Oeuvre poétique*.

Saint-John Perse has been so much written about that it is difficult to add anything fresh. He is the creator of a mythical world where the poet rules, often somewhat arbitrarily. His work can be of delphic obscurity, hieratic grandeur—and, not infrequently, of disconcerting flatulence. He himself is perhaps best described as a stoic turned rhetorician.

Main works (poetry and prose):
Eloges (vol. including *Images à Crusoé, Pour fêter une enfance, Récitation à l'éloge d'une reine* (1911, republished 1948); *Amitié du Prince* (1924); *Anabase* (1924, new edition 1948 with prefaces by Valéry Larbaud, Hugo von Hofmannsthal, T. S. Eliot and Giuseppe Ungaretti to the Russian, German, English and Italian translations); *Exil*, suivi de *Poème à l'étrangère, Pluies, Neiges* (1946); *Oeuvre poétique I* comprising *Eloges, La Gloire des rois, Anabase, Exil, Vents* (1953); *Amers* (1957); *Chronique* (1960); *L'Ordre des oiseaux* (1962); *Poésie* (1963); *Pour Dante* (1965).

Translations:
Eloges, translated by Louise Varèse (New York, 1944; revised version 1956); *Anabasis*, translated by T. S. Eliot (London, 1930; revised version London, 1959); *Exile*, translated by Denis Devlin (New York, 1949); *Winds*, translated by Hugh Chisholm (New York, 1953); *Seamarks*, translated by Wallace Fowlie (New York, 1958); *Chronique*, translated by Robert Fitzgerald (New York, 1961).

To consult:
Alain Bosquet, *Saint-John Perse* (1953, revised edition 1964); Roger Caillois, *Poétique de Saint-John Perse* (1964); Jacques Charpier, *Saint-John Perse* (1962); Pierre Guerre, *Saint-John Perse et l'homme* (1955); Albert Loranquin, *Saint-John Perse* (1963); Christian Murciaux, *Saint-John Perse* (1961); Maurice Saillet, *Saint-John Perse* (1952).

JEAN-PHILIPPE SALABREUIL

Born 1940 in Neuilly-sur-Seine, died 1970 in Paris. Began writing poems, of religious inspiration, at the age of fourteen. At the age of twenty, first symptoms of serious illness. He published his first collections of poems, *La Liberté des feuilles*, in 1963. A major operation which he underwent in 1965, and from which he recovered successfully, engendered a spiritual crisis leading to a new visionary outlook, which he celebrated in his second collection of poems, *Juste retour de l'ambîme*. Military service in Africa 1967–8: his third collection of poems, *L'Inésperé*, was written during two periods of leave.

Beginning under the spell of Jammes, Salabreuil had since progressed towards a more difficult and indeed contorted mode of expression, the clue to which is perhaps his own phrase about his desire for 'a language astonished by destiny'. At the core of his writing lies an ecstatic vision of spiritual dispossession, redeemed by love of women. He continues the tradition of the mystics of the seventeenth century into our own age.

Main works:
La Liberté des feuilles (1963), *Juste retour d'abîme* (1965), *L'Inésperé* (1968).

JUDE STEFAN

Born 1936 in Pont-Audemer (Eure). Lives in the Calvados region of Normandy. Prefers to remain reticent about the details of his life and circumstances: 'We are all, of necessity, born some place, and carry some name, but for the rest anything worth saying is contained in the poems themselves.' His first poems were published in December 1965 in *Les Cahiers du Sud*, and he has since contributed to the *Nouvelle Revue française*.

Within the comparatively brief space of time since his first poems appeared, Stéfan's reputation has established itself solidly in France, perhaps because his poems have a striking compactness and economy. Although sometimes reminiscent of Follain, he possesses greater range of mood and technique, and a saving sense of irony.

Main works:
Cyprès (1967), *Libères* (1970).

JEAN TARDIEU

Born 1903 in Saint-Germain-de-Joux (Jura). His father was a painter, his mother a musician. He acquired an arts degree in 1927. His first poems were published by Jean Paulhan in the *Nouvelle Revue française* that year. Military service in Indochina, where he met his future wife, 1927. Returned to France in 1930. His first collection of poems, *Le Fleuve caché*, was published in 1933. During the Occupation, active participation in the 'literary' Resistance, and friendships initiated with Eluard, Jean Lescure, Frénaud, Queneau. Appointed director of dramatic services of Radiodiffusion Française in 1944: from 1946 to 1960 director of the radio's 'Club d'Essai' sponsoring experimental and avant-garde programmes of all kinds, especially in the field of sound drama. In June 1955 the production in Paris of his *Six pièces en un acte* marked the beginning of his career as a playwright: since then, his short plays have been performed continuously in France and abroad. In addition to his poetry and what he calls his '*théâtre de chambre*', he has written prefaces for the work of a number of contemporary painters (Lapicque, Dufy, Hartung, Bazaine), a book on art (*De la peinture abstraite*, 1960), and translated Goethe (*Iphigénie en Tauride, Pandora*) and Hölderlin (*L'Archipel*).

Jules Supervielle said of Tardieu: 'A very diverse and always suggestive poet, he has several tones which come from the same voice. And as happens for the best writers, no one depicts him better than himself, as when he says to us, for example, 'that he loves all colours because his soul is "dark" '. Tardieu's diversity is still little appreciated outside France. As a poet, he first made his impact in England and America with the ironic humour of *Monsieur, Monsieur*, which is still, no doubt, his best-known collection outside France. Despite the baroque imagination which made him a founder member of the 'theatre of the absurd', his recent poems have returned to the more gravely lyrical mood with which he began his career.

Main works (poetry, prose poems, dramatic '*poèmes à jouer*'):
Le Fleuve caché (1933), *Accents* (1939), *Le Témoin invisible* (1943), *Figures* (1945), *Les Dieux étouffés* (1946), *Le Démon de l'irréalité* (1946), *Jours pétrifiés* (1947), *Un Mot pour un autre* (1951), *Monsieur, Monsieur* (1951), *La Première Personne de singulier* (1952), *Une Voix sans personne* (1954), *L'Espace et la flûte* (1954), *Théâtre de chambre* I (1955), *Poèmes à jouer* (*Théâtre II*) (1960), *Choix de poèmes 1924–1954* (1961), *Histoires obscures* (1961).

To consult:
To consult:
Martin Esslin, *The Theatre of the Absurd* (London, 1968); Philippe Jaccottet, *L'Entretien des Muses* (1968); Emilie Noulet, *Jean Tardieu* (1963).

TOURSKY (Alexandre Toursky, known as)

Born 1917 in Cannes, of a Russian father and a Provençal mother; brought up by his mother and her second husband, an Englishman. Childhood and secondary studies at Cannes. Established himself in Paris in 1938. Friendships with Francis Carco, Milosz, Godoy, Maurice Rostand. Entered the Operal Mundi press agency and worked on their children's newspapers—Mickey Mouse, etc.; has always retained an affectionate memory of this period of close contact with the world of 'fiction, the cartoon strip, pop'. Remained in the Midi during the war. In 1940 joined the group publishing *Les Cahiers du Sud* (Jean Ballard, Léon-Gabriel Gros, Jean Tortel, etc.) and remained a member of the magazine's Conseil de Rédaction until its demise in 1967. In 1942 joined the publishing house of Robert Laffont. In 1948 returned to Paris, and enjoyed the '*âge d'or*' of Saint-Germain des Prés' without participating in the movements it gave birth to. In 1951 returned to Marseilles, and the following year joined Radiodiffusion Française there: announcer, then producer, then television, in which he is at present the director of Public Relations.

Apart from his poetry, he has illustrated works by Marcel Brion and René Laporte, and writes a regular column of art criticism for the Marseille newspaper *Le Soir*.

As a poet, Toursky is the sworn enemy of rhetoric. He has described his poetry, over-modestly, as 'an attempt (vain, perhaps) to record the melancholy of never having made anything much of life, my life, and to approach the gloomy banks of Lethe in a state of mind as disarmed, as curious and as vaguely terrified as when I was ten years old. . . . I have never really understood the adventure of life in which I became involved. Without friendship it would long ago have seemed intolerable to me.' He has also referred to his poems as 'precise and melancholy notations', a phrase which describes perfectly his disciplined approach to his material, the choice of subject being nearly always motivated by a desire to redeem the quotidian without falsifying it.

Main works:
Enfances (1937), *La Suite à demain* (1938), *Les Armes prohibées* (1942),

406

Connais ta liberté (1943), *Ici commence le désert* (1946), *La Mort est naturelle* (1948), *Souvenir de Colette V.* (1949), *Christine ou la connaissance des temps* (1950), *Un Drôle d'air* (1963).

BORIS VIAN

Born 1920 in Ville-d'Avray (nr. Versailles), died 1959 in Paris. Trained as a civil engineer, but soon turned to other activities: these included jazz music and writing. As a trumpeter heading his own jazz band he played in various celebrated Paris *caves* during the immediate post-war period, as well as writing record reviews and articles for *Le Jazz Hot*. From 1945 onwards he acted in several films, and wrote a great number of songs and cabaret sketches. His first novel, *Vercoquin et le plancton*, was published in 1946, and his first play, *L'Equarissage pour tous*, was performed in 1950. Between 1946 and 1948, he also wrote a series of 'tough' American-style novels under the pseudonym of Vernon Sullivan. In addition to writing five novels, a short opera (with Darius Milhaud), many short stories, essays, articles on a variety of subjects, four plays, a study of contemporary popular music, and poetry, he translated plays, novels and memoirs into French.

The Protean activities of this brilliant and prolific young man, during a tragically brief life span, defy classification, though he must be placed in the direct line of descent from Rabelais through Jarry (who was the most important influence in his development). Although names as diverse as those of Swift, Lichtenberg, Ambrose Bierce, Ionesco, Alphonse Allais, Edward Lear, have been invoked in trying to find analogies with his written work, the poetry is perhaps the least complex and the most readily accessible part of his diverse *oeuvre*. Filled with the same romanticism, fantastication and gleeful humour as his novels, the poems blend an absolutely unforced joy at the wonders of life with a sad and poignant consciousness of the imminence of death. They are unpretentious (even casual), but carry a surprising impact.

Main works (poetry):
Cantilène en gélée (1950), *Je voudrais pas crever* (1962), *Textes et chansons* (1966).

To consult:
Noël Arnaud, *Les Vies parallèles de Boris Vian* (special number of the

review *Bizarre*) (February 1966); Henri Baudin, *Boris Vian, la poursuite de l'homme total* (1966); Jean Clouzet, *Boris Vian* (1966); Freddy de Vree, *Boris Vian* (1965); David Noakes, *Boris Vian* (1964); Michel Rybalka, *Boris Vian* (1969); Jacques Duchateâu, *Boris Vian* (1969).